Andrés Oppenheimer

THE ROBOTS ARE COMING!

Andrés Oppenheimer is a foreign affairs syndicated columnist with the *Miami Herald,* the anchor of *Oppenheimer Presenta* on CNN en Español, and the author of seven books. He is a cowinner of the 1987 Pulitzer Prize as a member of the *Miami Herald* team that uncovered the Iran-Contra scandal and a winner of the 2005 Suncoast Emmy Award. He won the Inter American Press Association Award twice (1989 and 1994) and is also the winner of the 1993 Ortega y Gasset Award of Spain's daily *El País* and the 1998 Maria Moors Cabot Prize of Columbia University. He was included in the 1993 *Forbes* Media Guide as one of the "500 most important journalists" in the United States. He lives in Miami, Florida.

Also by Andrés Oppenheimer

Innovate or Die!

Saving the Americas

Bordering on Chaos

THE ROBOTS ARE COMING!

THE ROBOTS ARE COMING!

THE FUTURE OF JOBS IN THE AGE OF AUTOMATION

ANDRÉS OPPENHEIMER

TRANSLATED FROM THE SPANISH BY EZRA E. FITZ,
EDITED BY THE AUTHOR

VINTAGE BOOKS
A Division of Penguin Random House LLC
New York

A VINTAGE BOOKS ORIGINAL, APRIL 2019

The Cataloging-in-Publication Data is on file at the Library of Congress.

Vintage Books Trade Paperback ISBN: 978-0-525-56500-0
Premium Edition ISBN: 978-1-9848-9891-3
eBook ISBN: 978-0-525-56501-7

www.vintagebooks.com

Printed in the United States of America
10 9 8 7 6 5 4 3 2 1

For Sandra

CONTENTS

THE ROBOTS ARE COMING!

PROLOGUE

Ever since a study by the University of Oxford predicted that 47 percent of U.S. jobs are at risk of being replaced by robots and artificial intelligence over the next fifteen to twenty years, I haven't been able to stop thinking about the future of work. How many people will become unemployed because of the increasing automation of jobs? This is not a new phenomenon, but never before has it developed at such a fast pace. Technology has been killing jobs since the Industrial Revolution in the late eighteenth century. But up to now, humans have always managed to create more jobs than those that were wiped out by technology. The question now is, can we continue creating more jobs than we are eliminating?

The media bring us one example after another of how technological disruption often creates new companies, though at the cost of decimating others that employed many more people. The Eastman Kodak Company, an icon of the photographic industry that employed 140,000 people, was pushed into bankruptcy in 2012 by Instagram, a start-up with just 13 employees that knew how to beat Kodak to the punch when it came to digital photography. Blockbuster, the giant movie rental chain that employed 60,000 people around the world, went bankrupt shortly before that because it could not compete with Netflix, another start-up with 30 employees that started shipping movies directly to people's homes. During its golden age, General Motors had a staff of some 618,000 workers, whereas now their number is down to 202,000. What's more, the car company is now being threatened by Tesla and Google, which are ahead in the development of self-driven cars and employ 30,000 and 55,000 people, respectively. Will GM's employees suffer the same fate as those at Kodak and Blockbuster?

Growing numbers of jobs are disappearing. We see this every day in our lives. In the very recent past, we've witnessed the gradual extinction of elevator attendants, telephone operators, factory workers, and garbage collectors who swept the streets with brooms in their hands, all of whom are being replaced by machines. In the United States, parking lot attendants and their collection booths are vanishing fast, as are airline tellers and their check-in desks at airports. At many restaurants in Japan, conveyor belts have taken the place of servers, and a number of sushi restaurants have replaced their chefs with robots. Today it's not just people performing manual labor who are seeing their jobs threatened, but also white-collar workers such as journalists, travel agents, real estate salesmen, bankers, insurance agents, accountants, lawyers, and doctors. Virtually no profession is safe: all are feeling the impact—at least somewhat—from the automation of work.

My own profession, journalism, is among the most threatened. *The Washington Post* is already publishing election stories written by robots, and almost all major American newspapers publish sports scores and stock market figures generated by smart machines. Journalists will have to ride the wave of this new reality and reinvent ourselves, or we will soon find ourselves out of the game. And the same thing will happen in almost every other profession.

Even those who are themselves responsible for the technological revolution—people like Microsoft founder Bill Gates or Facebook founder Mark Zuckerberg—are now admitting for the first time that unemployment caused by technological advances—technological unemployment—could become the biggest global challenge of the twenty-first century. As Zuckerberg said during his 2017 commencement-day speech at Harvard University, "today, technology and automation are eliminating many jobs," and "our generation will have to deal with tens of millions of jobs replaced by automation like autonomous cars and trucks." And long before many people were talking about this issue, in 2014, Gates was already admitting that "technology over time will reduce demand for jobs, particularly at the lower end of skill set . . . 20 years from now, labor demand for lots of skill sets will be substantially lower."

How are the big corporations responding to all of this? The vast majority of them are claiming that far from killing jobs, they are increasing productivity and hiring new people by automating their operations. Should we believe them, or are they just feeding us fairy tales and half-truths? And if what they're saying is in fact true, which are the jobs that will disappear and which others are going to replace them? Where will the effects of automation and artificial intelligence be felt the most, in the industrialized world or in the emerging countries in Asia, Eastern Europe, and Latin America? Most important, what should each of us be doing to prepare ourselves for this tsunami of labor automation that is sweeping across the globe?

To answer these questions, I followed the same methodology I used in my 2014 book *Innovate or Die!*: I traveled to major world innovation centers, interviewed some of the best-known creativity and business gurus, and then drew my own conclusions. This time, I started my journey at the University of Oxford in England, where I interviewed the two researchers who shocked the world in 2013 with their study predicting that 47 percent of current jobs will disappear in the near future. From there, I traveled to Silicon Valley, New York, Japan, South Korea, Israel, and several countries in both Europe and Latin America to study the future of some of the key industries of the twenty-first century.

What I learned in this journalistic voyage at once surprised and scared me. Fortunately, while history is rife with examples of technologies that have annihilated entire industries, these same technologies have created brand-new industries that produced more jobs than they erased. But there is no guarantee that this same trend will hold true going forward as automation and artificial intelligence take growing numbers of jobs and the rate of technological acceleration increases. I have little doubt that technological unemployment—and the question of what we will do with our lives in a world where robots will do much of the work—will be one of the world's most pressing issues in coming decades. Don't be fooled by the relatively low 2018 unemployment rates in the United States: it's an issue that—whether it's because of the disappearance of jobs or the gradual fall of wages—will affect each and every nation on earth.

In many ways, it's already upon us. Growing disaffection among workers in traditional twentieth-century industries has led to the emergence of nationalist, protectionist, and anti-globalization movements in the United States and a number of European nations. Donald Trump won the 2016 U.S. presidential election in part by exploiting the anxieties of workers in technologically threatened industries and blaming undocumented immigrants for taking American jobs or driving American wages down. But it wasn't immigration that was killing jobs and reducing wages: it was the automation of labor. In fact, the number of undocumented immigrants had declined significantly since the 2008 financial crisis. And the impact of growing automation and artificial intelligence will become only more visible as time goes on. If we do not find a solution to the coming disruption of key industries, the world will become an even more tumultuous place. My hope is that this book will help create a greater awareness of the challenges that new waves of technological unemployment will bring about and help us better prepare ourselves to face this new reality, both as individuals and as nations.

1

A JOBLESS WORLD?

OXFORD, ENGLAND

As I started working on this book, the first stop I made was to the University of Oxford to interview Carl Benedikt Frey and Michael A. Osborne, the two researchers at the Oxford Martin School who raised alarm bells in 2013 when they published a study predicting that 47 percent of jobs could disappear over the next fifteen to twenty years due to automation. The study landed like a bomb in the academic and economic worlds, not simply because of its premise but more so because the two researchers accompanied their work by ranking 702 occupations and their respective possibilities of being eliminated over the next two decades. It marked the first time in recent memory that an academic paper had forecast the possible disappearance of hundreds of specific jobs, and it spread like wildfire, leaving many of us who work in offices—lawyers, accountants, doctors, bankers, business executives, and journalists, among others—shocked to learn that our own positions were at risk of disappearing, either completely or in part, in the coming years.

Frey and Osborne's study coincided with a number of

reports predicting a new revolution in robotics and artificial intelligence that would eliminate tens of millions of jobs across the workforce. Meanwhile, Google announced that it had bought eight robotics companies, including Boston Dynamics, which produced military-grade metallic monsters such as BigDog and Cheetah. These acquisitions were the "the clearest indication yet that Google is intent on building a new class of autonomous systems that might do anything from warehouse work to package delivery and even elder care," *The New York Times* warned in 2014. In May 2013, the global consulting firm McKinsey had published an extensive report titled "Disruptive Technologies: Advances That Will Transform Life, Business, and the Global Economy," which warned that new technologies would leave unemployed not only millions of manufacturing employees but also between 110 million and 140 million office workers and business professionals by the year 2025. All of a sudden, people were starting to ask themselves, are we heading for a jobless world?

From that moment forward, the headlines became increasingly dramatic. "Forrester Predicts That AI-enabled Automation Will Eliminate 9% of US Jobs in 2018," read one in *Forbes.* "Automation Could Kill 73 Million U.S. Jobs by 2030," said another headline, in *USA Today.* "Robots will destroy our jobs—and we're not ready for it," predicted the British daily *The Guardian*.

FREY, A SKEPTIC OF TECHNO-OPTIMISM

The first thing that struck me when I arrived in Oxford, which is an hour outside London by train, was the disparity between the futuristic research of Frey and Osborne and the medieval environment in which they had conducted it. Oxford is a monastic city dating back to the twelfth century, and it was saved from destruction during World War II because Hitler wanted to convert it into his capital city in England had he won the war and therefore had ordered his air force not to bomb it. In the fourteenth century, many of its monasteries had already become universities. Today the city includes thirty-eight institutions of higher education linked by a sort of academic federation known as the University of Oxford, which operate largely in medieval convents, as if they had been frozen in time.

In that atmosphere, just a few steps from the Oxford Divinity School, built in the mid-fifteenth century, is the Oxford Martin School, a futuristic research center founded in 2005 so that all professors of the Oxford academic community could conduct studies designed to help bring long-term improvements to the world. James Martin, the British billionaire who donated the funds to create this institute, had specified that its mission would be to tackle issues of global significance by supporting programs that "have an impact beyond academia" and haven't been funded by public or private sources. Since its inception, the Oxford Martin School has sponsored nearly fifty studies by some five hundred Oxford professors. Most of these studies have been focused on the future, as well as on the social challenges that new technologies will bring about once the robots—as we've seen in science fiction movies—begin to think for themselves.

Carl Benedikt Frey is a Swedish economist and economic historian who has been studying the process of technology's "creative destruction" for several years. He told me he'd been eager to study whether the technological optimism radiating from Silicon Valley was justified. He had wondered about the accuracy of the widespread belief in academic, business, and political circles that technology would inexorably improve the world. Something told him that while this had been true in the past, it might not be the case in the future, because robots and artificial intelligence may begin to replace growing numbers of jobs and cause a serious social problem.

TECHNOLOGICAL UNEMPLOYMENT

Before Frey and Osborne, a number of economists had already been warning about the potentially disruptive effects of robots and artificial intelligence. Their argument was that unlike in the past, technology today is growing exponentially, or at an increasingly accelerated rate. According to what's known as Moore's law—which is based on an article written by Gordon Moore, a cofounder of Intel, in 1965—the processing power of computers increases by 100 percent every eighteen months. A decade from now, computers will be 10,000 percent more powerful than they are today. And according to Lin Wells, in his November 1, 2014, essay "Better Outcomes Through Radical Inclusion," this will change the world much more significantly than it has in the past, because technological acceleration will be taking place not only in the field of computing but also in robotics, biotechnology, and nanotechnology.

By 2003, economists like Maarten Goos and Alan Manning of the London School of Economics were already warning that the exponential advancement of technology was beginning to polarize the labor force, and that the only workers whose jobs would be safe would be the better and the lesser educated. The majority of those in the middle, they argued, would be left without work. In their paper "Lousy and Lovely Jobs: The Rising Polarization of Work in Britain," Goos and Manning predicted that smart machines would soon be able to react to unexpected situations, allowing them to replace not only those who do routine work but also those who perform complex tasks. And in 2011, MIT economists Erik Brynjolfsson and Andrew McAfee had written a book titled *Race Against the*

Machine, in which they also warned about the growing advantage that intelligent machines had over humans.

However, Frey wanted to dig a bit deeper and proposed a study of the 702 jobs listed by the U.S. Department of Labor that would rank them in accordance with their relative risk of being eliminated by new technologies. He contacted Michael Osborne, a young engineer specializing in robotics and artificial intelligence who taught just a few blocks away at the Department of Engineering Science, and asked him for help creating an algorithm that could classify jobs according to their risk of disappearing in the near future.

Osborne, who had yet to turn forty when I interviewed him, is a tall, thin man who seemed to have permanently disheveled hair. He has the classic look of an absent-minded genius. Not only does he teach his students at Oxford how to create algorithms, he also uses algorithms to guide his private life. When I asked him, only half-jokingly, if he would describe himself as a nerd, or as somebody who used technology to manage the most trivial details of his personal life, he smiled affirmatively. He told me, as an example, that he had even created an algorithm to plan his wedding party, organizing seating arrangements for the guests according to their ages, occupations, and interests.*

For their study on the future of jobs, Frey and Osborne created an algorithm into which they fed examples of what kinds of jobs were already being displaced by automation, and asked it to compare them with the 702 jobs on the U.S. Department of Labor list. The results surprised even themselves, as they told me in separate interviews.

* "It worked great; everyone had a wonderful time," Osborne assured me with pride. "We asked each of the wedding guests to fill out an online questionnaire asking them about their personality and interests, and we asked the algorithm to seat those who had similar interests together and to keep them separated from people they already knew."

THE RANKING OF THE MOST THREATENED JOBS

Frey and Osborne's algorithm produced a ranking that begins with jobs that have a 99 percent chance of being replaced by robots, drones, autonomous vehicles, and other intelligent machines. According to their study, this most-at-risk category includes telemarketers (who in many countries have already been replaced by robocalls), insurance underwriters, new accounts clerks, library technicians, and cargo and freight agents, all of whom are at risk of being replaced by computer programs capable of accumulating and processing data and making future projections much more accurately than humans.

The jobs with a 98 percent chance of being replaced in the next fifteen to twenty years include administrative employees, bank loan officers, and many insurance agency workers, whose routine tasks can be easily replaced by artificial intelligence. Interestingly enough, also included in this category are sports umpires, whose calls on controversial plays will be increasingly replaced by drones and video replay systems that can make much more precise judgments than humans.

Jobs with a 97 percent risk of being killed in the near future include phone operators and store salespeople, who in many cases are already being replaced by e-commerce or humanoid robots that can answer questions from customers in much the same way that Siri, Alexa, Google Assistant, Cortana, and other virtual assistants can respond to whatever we want to ask them. Other jobs that, according to this same study, run a 97 percent risk of disappearing include real estate brokers, who like travel agents are being replaced by Internet websites that allow us to virtually visit homes for sale, and cashiers, who are already being replaced by self-checkout stations at many stores and supermarkets.

To my surprise, another kind of job that is on the way out

is that of restaurant waiters. How could that be? I asked the study's authors. Well, it's already happening, they replied. In many U.S. fast food restaurants, including McDonald's, Chili's, Applebee's, and Panera, it is already common to order and pay for your food with a tablet or on your own smartphone. Soon enough, robots won't just be replacing the waiters, but will be replacing many of the chefs as well.

"We were surprised to see that servers were among the most likely people to have their jobs automated," Osborne told me. "When we designed the algorithm, which learns from examples just like children do, we ran thirty-five examples of jobs we thought weren't very susceptible to automation, followed by another thirty-five we considered to be more at risk. We included servers with the latter group, because we thought that personal engagement in restaurants was an essential part of their work and couldn't be replicated by a machine. But when the results were calculated, it turns out we were wrong, and that waiting tables is a routine job that could easily be automated."

Among the jobs listed as having a 96 percent risk of disappearing are chefs—who are already being replaced by robots, as I witnessed in Japan's sushi chains—secretaries and administrative assistants, receptionists, information clerks, and bank or department store tellers, all of whom are being increasingly replaced by tablet computers or humanoid robots. According to the study, other jobs at high risk of replacement include taxi drivers, truck drivers, and messengers—who will be displaced by autonomous vehicles—tourist guides, dental technicians, pharmacy technicians, butchers, legal clerks, and accountants.

THE JOBS THAT WILL SURVIVE ARE THE ONES THAT ARE HARD TO EXPLAIN

According to Frey, "Anything that relies on storing and processing information, something that computers are relatively good at, is highly automatable. That includes anything from basic administrative back-office work to basic assembly production jobs, to even some types of sales and service jobs. The list is endless." And according to Osborne, "The new thing about technology is that it's able to substitute routine clerical work the way it used to be able to replace routine mechanical work." When I asked him if he could give me a general rule about who is most at risk of losing a job due to automation, he responded that "the probability of automating an occupation is closely related to the level of skill or education. . . . Highly skilled people tend to be sufficiently well-equipped to keep pace with technological change, to be able to move to whatever new occupations emerge, and to use new technologies, whereas at the bottom of the spectrum, we see the kind of skills that can be replaced entirely by technology."

Other futurologists I interviewed agreed that academic training and skills like creativity, originality, and social and emotional intelligence—which should also be taught at colleges and universities—will be key to the jobs of the future. And academic training will have to go far beyond current one-dimensional careers like law, medicine, and business administration. New careers will be increasingly interdisciplinary and will include technological, critical thinking, and problem-solving capabilities, as well as social skills. Furthermore, tertiary education will be intermittent, in the sense that it will be constantly updated over time. For example, today's dermatologists study medicine, specialize in dermatology, and spend a significant part of their time examining brown spots on their patients' skin to determine whether they could potentially be cancerous. But in the future, growing numbers of patients will be using applications on their smartphones that can take a picture of a dark spot on the skin and instantly tell them whether it's dangerous or not.

Doctors who want to work in dermatology will have to specialize in skin cancer treatments that will increasingly rely on the diagnostic of algorithms and robots. And to do this, they will have to study previously unrelated subjects like statistics and perhaps even robotics. We will always need good doctors who provide humane treatments, who can empathize with their patients, and who can explain a diagnosis made by an intelligent machine, but those who best understand the new technologies will be the most successful. If a cardiologist, for example, also studied engineering and can manufacture pacemakers using a 3-D printer, tailoring them to each individual patient, he or she will be in much greater demand than their average colleagues.

Anders Sandberg, a Ph.D. in computational neurosciences who was also involved in the Oxford study on the future of jobs, summed it up for me this way: "It's quite simple: if your job can be easily explained, it can be automated. If it can't, it won't." In other words, algorithms and robots are better than humans at doing repetitive, predictable tasks. An algorithm learns the same way a child does, based on examples or behaviors that are taught. If you can show another person a detailed list of the tasks he or she performs and if most of these tasks are relatively predictable, sooner or later that job will be replaced by an algorithm or a robot. And to take it one step further, just about every job has at least a few chores that will end up being automated.

RECENT HISTORY SHOWS US THAT THE IMPOSSIBLE IS NOW POSSIBLE

At first glance, the Oxford researchers' algorithm seemed somewhat ruthless. Is there really a greater than 90 percent chance that the jobs of waiters, receptionists, truck drivers, tour guides, and real estate agents won't exist in the near future? I asked them. Don't waiters do a job that, in addition to providing a human touch, requires a high degree of improvisation and creativity when it comes to responding to unexpected situations? How would a humanoid waiter deal with a customer who wants to exchange one dish for another? And when it comes to truck drivers, will an autonomous truck be able to react quickly enough to unexpected events like a dog running across a road?

They both responded with resigned smiles. It might be hard to believe, but this won't be the first time in history that common jobs disappear only to be replaced by others, they said. Until recently, in many countries around the globe, agriculture employed more people than any other industry. Now it's far from the main source of work. For example, the number of people working in agriculture in the United States fell from 60 percent of the population in 1850 to less than 2 percent in the early twenty-first century. There were only 700,000 farmers in the United States in 2010, down from 12 million a century earlier in 1910, despite the fact that the overall population had tripled during that period. But the world didn't come to an end. On the contrary, average Americans saw their standard of living rise. If agriculture could be revolutionized by tractors and computers, thus forcing millions of people to seek new occupations, they argued, why not expect something similar from the current revolution in robotics and artificial intelligence?

It's a fair question. Plus, recent history shows us that skepticism is a bad method of predicting the future. Many ideas that seemed preposterous just a decade ago are now part of our daily lives, which we now accept as completely normal. After all, if someone had told me ten years ago that I would have a virtual assistant named Siri on my cell phone and that I could ask her to tell me the capital of Afghanistan and receive the correct answer, I would have considered the whole idea to be insane. The same thing would have happened if someone had told me an application called Waze could tell me, loudly and in the language of my choice, the shortest and quickest route to my destination, or that I could buy plane tickets online, or that supermarket cashiers would be replaced by self-checkout stations. But all that—in fact, much more—is already happening.

Technological advances happen so quickly that they numb our capacity for amazement. New innovations might stun us for a few minutes, but soon enough we incorporate them into our lives as if they've always been with us. Not many people would remember that the iPhone as we know it today didn't exist before 2007, or that Waze—the app that calculates traffic and driving time to a destination—went into worldwide use only after the company was bought by Google in 2013. But today many of us wonder how we had ever lived without them.

IN JAPAN, SOME HOTELS ARE ALREADY BEING RUN BY ROBOTS

When I traveled to Japan to conduct interviews for this book, the first thing I did was book a room at the Henn na Hotel, which had attracted a great deal of attention for becoming the first hotel in the world operated by robots. I had read that the concierge, receptionists, bellhops, and even the waiters at the hotel are fully automated, and I wanted to experience firsthand how that worked. When I arrived at the hotel, located in a suburb near Tokyo's Disney Resort, I found that, yes, several of the employees had been replaced by robots and intelligent machines . . . although, as you will see, some of them were not terribly smart, or at least were in the process of learning.

Behind the reception desk were two giant robotic dinosaurs that looked quite real and were wearing green hats like those used by concierges at traditional Japanese hotels. Apparently excited to see me enter, they started making guttural grunts and swinging their heads from side to side. Since there were no human beings behind the counter, I had no choice but to deal with them. As I later learned, other branches of the hotel chain have robotic receptionists who look like men and women, but because of its proximity to Disney, the Tokyo branch had opted for dinosaurs to delight its younger guests. At the other end of the lobby was an aquarium about six feet across in which three large goldfish were swimming in circles, rising and diving in their irregular paths. It was only when I approached it that I realized they were also robotic, driven by some sort of internal motor.

"Welcome to the Henn na Hotel," the reptilian concierge said in a raspy voice, which is what you might expect from a dinosaur, though it was pleasant enough not to frighten anyone. Using his claws to point to a tablet on the counter in front of him, the dinosaur continued: "Please select your language of preference." Once I did that, his head continuing to sway from side to side, he added, "Please place the first side of your passport on the screen and press the start button."

Then I asked the robotic dinosaur, "What's your name?" But the robot didn't seem prepared to answer that question. Shaking his head more excitedly than before, he began to growl. "*Grrrrrrrrr! Grrrrrrrr! Grrrrrr!*" "You have a name, don't you?" I pressed, rather enjoying the exchange. The giant robotic reptile became even more agitated, swaying from side to side as if desperately seeking an answer, before finally releasing a prolonged "*Grrrrrrrrrrrrrrr!*" Obviously, this particular robot didn't have much of a sense of humor. Either that, or he didn't like being taken out of his preprogrammed dialogue routine.

"Are you angry?" I asked him. Then the reptile with the concierge hat seemed to lose patience and said, "One moment, please. An assistant will be here shortly to help you." A few seconds later, a young lady in the hotel's uniform emerged from a little door behind the counter and, after greeting me with the customary Japanese reverence, explained to me with the utmost seriousness that the dinosaurs were new at their jobs and were currently only able to help guests check in and out of their rooms. In other words, these were not fully conversational dinosaurs.

"Okay," I said, a bit disappointed. I placed my passport on the little screen, hit the start button, and followed the reptile's instructions to the letter. I filled out the form on the tablet with my name, address, and signature. Then, gesturing with his claws, the dinosaur asked me to move over to the next machine "to finish the registration process." This small tower resembling an ATM asked for my credit card and in return gave me a plastic key and a receipt with my room number on it. As soon as I took the key, the dinosaur—now visibly happy—proclaimed, "The registration process is complete." He raised his arms, and with what looked like a smile on his face, he concluded with "Please proceed to the elevator, and enjoy your stay at our hotel."

I WILL BE YOUR PERSONAL ASSISTANT.
LET ME KNOW WHAT YOU NEED.

When I entered my room, number 611, I was greeted by the voice of another robot. This one looked like a big egg, was the size of a soccer ball, and was perched on top of one of the dressers. It was painted with colorful dots and had an electronic tablet on its front that showed two cartoonish eyes that looked from side to side when the machine talked. "Welcome to our hotel, Andrés-san. My name is Tapia," it said, introducing itself and talking in a girl's voice. "Let me show you all the things I can do for you." Immediately, a menu popped up on the screen displaying a variety of options, including games, news outlets, weather reports, music stations, and commands for controlling the TV, lights, and air conditioning, all of which could be activated vocally. I set out to test Tapia, and indeed, when I asked her to turn off the lights and turn on the television, she did so immediately.

Tapia was much smarter than her dinosaur colleagues on the ground floor. Plus she had a sense of humor and was programmed to have conversations unrelated to her functions. When I told her jokingly that she was a very cute robot, Tapia replied, "Thank you very much, I hope you don't say the same thing to other robots besides me." Tapia was more comfortable communicating in English than the reptiles at the reception desk. She probably had more experience speaking languages, because robots learn from each and every interaction, adding new data to their memory. She had obviously been at her job longer than the robots downstairs.

When it was time for dinner, I called the desk to ask where I could find the restaurant, only to be informed by the human assistant to the robotic concierges that unfortunately there was none. The hotel had only vending machines that offered warm meals, which were located on the ground floor. Since it was late and very cold outside, I had no choice but to buy a bowl of Japanese noodles from the vending machine, which was not unlike those that sell soft drinks. I put the money into a slot, pressed a button showing an image of the noodles, and a box with my dinner dropped into a small microwave in the lower part of the machine, which automatically turned on, heated the food, and dispensed it for me. The noodles, by the way, were dreadful.

Since I was already in the lobby, I decided to knock on the door of the human assistant to the dinosaurs and to try to interview her. After a question or two about the hotel, I asked her almost in passing how many actual humans worked there. The young woman, Saki Kato, seemed delighted to practice her English, which was pretty good. She told me that there were only two people working that night: the manager and her. Together they were in charge of the entire hotel—a hundred rooms in all—almost all of which were occupied. Maids are there during the day, but almost all other functions, down to cleaning the windows and washing the floors, are handled by robots, Saki told me. "And, well, we also have people to service the robots, because they often break down and have to be reprogrammed," she added with a mischievous grin.

The next day, once my curiosity was satisfied, I relocated to another hotel in Tokyo. At $400 per night, the Henn na Hotel was quite expensive, and the room was tiny, even by Japanese standards. There was barely enough room to walk between the bed and the wall. And I didn't like the idea of having another dinner of reheated noodles from a vending machine in the lobby. I concluded that the dinosaur concierge was doing about the same thing as an airport check-in kiosk, though it did make the experience a bit more fun. And Tapia, the egg-shaped robot, was simply a personal assistant with voice recognition software, not unlike Siri on my smartphone.

But while there weren't any extraordinary technological advances at the hotel, there was little doubt in my mind that the automation of the hotel industry is just around the corner. When I checked out, the dinosaur concierge asked me to return my plastic room key to a slot, said goodbye, and thanked me in Japanese with a bow that made me smile. As I was leaving, I concluded that perhaps the only reason why more hotels haven't started using robots yet is due to fears that customers would find the machines too cold and lacking in human warmth. But if the Henn na Hotel was able to overcome this challenge by turning the robotic registration into a fun experience through dinosaurs wearing concierge hats instead of metallic robots, others in the industry are likely to follow its steps soon. The Henn na Corporation has announced that it will be opening six new automated hotels in Tokyo and three in Osaka in 2018 and that in the long term, it is planning on opening a hundred more worldwide. It will be difficult for other hotel chains to compete with that or to resist the temptation of running a hundred-room hotel with just two regular employees, a cleaning staff, and a team of robots that can work twenty-four hours a day, take no vacations, and never ask for raises.

ROBOTS WILL BE EVERYWHERE

Soon enough, robots won't be seen just in hotels but also in the streets, schools, hospitals, law firms, and almost everywhere else. Industrial robots have been used since the 1960s to perform repetitive and relatively simple tasks, especially in the auto industry. But until now they had not spread much beyond the manufacturing floor. Despite the futuristic predictions of cartoons like *The Jetsons* and science fiction films that have been predicting the emergence of robots as domestic servants, drivers, and even as pets, the science of robotics had remained stagnant for decades.

But now robotics is growing by leaps and bounds, thanks to the fact that robots are getting cheaper and smarter. Artificial intelligence and cloud computing (the massive online database commonly known as the cloud) is allowing each individual robot to learn from the experiences of all others. Before, a robot was an individual machine that carried its own information internally, sharing it with a small group of similar automatons, if at all. But now every robot connected to the cloud has immediate access to an almost unlimited amount of data and the experiences of the entire globe's robotic population, allowing them to be constantly learning from one another. And that is revolutionizing the world of work.

Ever since the supercomputer Deep Blue defeated world chess champion Garry Kasparov in 1997, robots have been taking down one challenge after another. In 2002, a software program beat the world's best Scrabble players. In 2010, another program took down some of the greats at the game of bridge. In 2011, IBM's Watson supercomputer beat two champions of the popular TV game show *Jeopardy!* And in 2016, AlphaGo, a computer Go program developed by Google's DeepMind program, made headlines around the world by defeating South Korea's Go champion Lee Sedol. Until then, the game of Go was considered unwinnable for a machine, because in addition to intelligence, it requires a good amount of intuition and creativity.

Some scientists, including Vernor Vinge, who is also an accomplished science fiction author, have predicted that intelligent machines will surpass all human capabilities by 2023. Others, such as Google's futurologist and engineering director Ray Kurzweil, predicted that singularity—that moment in time when artificial intelligence surpasses human intelligence—will occur in 2045. With technology advancing at the rate that it is, it would not be surprising for it to happen sometime in between. Recently, a robot named Michihito Matsuda ran for mayor of the Japanese city of Tama, on the outskirts of Tokyo, with the campaign slogan "Artificial intelligence will change Tama City." Matsuda, who according to press reports was created by two big-tech executives, got 4,000 votes and finished in third place. But how long will it take before another robot runs a better campaign and convinces voters that it can make more levelheaded decisions than a human?

It's no longer a question of whether technology will surpass human intelligence, but of when. That's why, when asked how he would prepare for the next chess match against a supercomputer like IBM's Deep Blue, the great Dutch chess master Jan Hein Donner replied, "I would bring a hammer."

ROBOTIC RECEPTIONISTS ARE ALWAYS IN A GOOD MOOD

During my recent trip to Japan, I encountered robots in restaurants, retail stores, banks, and office buildings. I met a robot named Pepper at one of the Hamazushi sushi restaurants in Tokyo, and another one at the entrance of a branch of Mizuho, one of the largest banks in Japan. They were welcoming customers and directing them to the appropriate offices, always with a smile and a bow. Robots are also currently being trained to work as car dealers at Nissan branches in Tokyo and to serve customers in shopping centers in a number of cities throughout the country.

Pepper, a doll-like little humanoid robot with big black eyes and a white plastic body, costs less than the annual salary of a Japanese receptionist and provides many more years of useful service. But most important, Pepper can work for twenty-four hours a day, seven days a week, and never asks for vacation time or pay increases. When he operates well—which isn't always the case, though eventually it will be—he is the ideal employee for companies that want to lower labor costs and avoid union problems. While looking for a place to exchange some currency at Tokyo's Haneda Airport, I wandered past the entrance of a Bank of Tokyo-Mitsubishi branch, where I was greeted by another robot, named Nao. Like Pepper, Nao was armed with cameras, sensors, and microphones with which he could interact with customers. Nao proudly assured me that he could understand and speak nineteen languages and give customers the daily rate of the yen against any other currency. As the branch manager would later explain to me, Nao was being trained to serve the tourists who would be coming from all over the world for the 2020 Tokyo Olympics.

I spoke into the robot's microphone, and indeed it was able to recognize the language being spoken to him and reply in kind. In Singapore, a humanoid robot named Nadine is already working as a receptionist and assistant at the Nanyang Technological University, and—using the same technology as other personal assistants on the market, like Siri—she can answer any question someone might ask, whether it's related to the university or a recommendation for the best restaurant in the area. And as I experienced several times, many of these robots are programmed to have a sense of humor. At the entrance to a men's clothing store near the Akihabara train station in Tokyo, I saw a robot that sang, danced, and waved its arms, inviting passersby to enter the establishment. Unlike some other human receptionists, he seemed genuinely happy, smiling from ear to ear.

THE END OF RESTAURANT WAITERS?

Automation in the restaurant industry is advancing at full speed. I came across this phenomenon for the first time in Miami in 2016, when I had lunch at one of Panera's 1,800 U.S. locations. McDonald's, Wendy's, Pizza Hut, and virtually every other fast-food chain in America and Europe are using touch screens to allow customers to place their orders electronically instead of having to interact with a human waiter. As soon as I entered the Panera, I saw five small metal towers topped with tablets displaying the menu, images of all the items, and their respective prices. I swiped through the various dishes with my finger, and—as with any online shopping site—I hit *okay* to confirm my purchase and inserted my credit card.

"Thank you, Andrés," the machine instantly replied. I was stunned for a moment, wondering how Panera knew who I was, because the tablet had never asked me for my name. But of course it had picked it up from my credit card and treated me as if we were old acquaintances. Then I walked a few steps over to an area where other customers were waiting to pick up their orders, and I realized that there weren't any employees to let me know when my food was ready. Instead there was a TV screen on the wall with a chronological list of pending orders along with the names of the people who had placed these orders. When a name reached the top of the list, his or her order was ready to pick up. But what amazed me most about the whole process was the fact that there was a restaurant employee standing at the counter, ready to take orders, but very few customers ever approached her. They seemed to prefer to interact with the tablets.

According to industry spokespeople, the main reason restaurants are becoming more and more automated isn't to save costs but to satisfy their customers: growing numbers of people—especially the younger generations—would rather place their orders through tablets or on their cell phones. I asked several industry representatives why they preferred this to interacting with a person, and the reason was simple: young people don't to want to spend time waving a hand or trying—often unsuccessfully—to make eye contact with a waiter to get his or her attention. Why go through all that trouble when you can simply order your food electronically? Why sit at a table for ten minutes for a waiter to bring you your bill when you can swipe a card and pay it directly whenever you're ready? All of this is causing many restaurants to reduce their number of waiters, whose job is now mostly limited to delivering food to customers' tables. And soon enough, even that could change, with robots or conveyor belts performing that task.

While in Japan, I ate at a number of sushi restaurants that have neither hostesses, waiters, nor cooks. Even the chef who prepares the sushi is a robot. And judging by the success they're having, they will likely be joined by restaurants serving other kinds of food. Japanese customers, attracted by the low prices and the speed at which automated restaurants operate, are turning to them in ever-growing numbers, often without even realizing that the chef preparing their sushi is a machine. Hamazushi, one of several automated sushi restaurant chains, already operates in 454 locations across Japan. Customers line up in front of a robot hostess who assigns them a table, and then they sit next to a conveyor belt that brings the sushi plates to each and every table. Each of these tables is topped with a tablet computer displaying the menu, a hot water tap for making tea, place settings, chopsticks, and several varieties of soy sauce.

When customers sit down, they choose their preferred dish—there is a picture of all the options, along with their respective prices—and after a few minutes, the tablet bleeps out a little tune and flashes a message that reads "Your order is about to arrive." And indeed, within a few seconds, a plate with a sign indicating the specific table arrives on the conveyor belt. When their meal is over, customers swipe their credit card through the tablet, and leave.

JENKINS: HALF OF ALL BANK EMPLOYEES WILL DISAPPEAR

Just as robots are threatening the jobs of hotel and restaurant industry workers, the Internet and artificial intelligence are challenging bank employees by creating new ways of investing, lending, and transferring money. Virtual banks, such as Betterment.com, have no physical headquarters, which allows them to reduce costs and charge lower fees than traditional banks. And while these virtual banks are handling more and more private investments, they also face growing competition from other online payment platforms that are increasingly performing routine transactions such as money transfers that, until recently, were carried out only by brick-and-mortar banks. Growing numbers of people are moving money around through their computers and cell phones, and many of the companies that are performing these transactions, including Square, Google Wallet, Apple Pay, and Venmo, are not—nor were they ever—in the banking industry.

Former Barclays CEO Antony Jenkins shook the banking industry to the core in 2015 when he predicted that by 2025, banks will have cut their number of branches—and the number of employees—in half. Jenkins, who had already begun executing a layoff plan for some 19,000 employees when he left the bank, said in a speech that the "Uber moment" had come for the financial world. He said technology is "an unstoppable force," and predicted that many of the large, traditional banks would either merge or disappear in the coming years because they wouldn't be able to compete with the new virtual banks or payment systems like PayPal in the United States or Alipay in China.

He wasn't exaggerating. In northern Europe, the number of bank branches has already started to plummet. Whereas in 2004 there were twenty-five banks per 100,000 citizens in Scandinavian countries, that number dropped to seventeen by 2014, and is projected to fall to eight by 2025, according to predictions by the World Bank and a Citi GPS report. In the United States, the number of bank branches is expected to fall by 33 percent during that same period, and by 45 percent in Latin America, according to the Citi GPS report.

"The return on having a physical network is diminishing," says Jonathan Larsen, Citigroup's former global head of retail and mortgage, in that report.

> Branches and associated staff costs make up about 65% of the total retail cost base of a larger bank and a lot of these costs can be removed via automation. The pace of staff reductions so far has been gradual (~2% per year or ~11–13% from peak levels pre-crisis). We believe there could be another 30% reduction in staff between 2015 and 2025, shifting from the recent 2% per year decline to 3% per year, mainly from retail banking automation.

Bank CEOs are asking themselves: Why maintain a network of brick-and-mortar banks with human tellers to make cash deposits and handle checks when these transactions can be easily automated and growing numbers of clients are choosing to go paperless? Cash—the bank's raw material, which was already affected by the advent of credit cards—is becoming even more obsolete in the age of electronic payments. Some countries, like Denmark, are seriously considering eliminating cash altogether. In Europe's Nordic countries, even beggars have gone online: since they know most people don't carry cash anymore, they ask for transfers to their cell phones. "Could you transfer me a few cents?" they ask.

REAL ESTATE AGENTS REPLACED BY ALGORITHMS

In California, more and more home buyers are looking for properties using algorithms, which charge a 2 percent commission on each sale, rather than real estate agents, who charge 6 percent. REX Real Estate Exchange, an automated real estate company, uses artificial intelligence to locate potential buyers in a matter of seconds, making it much more efficient than the massive listings used by traditional real estate agencies.

Instead of putting the information on a general sales listing that goes to everybody in the hopes that someone out there will be interested in the property, REX analyzes hundreds of thousands of consumer data points to identify specific people who might be interested in that specific house. For example, the company's computers identify young couples who are buying baby clothes, because if they're having a child, they might be needing a larger home. Or if someone is constantly buying construction materials and home repair products, they might be ready for a newer property. On the other hand, the REX algorithms will automatically ignore someone who just bought a massive flat-screen television, because there's little chance that this person will be moving anytime soon. All this information is for sale, and it represents the daily bread of data analysts.

"The fact that you bought a hammer itself isn't very informative to us," says Jack Ryan, CEO of REX. "The changes in the rate at which you're buying home supplies is very important to us." Next, REX emails a first round of ads to thousands of potentially interested parties. Then if some five hundred people click on these ads in their email, the computer can find, in real time, the common characteristics among them, and email the ad to thousands of other people who share their profile.

As of 2018, REX was employing twenty-two human real estate agents in its offices in New York, Austin, Denver, and California to help clients navigate the company's website or show a property in person, CNBC reported. But these agents are often accompanied by a robot programmed to answer some seventy-five questions that an agent would be hard pressed to know off the top of his or her head. If a client wants to know when was the last time that the property's roof was replaced or the pool was resurfaced, the robot is there to provide answers. How long will it be before the robots are showing houses on their own, without their human companions?

AUTOMATED GUARDS AND INSPECTORS

Even security guards at department stores, banks, and apartment buildings are being automated. Advances in sensors and their abilities to detect anomalies are increasingly replacing human surveillance systems. But what, you might ask, about the security guards who sit surrounded by screens streaming feeds from closed-circuit TV cameras and monitor what's happening on these screens? We are still seeing such guards in supermarkets and office buildings, but that isn't likely to last much longer. Computers have a distinct advantage over humans because—unlike people—intelligent machines don't take breaks, have lapses in concentration, or spend time chatting on their cell phones. Plus their memories are easily searchable.

And what about the inventory inspectors who, with little notebooks in hand, visit vending machines at the end of the day to determine how much merchandise has been sold and needs to be replaced? This task has ceased to exist in many places. Thanks to the so-called Internet of Things—the new technology that allows things to be connected up with one another online—today's vending machines have sensors that detect for themselves how many items are missing; they then communicate that information directly to the distributor without the need for human intervention. And in a matter of years, the delivery truck will be an autonomous vehicle, and the person in charge of restocking the vending machine won't be a flesh-and-blood human but a robotic arm that will come out of the truck.

The same will be true of water, electricity, and machine inspectors. New automatic sensors connected to the Internet will replace human inspectors of all kinds. In cities like Doha, São Paulo, Beijing, and Barcelona, for example, water pipes have already been equipped with sensors that track the flow and detect leaks, allowing them to save huge amounts of money. In the near future, it will be possible to place cheap sensors on light poles near sidewalks and in other public places to detect sounds and images, which will reduce the need for actual guards, inspectors, and police officers.

WILL ROBOTS REPLACE DOCTORS?

Even medical doctors will have to get used to working with robots. According to Silicon Valley multimillionaire innovator Vinod Khosla, technology will replace 80 percent of the work done by doctors, starting with diagnostics. Today, in some of the best U.S. hospitals, many diagnostic tests are being performed by IBM's Watson supercomputer, which can analyze far more data than any single doctor. While a physician makes his decisions based on his own experience and acquired knowledge, the Watson computer at Memorial Sloan Kettering Cancer Center in New York makes its diagnostics based on the medical histories of 1.5 million patients and 2 million pages of academic articles published in scientific journals.

What doctor could compete with that? Watson can take the symptoms, genetics, and medical histories of each patient and compare them with hundreds of thousands of similar cases, some successful, others not, and make a decision based on solid statistics as to what treatments work best in each and every case. Who should we trust more, a doctor with the experience of a few thousand patients, or a computer with access to millions of clinical cases? If our grandchildren or future anthropologists come across the television show *House*—in which the main character, a diagnostic medicine specialist named Dr. Gregory House, imposes his diagnoses on his colleagues based mostly on his instincts and beliefs—they may raise their eyebrows and scream, "*What?* Is that how medicine was practiced in the early twenty-first century?"

As we will see in the chapter dealing with the future of medicine, the gurus of medical technology agree that medicine is no longer a practice based on the personal experience of professional doctors being able to sniff out a solution, but a science based on data provided by smart machines. Instead of doctors listening to the heart with a stethoscope, eyes closed so they can concentrate, and measuring blood pressure with a rubber cuff around the arm, as has long been the practice, digital devices with more precise technologies will be used. Some of them are already on the market. And when it comes to surgeries, which in many cases are already being performed by robots, they will be handled almost exclusively with robotic hands, which tremble much less than human ones.

SIRI, I HAVE A HEADACHE

New technologies will allow us to perform growing numbers of medical tests at home, resulting in fewer trips to a doctor's office or a hospital. Many of us are already using search engines like Google, or the personal assistants on our phones, like Siri, or virtual assistants such as Alexa or Cortana, to ask for medical advice. And thanks to artificial intelligence, these personal assistants will soon be able to respond to medical queries as well as or even better than many doctors. Alexa, Amazon's virtual assistant, a little intelligent loudspeaker that I have in my own home, can already give me precise instructions on what to do when I have anything from a headache to a heart attack, or how to perform cardiopulmonary resuscitation on a person in an emergency.

As we move forward, we will be increasingly relying on Siri, Alexa, or their successors for answers to our medical questions. If our children have a fever, the first step won't be to go to the doctor's office. Instead, it will be to consult a robot, which—based on the information we give it, plus what it receives from its sensors—will decide whether to recommend an aspirin or a trip to the nearest emergency room. What tasks will be left to the doctors? I'll talk more about that later in the book, but here's a preview: it will have a lot to do with explaining intelligent machines' diagnoses to patients and holding people's hand during the process.

As robots become more highly skilled and less expensive, even anesthesiologists will be replaced by robots. In the United States, an automatic sedation system called Sedasys, from Johnson & Johnson, was approved in 2013 for patients undergoing a colonoscopy. The system allowed one doctor to monitor up to ten patients simultaneously, instead of a one-to-one doctor-to-patient ratio, thus dramatically reducing hospital costs. While sales of Sedasys were recently discontinued, among other things because of pricing issues and anesthesiologists' objections, it's only a matter of time until a new version of it becomes a must for most hospitals.

What about pharmacists? you may be asking yourself. They will have to reinvent themselves as much or more so than doctors. For the past several years, the University of California at San Francisco has been using a pharmaceutical robot that has filled over 2 million prescriptions without a single mistake, and its example is being followed by many hospitals across the United States. By comparison, average human pharmacists make a mistake in about 1 percent of prescriptions they fill.

ROBOTS WILL BE LAWYERS AND EVEN JUDGES

Robots are handling growing numbers of chores at law firms and are increasingly offering legal advice to the outside world. In 2016, the giant U.S. law firm DLA Piper, with over four thousand attorneys across thirty countries, used a computer program designed by the artificial intelligence company Kira Systems to analyze corporate contracts and propose changes, which were tasks ordinarily assigned to young lawyers who had just joined the firm. Meanwhile, many other firms are starting to use online legal services platforms such as LegalZoom and Rocket Lawyer to collect data, something that used to be done by young associates or paralegals.

These same online platforms are also offering customer services such as writing deeds, commercial contracts, and even divorce papers. In other words, the algorithms they use are skipping right past the lawyers, resulting in automated legal services that end up being much cheaper for their clients. Just as online websites have replaced many travel agencies, legal websites are replacing many attorneys who used to handle routine tasks like preparing real estate rental contracts or prenuptial agreements.

THE CASE OF THE ISRAELI APPEALS COURT JUDGES

Even judges—members of a highly prestigious profession demanding skills we wouldn't normally associate with computers, like the ability to use good judgment and common sense—are at risk of being replaced by much more efficient algorithms. According to their advocates, these computer programs are not prejudiced and can issue far more impartial verdicts than humans. This is no joke: a study done by Professor Shai Danziger, now at Tel Aviv University in Israel, which examined the rulings by eight Israeli judges over a ten-month span, found that they handed down more generous judgments after having lunch.

According to this study, published in the American journal *Proceedings of the National Academy of Sciences* in 2011, the eight judges—who were in charge of accepting or rejecting prisoners' requests for paroles or sentence reductions—approved roughly two thirds of the requests they handled early in the morning. But later in the morning, the number of applications they approved fell dramatically . . . until lunchtime. After eating, the judges again tended more toward clemency.

Danziger and his coauthors concluded that the judges' grumpiness increased as time passed since breakfast, affecting their verdicts. They speculated that it could be attributed to two factors. The first had to do with the judges' blood sugar levels, which decreased progressively as the hours went on since their last meal. The second key factor didn't have to do with the amount of time that had passed, but rather the number of cases over which they had presided. According to this latter explanation, decision-making is an arduous and exhausting task, and it was the caseload that made them crankier and led them to issue harsher verdicts. Whichever the case may be, the study concluded that the judges hadn't shown a racial or gender-based bias in rendering their rulings. The primary constant among their verdicts was simply the time of day. In other words, robotic judges could be much more impartial than humans.

ROBOTIC PROFESSORS ARE ALREADY TEACHING CLASSES

When it comes to education, there are already robots in the marketplace that promise to carry out a number of tasks currently performed by teachers. According to their manufacturers, these robots have several advantages over human educators, including the fact that they have infinite patience when it comes to explaining things. Unlike human teachers, who tend to get exasperated after several unsuccessful attempts to explain something to their students, a robotic teacher can explain things in hundreds of different ways. If a student doesn't follow a particular explanation, the robot can move on to the next one, and the next one, and so on.

One of the most charming robot professors I met, and who I'll describe in detail later in the book, was Professor Einstein, a smart doll standing fifteen inches tall with the face and white hair of the world-known Nobel Prize–winning physicist. The doll has multiple facial expressions and gestures, and when it says something mischievous, it even sticks out its tongue. The creators of Professor Einstein claim the robot is able to explain physics and mathematics to students better than most human teachers because it has dozens of alternative teaching methods, depending on whether the student learns better verbally or visually, from playing or by solving problems. In other words, if the student doesn't understand the lesson as it's being explained orally, Professor Einstein can explain it in a visual manner by showing a video or illustration. And while robotic teachers aren't about to replace their human counterparts, they can at least help children with their homework. If young people now prefer interacting with tablets rather than human beings in a restaurant, why should it be any different when it comes to a classroom or doing their homework?

BIONIC SOLDIERS: HALF HUMANS, HALF ROBOTS?

The field of robotics is advancing at such a pace that even cyborgs—those half-human, half-robot warriors we saw in Arnold Schwarzenegger movies—could come true. I saw evidence of this with my own eyes when I interviewed Dr. Hugh Herr, also known as the Bionic Man. Herr is currently serving as director of the Biomechatronics group at MIT's Media Lab, and I had him as a guest on my television show. While I knew his personal story well (he had been the cover story in many major magazines) I had never thought about the potential impact his discoveries might have for the future of humanity.

Herr had been an avid mountain climber from a very young age, and was considered something of a child prodigy in the climbing world. When he was seventeen, he and a partner were climbing in the northeastern United States when they became trapped for four days during a blizzard; he suffered severe frostbite, and doctors were forced to amputate both his legs below the knee. When he was fitted with artificial limbs, Herr couldn't understand how, with all the new technology available to us, the prosthetics being used were still nothing more than the same stiff pieces of metal that had been used for centuries. So he set out to create his own prosthetic limbs: he studied mechanical engineering at MIT and completed his doctorate in biophysics at Harvard. After that, he set up his laboratory on the MIT campus and began exploring new technologies for increasing the physical capabilities of human beings, starting with his own body. His dream was, quite literally, to be able to climb mountains again.

Today Herr uses his own bionic legs to climb everything from stairs to mountains more easily and more powerfully than anyone with natural limbs. While spring-based prostheses like those used by South African sprint runner Oscar Pistorius are passive extensions of the human body, Herr's legs are intelligent, with their own power supply, six computers, and twenty-four separate sensors. They allow him to walk and run much more naturally and powerfully. During our interview, he told me that while the rest of us may keep a dozen or so pairs of shoes in our closet, he has more than a dozen different pairs of legs that he uses for walking, running, and every sort of rock or ice climbing imaginable.

According to Herr, his inventions will allow us to put an end to physical impossibilities and delete the word *disabled* from our vocabulary. With bionic arms or legs, people with physical limitations can be as able as any other, and perhaps even more so. "You cannot, with a straight face, label me as disabled," he told me. "My ultimate dream for the world is that disability is no more, and I believe that this will come to pass in this twenty-first century . . . I think fifty years from now, most disabilities will have been eliminated. Blindness, paralysis, severe depression, all these disabilities of today will be eliminated."

But isn't all this potentially dangerous? I asked. Couldn't it lead to a world of half-human, half-robot supersoldiers who could overpower the world with their bionic arms and legs? Herr shrugged, and replied that since the Stone Age, the armies with more advanced technology have held an advantage over those with more primitive tools. "I call that 'augmentation,'"

Herr explained. "Augmentation is a technological enhancement that enables us to overcome our normal physiological levels. You know, augmentation technology has been here for a very long time. It's actually pervasive in society. It's so pervasive that it's commonplace, and we often don't recognize it as such. The bicycle is an example: I can hop on a bicycle and go from point A to point B much faster and with much less energy than by using my own legs. The automobile is another profound example. So there's augmentation all around us. It's pervasive. So as we march into the future, there will just be more and more levels and forms of augmentation."

THE SOLDIER ROBOTS OF SOUTH KOREA

In South Korea, I got a bit of a preview of the world Herr was describing to me. While for years the United States has been using unmanned aerial vehicles known as drones to fight terrorists in the Middle East, and is increasingly automating its armed forces, few countries are developing robotic soldiers as quickly as South Korea. Faced with constant threats from its neighbor to the north, South Korea is thinking about replacing a significant number of troops along the demilitarized zone with robots.

"Our soldiers are currently hunkered down in a bunker, their rifles aimed permanently north, but they're freezing to death," Junku Yuh, director of robotics at the prestigious Korea Institute of Science and Technology (KIST), told me. "But very soon we will be replacing them with robots, which our soldiers will be operating remotely from a heated building. So we will need far fewer soldiers, and if the enemy attacks us, they will be attacking robots, not men."

A South Korean arms company has already produced a robotic machine gun turret known as the Super aEgis II, which has a firing range of 2.5 miles and is paired with a loudspeaker whose voice has a range of nearly 2 miles. The sound is delivered with extraordinary precision, issuing a warning to a potential target advancing from the north before they are fired upon. "Turn back," it says in rapid-fire Korean. "Turn back or we will shoot." And the *we* is important, because there is a human being supervising the robotic turret from a remote location who must manually enter a password and give the order to shoot before the machine gun will open fire. However, as the manufacturer says, human supervision is simply there to calm the public, because the robot is perfectly capable of fulfilling its mission without the need for human approval. The most important thing about the robot—which has already been sold to the armed forces of Dubai, Abu Dhabi, and Qatar—is that it identifies potential threats through cameras and sensors that the company claims are so acute that they can even detect whether a suspect is carrying explosives underneath his clothing. That's something that robots can do much better than humans, the company says.

In 2017, another South Korean company, Hankook Mirae, publically debuted a gigantic thirteen-foot-tall robot soldier known as Method-2 that is eerily reminiscent of the ones in science fiction movies. According to the company, the massive robot can cross all kinds of terrain where human soldiers can't venture without protection, such as the demilitarized zone along the border with North Korea.

I asked several engineers and manufacturers in South Korea whether there was any danger that the robots could be hacked or make mistakes that end up killing innocent people. Most replied that the danger is no greater than the dangers posed by machines operated directly by humans. A number of them cited the case of the Germanwings air disaster in 2015, in which the copilot, Andreas Lubitz, deliberately crashed his plane into the Alps, resulting in the death of 150 passengers.

Couldn't that tragedy have been averted, they asked me, by prohibiting humans from overriding computers in the navigation decision-making process?

FOR THE FIRST TIME, TECHNOLOGY IS GROWING FASTER THAN EMPLOYMENT

Techno-skeptics have serious doubts as to whether all these technological advances will actually result in a happier world. Instead, they're predicting a huge increase in unemployment, arguing that the old axiom that technology always creates more jobs than it eliminates is no longer valid. While it was true in the past, it doesn't hold up today, because—as stipulated by Moore's law—technological advances are now happening so quickly that they aren't leaving enough time for the new jobs to be created, they say.

Primitive humans took tens of thousands of years to spread technological advances such as fire and the wheel around the world. That allowed for the creation of new applications and new jobs for newly discovered technologies. But since then, the time frames of technological progress have shrunk drastically. In the eighteenth century, it took humanity 119 years before the sewing machine spread outside Europe, whereas in the twentieth century, it took only seven years for the Internet to spread from the United States across the globe. Today, in the twenty-first century, WhatsApp—the cell phone messaging program invented by two people in their twenties—had 700 million followers in just six years of existence. It took Christianity nineteen centuries to achieve that same number of followers.

Another example of today's technological acceleration is the number of years it takes for technologies to reach 25 percent of Americans. While the United States began using electricity in the early nineteenth century, it took forty-six years before the service reached 25 percent of the population. When the telephone was invented, it took thirty-four years for it to be adopted by the same number of people. With radio, the figure went down to thirty-two years; with television, twenty-six years; with personal computers, fifteen years; with cell phones, twelve years; with the Internet, seven years; and with Facebook, just four years.

The people in the nineteenth century whose job it was to light gas streetlamps had several decades to change their jobs while the use of electric lighting was expanding. Today, salespeople, security guards, cashiers, and even surgeons are finding their jobs threatened by robots and algorithms almost overnight. They have much less time to reinvent themselves.

AT&T EMPLOYED 758,000 PEOPLE, GOOGLE EMPLOYS 55,000

According to the techno-pessimists, one of the driving forces behind growing technological unemployment is that many of the current advances are in the field of software, an industry that generates far fewer jobs than the manufacturing industries of the nineteenth and twentieth centuries. Many of the technological innovations of the twentieth century in the automotive, aeronautical, and computer industries resulted in producing a machine—like a car—that required a large amount of labor to be manufactured and that would have to be replaced every so often. Software, on the other hand, takes far fewer people to create, requires much less maintenance, and can be updated without being thrown away.

In the 1980s, 8.2 percent of U.S. jobs were created by new technology companies that were born during that same decade. In the 1990s, that percentage fell to 4.2, and in the 2000s it was down to 0.5 percent, according to some studies. It can be no coincidence, then, that some of the world's largest technology companies have far fewer employees than manufacturing companies did a few decades ago. In 1964, when AT&T was the most valuable company in America, it employed 758,000 workers. Today, however, Alphabet—Google's mother company, which at the time of this writing has the highest market value in the world—employs 75,000 people, less than 10 percent of the number of people who worked for AT&T in its heyday.

BLOCKBUSTER HAD 60,000 EMPLOYEES, NETFLIX HAS 5,400

There are plenty of examples of new technologies created by people in their twenties taking down massive corporations, though it is also true that many of these new technologies made the cost of products cheaper, leaving people with more disposable income with which to buy more things and therefore create jobs in other industries. Blockbuster, the video rental chain that employed 60,000 people in 2004, went bankrupt in 2013 after being wiped out by Netflix, a company that started with a mere 30 employees. Netflix started with DVD rentals delivered straight to your door, and later brought movies directly into our bedrooms with streaming videos and movies on demand. Their subscription service gives us the convenience of enjoying movies at home without having to go to a rental store and get them. But while Blockbuster had tens of thousands of employees, Netflix—which has 87 million subscribers in 190 countries and generates much more income than Blockbuster did—has a mere 5,400 full-time employees, though it does generate thousands of other indirect jobs through the television shows it produces.

Likewise, Kodak—the emblematic photography company that had been in existence for more than a century and employed 145,000 people in 1988—went bankrupt in 2012 for not innovating fast enough and failing to become a leader in digital photography. It was largely disrupted by Instagram, a start-up of just thirteen employees that popularized the sharing of photographs from one cell phone to another.

It's no secret that new technology companies employ far fewer people than traditional manufacturing firms. According to the World Bank, the computing and telecommunications industries employ, on average, only 1 percent of workers in developed countries. Even in the United States, the country that produced Google, Amazon, and Facebook, tech jobs represent only 0.5 percent of total employment.

"THE FACTORIES OF THE FUTURE WILL HAVE TWO EMPLOYEES: A MAN AND A DOG"

One of the most vocal techno-pessimists is Martin Ford, a former Silicon Valley entrepreneur who wrote *The Rise of Robots: Technology and the Threat of a Jobless Future.* He is convinced that smart machines will kill many more jobs than they will create in the future. When I interviewed him, he assured me that he is not anti-tech, but that we must have economic and political responses in place before the coming wave of technological unemployment takes us by surprise. Ford has become a passionate spokesperson for establishing a universal basic income for everybody so that people can cope with the coming job disruption.

According to Ford, in the past, automation was a phenomenon that used to be concentrated in one industry at a time. This allowed workers displaced by technology in one field to move into another emerging industry. But our current situation is quite different because artificial intelligence can be utilized in every field of work, and automation is being incorporated simultaneously in virtually all industries. A robot that knows how to answer a phone, take dictation, transcribe, and translate a text will not only replace secretaries and translators but potentially every other job. That's why virtually every industry that exists today will need fewer workers going forward, and why that transformation could happen much faster than many people expect, Ford told me.

"While innovations in robotics produce tangible machines that are often easily associated with particular jobs (a hamburger-making robot or a precision assembly robot, for example), progress in software automation will likely be far less visible to the public; it will often take place deep within corporate walls, and it will have more holistic impacts on organizations and the people they employ," Ford wrote.

As the algorithms become more and more intelligent, this process will accelerate. For example, it was once thought that most executives are irreplaceable because they are constantly making decisions and implementing them. But artificial intelligence is already learning to do exactly that. The education of intelligent machines takes place in two stages, Ford explains. First, an algorithm is created and fed with known data, and then it is asked to solve a similar problem. For example, the computer program that determines which emails land in our inbox and which are diverted into our junk folder was trained by the millions of emails that we respectively classified as either important or trash. And after having been fed with examples of both classes of emails, the algorithm begins to decide for itself which emails to send to which mailbox.

In much the same way, the company algorithms that read an executive's emails are learning what kinds of decisions they make and why they do it, and—according to Ford—they'll soon be able to replace a fair number of business managers. In

2013, Google filed a patent application for a computer program that can automatically generate personalized emails and hold conversations over social networks. In other words, this software can answer our emails for us. It can generate responses based on our history of posts and comments on Twitter and Facebook, and it can even match our writing style. "The predictions that can be extracted from data will increasingly be used to substitute for human qualities such as experience and judgment," Ford writes, adding that this will result in fewer executives within corporations. "Whereas today there is a team of knowledge workers who collect information and present analysis to multiple levels of management, eventually there may be a single manager and a powerful algorithm." A well-known joke in Silicon Valley puts it in a more dramatic way. According to it, the factories of the future will have two employees: a man and a dog. The man will be there to feed the dog, and the dog will be there to prevent the man from touching the machines.

FEWER WORKERS COULD MEAN FEWER CONSUMERS

When Ford gave me his pessimistic view of technological advances, I responded with a question that any techno-optimist would ask. Where is it written that replacing many routine and repetitive tasks with intelligent machines is something negative? According to virtually all economists, I argued, technology has helped the world economy grow and has lowered the cost of goods, making it possible for most of the population to live longer and better than our ancestors. Over the past few decades, technological innovations have coincided with a reduction—not an increase—of poverty around the world, I reminded him. According to data from the United Nations, in 2015, there were 836 million people across the planet living in extreme poverty, or on less than $1.25 a day, down from 1.9 billion in 1990.

I also reminded Ford that people are working less than before. In the agricultural age, our ancestors worked from sunrise to sunset in order to eat, and it wasn't until the twentieth century that most countries settled on a forty-hour workweek. Now, some highly developed nations like the Netherlands are already implementing the twenty-nine-hour workweek. Why shouldn't we expect this trend to continue into the future? I asked him. Why not look forward to a time when we could work fifteen or twenty hours a week and let technology continue reducing the price of all the products we need to enjoy that life?

"That's the outcome that I hope for," Ford replied. "But ask yourself: suppose you are working a minimum-wage job in the United States and right now you might be struggling to even get full-time work and now we're saying, Okay, in the future you're gonna work fifteen hours a week. That sounds great, but how are you gonna survive? Something else has to happen, right? You'll need to get paid a lot more. Technology is making some things cheaper, but the things that really matter, like housing, are not becoming cheaper. Some things are not driven so much by the efficiency of production; they're driven by scarcity of land and so on."

Ford went on to explain that computers, cell phones, and television sets are becoming cheaper thanks to ever-more-efficient production processes. Housing, on the other hand, depends on available square footage and other external factors. "It's kind of hard to imagine that the cost of housing in the United States is gonna collapse and get really cheap all of a sudden because of technology," he said, stressing that it was not entirely true that technological advances will help reduce the costs of everything and allow us to work less across the board.

The other serious problem will be that, with fewer people working—or at least working fewer hours, as they are replaced by smart machines—the global economy could potentially shrink. "In order for the economy to thrive, you gotta have consumers out there who are capable of buying what's being produced. Companies can't just sell into thin air, they need people to buy, and that's ultimately what drives the whole economy. So, if we get into a situation where there might be lots of unemployment, or where wages are driven lower and lower because it's hard to find jobs and people have to compete for those jobs, it means that people will have less to spend. The risk you face is that you get into a downward spiral where there are few people out there to buy things being produced and companies are competing and we get into a deflationary scenario," Ford explained.

TECHNO-OPTIMISTS: IT'S ALL FOR THE BEST

Does technological unemployment really warrant such concerns? Techno-optimists have always dismissed the naysayers outright, arguing that the techno-pessimists have been sounding the alarm for centuries—warning that the latest technologies would eventually result in a jobless world—and that the techno-skeptics have been consistently wrong. During the Industrial Revolution in the late eighteenth and early nineteenth centuries, textile workers in the United Kingdom burned their sewing machines to protest the new automatic looms, which were beginning to replace human workers. A protest in Nottingham in 1811, now referred to as the Luddite rebellion, became a rallying cry against technological unemployment. But what happened? According to the optimists, it was the exact opposite of what the Luddites had feared: the new automatic looms greatly reduced the cost of clothing, which left people with more disposable income they could spend on other goods and services, generating greater employment and well-being for all.

Also contrary to the textile workers' concerns is the fact that new technology created new jobs that did not exist before. Thanks to the new automatic looms, the huge increase in global clothing consumption created a demand for designers, textile engineers, machine operators, distributors, marketing managers, and many other jobs that either didn't exist or weren't previously necessary to the industry. According to a study by Boston University economist James Bessen, the number of textile workers actually quadrupled between 1830 and 1900, and the increase in jobs generated by other industries thanks to higher levels of disposable income was equally impressive.

KEYNES WAS WRONG ABOUT TECHNOLOGICAL UNEMPLOYMENT

As early as 1858, in *Grundrisse: Foundations of the Critique of Political Economy,* Karl Marx had written that "the means of labour passes through different metamorphoses, whose culmination is the machine." A 1928 headline in *The New York Times* read, "March of the Machines Makes Idle Hands." The world-renowned economist John Maynard Keynes had warned of technological unemployment in the 1930s when he predicted that the world would suffer from high industrial unemployment "due to our discovery of means of economising the use of labour outrunning the pace at which we can find new uses for labour." And in the 1960s, President John F. Kennedy noted that computers and robots were spreading through offices and factories, and that one of the main challenges of the coming world would be "to maintain full employment at a time when automation, of course, is replacing men." However, all these predictions proved to be wrong, because—according to the optimists—technology always ended up creating more jobs than it eliminated.

THE PRINTING PRESS AND THE AUTOMOBILE CREATED MORE JOBS

The textile workers' rebellion in the early nineteenth century reverberated through just about every other industry. In 1814, when workers at *The Times* of London learned that the paper was to be printed by an automated steam press invented by a German engineer named Friedrich Koenig, they went on strike. They went back to work only when the company assured them that—for the time being—they would not be losing their jobs.

But their fears proved to be unwarranted, at least in the nineteenth century. When these workers went on strike, the prototype of the new printing press—which was powered by steam generated by a coal-fired boiler—could print 1,100 pages an hour, which was five times the capacity of a manual press. A few years later, in 1820, the steam printer had been refined and could put out 2,000 pages an hour. By 1828, the capacity had doubled to 4,000.

A few decades later, with the invention and proliferation of the rotary press in the 1860s, printers were turning out more than 30,000 pages every hour. And by the 1890s, with the arrival of electricity and new Linotype machines and photomechanical processes that allowed for the publication of photographs, *The New York Herald* could produce 90,000 copies, complete with color illustrations. "This stream of innovation, combined with greater press freedom, drove the growth of a vibrant and fast-growing newspaper industry in the United States and Europe, creating millions of jobs in printing, journalism, and other related fields," says a study by the McKinsey Global Institute.

The same thing occurred in the mid-twentieth century, when Henry Ford began mass-producing cars, and people who operated horse-drawn carriages protested out of fear that these new rolling machines would leave them jobless. And indeed, the automobile industry left many carriage drivers, stable masters, and blacksmiths without work. But not many people at the time anticipated that the advent of the car would generate millions of new jobs in auto factories, gas stations, and mechanics shops, and in the building and maintenance of asphalt roads. Today, there are millions more people working in the automotive industry than there were driving horse-drawn carriages more than a century ago. The big question is whether that will continue to be the case in the future. With growing numbers of us using private taxi services like Uber, or if autonomous cabs become more economically viable and convenient than having our own car, we will have to see what happens to the number of car industry workers.

ATMS DIDN'T MAKE BANK TELLERS GO EXTINCT

The classic example put forth by techno-optimists is that of ATMs. In the 1980s, when ATMs began to proliferate across the country, a panic broke out among bank employees. Many predicted that these new machines would soon put an end to the jobs of traditional bank tellers. But what actually happened was that ATMs allowed for human employees to take on more sophisticated tasks such as offering loans, mortgages, and other customer service duties. This allowed banks to expand their business, open more branches, and employ more people.

While in 1985 there were 60,000 ATMs and 485,000 customer service bank employees in the United States, by 2002 the number of ATMs had grown to 352,000 and the number of bank jobs had risen to 527,000 employees. And, techno-optimists note, this figure doesn't include the thousands more who work to maintain and repair the ATMs themselves.

"Why didn't employment fall?" asks James Bessen, the author of one of the best-known studies on the effects of ATMs. "Because the ATM allowed banks to operate branch offices at lower cost. This prompted them to open many more branches, offsetting the erstwhile loss in teller jobs. At the same time, teller skills changed. Non-routine marketing and interpersonal skills became more valuable, while routine cash handling became less important. That is, although bank tellers performed relatively fewer routine tasks, their employment increased."

Bessen cited several other recent examples in which automation has not reduced employment. In supermarkets, "bar-code scanners reduced cashier's checkout times by 18–19%, but the number of cashiers has grown since scanners were widely deployed during the 1980s," and "e-commerce has also grown rapidly since the late 1990s, now accounting for over 7% of retail sales, but the total number of people working in sales occupations has grown since 2000," Bessen argues. Still, though, as we have previously noted, the expansion of banks is coming to an end, and many financial institutions are beginning to close subsidiaries that aren't able to compete successfully with virtual banks and online platforms.

Another example Bessen cites has to do with automated answering services like voicemail, which, he argues, haven't wiped out the jobs of telephone operators but rather have changed what they do. Today, he argues, receptionists perform a number of different tasks, and many of them have become all-purpose receptionists. While the number of telephone operators has fallen dramatically, from 317,000 in 1980 to 57,000 today, the number of receptionists has grown from 438,000 to

1,035,000. There are still receptionists who answer the phone and take messages, but they're also doing many other things. So far the net balance between these jobs and technological advances has been positive, both in the quality and quantity of work, Bessen says in his study. Again, the big question is what will happen in the future when robotic receptionists become popular.

AMAZON BUYS MORE ROBOTS AND HIRES MORE PEOPLE

The most recent case of job creation resulting from technological disruption is that of Amazon, techno-optimists say. In 2016, Amazon increased its number of transport and cargo robots by 50 percent—from 30,000 to 45,000—in order to streamline its operations. When news of this broke, there was speculation that the automation of Amazon warehouses would result in the loss of 15,000 jobs. However, it had the opposite effect. Amazon hired 50 percent *more* people during that same time frame and announced in its 2016 fourth-quarter report that it planned to add 100,000 new jobs in the next eighteen months.

Amazon explained that thanks to the robots—which are much more efficient than humans when it comes to loading and unloading distribution trucks—the company managed to significantly reduce its storage and transportation costs. That, in turn, allowed the company to reduce prices, which led more customers to buy products via Amazon, producing a greater demand, which forced the firm to hire more sales and distribution employees. Before, Amazon workers had to roam from one end of a massive warehouse to the other, looking for product locations and climbing mobile staircases to load or unload packages, all of which took a good deal of time. When the website SingularityHub reported on this case, it titled the article—perhaps with a bit of exaggerated optimism—"How Robots Helped Create 100,000 Jobs at Amazon."

ACCORDING TO THE TECHNO-OPTIMISTS, THE KEY LIES IN INDIRECT JOBS

Techno-optimists argue that comparisons between the 758,000 employees AT&T had a few decades ago and the current 55,000 employed by Google or the 76,000 at Apple are misleading. They argue that such a strict, focused comparison doesn't take into account the huge number of jobs indirectly created by Google, Apple, and other technology firms. Since the release of its iPhone in 2007, Apple has built a platform where entrepreneurs from around the world have created hundreds of thousands of applications, generating jobs for 1.9 million people in the United States alone, according to figures from Apple's website. So, the optimists suggest, a more accurate employment figure for Apple would be 1.9 million, not the 76,000.

New technologies increase employment in three ways, according to a study by economists Michael Mandel and Bret Swanson commissioned by the Technology CEO Council. First, they generate direct jobs for the workers who manufacture their products; second, they generate indirect jobs by creating a favorable atmosphere for platforms such as the iPhone, which allow millions of entrepreneurs to invent applications that in turn become new companies themselves; and third, they increase productivity, which makes costs lower and frees up capital so that companies and consumers can invest in other things.

"There is good news," the study says. "With the arrival of powerful new technologies, we stand on the verge of a productivity boom. Just as networking computers accelerated productivity and growth in the 1990s, innovations in mobility, sensors, analytics, and artificial intelligence promise to quicken the pace of growth and create myriad new opportunities for innovators, entrepreneurs, and consumers."

SWANSON: "THERE WILL BE A BOOM IN EMPLOYMENT, NOT UNEMPLOYMENT"

Mandel and Swanson predict that over the coming years, millions of jobs will be created in the manufacturing sector. According to them, this sector has grown very little in recent years because the vast majority of technological investments have taken place in digital industries, which account for barely 25 percent of private-sector employment. There have been relatively few technological investments in factories or in the construction or transportation industries, which account for roughly 70 percent of private-sector employment. According to Mandel and Swanson, the next stage of the information revolution will be new Internet platforms that will allow entrepreneurs to create new companies in manufacturing, transportation, education, and agriculture, among a number of other industries.

When I asked Swanson to give me an example of how jobs might be generated in the manufacturing sector, he told me that 3-D printers and virtual reality headsets will create millions of new jobs. Just as the 2007 emergence of the iPhone opened the door for millions of people who weren't computer programmers to use computer programs, the same thing will happen with 3-D printers, he said. We'll have 3-D printers in our homes, and with them we will be able to make products for ourselves and for selling to others. There will be a boom in employment, not unemployment, he said.

"With a 3-D printer in our house, we could start a new business, we could make clothing or sporting equipment with built-in sensors, smart furniture, parts for drones . . . the possibilities are endless," Swanson told me. "Steve Jobs and the other inventors of the iPhone had no idea of the millions of applications that were made possible by the smartphone. The fascinating thing about these platforms is that they release an amazing wealth of creativity."

"WE'LL BE GARDENERS ON MARS"

One of the most optimistic futurologists I have ever met—so optimistic, in fact, that he founded a company to freeze the brains of dead people in the hopes that, by 2045, scientists will have discovered how to revive them—is José Luis Cordeiro, a Venezuelan researcher affiliated with Singularity University in Silicon Valley, a mecca for techno-optimists from around the world. Like Swanson, Cordeiro is not worried about the possibility of a jobless world.

Over breakfast in Buenos Aires, where we were invited speakers at a conference on innovation, Cordeiro told me that it's impossible to know how technologies will evolve, and that therefore—as was the case with the thousands of apps that emerged from the iPhone—there is no real way to predict what jobs might arise from them.

Not convinced by his argument, I asked him, "So what do you think most of us will be doing in a decade or two? What will the journalists, professors, office workers, lawyers, doctors, and manufacturing workers be doing once the robots have taken our jobs?" Cordeiro gave me the boldest—and wittiest—answer I received out of all the interviews I conducted for this book. "I don't know, maybe we'll be gardeners on Mars," he said with a shrug and a smile.

ANOTHER REASON FOR OPTIMISM: EVERYTHING WILL BE CHEAPER

If there were a pope of techno-optimism, it would probably be Peter Diamandis, the cofounder of Singularity University and the author of the book *Abundance: The Future Is Better Than You Think.* In it, he and his coauthor, Steven Kotler, predict that we will be shifting from a world of scarcity to one of abundance in which there will be more resources and greater prosperity. Thanks to advances in technology, mankind will be able to overcome its biggest current problems, including shortages of oil and drinking water, as well as manufacture cheaper products, making them available to growing numbers of people. As they write:

> Today 99 percent of Americans living below the poverty line have electricity, water, flushing toilets, and a refrigerator; 95 percent have a television; 88 percent have a telephone; 71 percent have a car; and 70 percent even have air-conditioning. This may not seem like much, but one hundred years ago men like Henry Ford and Cornelius Vanderbilt were among the richest on the planet, but they enjoyed few of these luxuries.

Diamandis, who earned a medical degree from Harvard and studied molecular genetics and aerospace engineering at MIT, said in the book that he isn't terribly concerned about technological unemployment because the world economy continues to grow, and he expects the cost of living for everyone to fall dramatically in the next twenty years. "People are concerned about how AI and robotics are taking jobs, destroying livelihoods, reducing our earning capacity, and subsequently destroying the economy," he wrote in a blog post for SingularityHub.

"But what people aren't talking about, and what's getting my attention, is a forthcoming rapid *demonetization* of the cost of living. Meaning—it's getting cheaper and cheaper to meet our basic needs."

HOUSING, TRANSPORTATION, AND FOOD WILL ALL BE CHEAPER

For much of human history, a person's entire income went to paying for shelter, food, and clothing. But now, thanks to advances in technology, the costs of transportation, food, medicine, clothing, and education have fallen significantly, and Diamandis expects them to fall even further. "In the U.S., in 2011, 33% of the average American's income was spent on housing, followed by 16% spent on transportation, 12% spent on food, 6% on healthcare, and 5% on entertainment," he writes. "In other words, almost 75% of Americans' expenditures come from housing, transportation, food, personal insurance, health, and entertainment." The figures are similar in other countries, like China. Thanks to new technologies, there is something of a worldwide "technological socialism" on the horizon, in which "the costs of housing, transportation, food, health care, entertainment, clothing, education, and so on will fall, eventually approaching, believe it or not, zero," Diamandis says.

Furthermore, Diamandis points out that "twenty years ago, most well-off U.S. citizens owned a camera, a video camera, a CD player, a stereo, a video game console, a cellphone, a watch, an alarm clock, a set of encyclopedias, a world atlas, a Thomas guide, and a whole bunch of other assets that easily add up to more than $900,000. Today, all of these things are free on your smart phone."

And this trend will only accelerate as we move into the future. Recalling Martin Ford's argument that the cost of housing will continue to rise because of the limited amount of space in cities, Diamandis argues that one of the main reasons for this—"location, location, location," or the advantages of living close to work—will disappear in coming years, thanks to self-driven cars and the ability to work remotely through virtual reality or the Internet.

"Think about what drives high housing costs," Diamandis writes. "Why does a single-family apartment in Manhattan cost $10 million, while the same square footage on the outskirts of St. Louis can be purchased for $100,000?" The answer is quite simple: their respective locations. People are willing to pay much more for the privilege of being close to their jobs and not having to deal with traffic jams. But all that will change when autonomous cars are ready to drop us off and pick us up from work. If you can spend your commute either working, reading, sleeping, or watching a movie, what does it matter if it takes an hour and a half? Diamandis predicts that more and more people will be moving out of the cities and into the suburbs, and that housing prices will fall. In addition to that, virtual reality will make the location of your home even more irrelevant, he adds. If you can interact with your coworkers through a virtual reality headset, why not work from home? And finally, building costs will be driven down thanks to 3-D printers and robots, which will be doing more and more of the actual work of construction.

When it comes to transportation, which is just behind housing in terms of what we spend the most amount of our money on, costs are already being reduced by Uber, Lyft, and other applications that offer private, low-cost taxi services. And the cost of transportation will fall even further when these services start using autonomous cars. "When Uber rolls out fully autonomous services, your cost of transportation will plummet," Diamandis writes. "Think about all of the related costs that disappear: auto insurance, auto repairs, parking, fuel, parking tickets. Your overall cost of 'getting around' will be 5 to 10 times cheaper when compared to owning a car."

With food, the cost as a percentage of our income has already plummeted in the past century thanks to the green revolution, and it will continue to decrease thanks to advances in genetics, biology, and vertical agriculture. Today, 70 percent of what we pay for food comes from transportation, storage, and packaging. But, according to Diamandis, when transportation is handled by autonomous trucks—which could begin happening as early as in the next five years—and the storage and packaging is handled by robots—which is already happening in some supermarkets—the price of food will fall even more rapidly. It is true that intelligent machines will eliminate many jobs, but techno-pessimists forget to acknowledge that everything will be cheaper, and that many more new jobs will be created, Diamandis said.

ONE THING SEEMS CERTAIN: THERE WILL BE MORE INEQUALITY

Regardless of whether new technologies will create more jobs or not, we are likely to see greater social inequality, because people with higher levels of education will be better prepared to adapt to technological change and to work in the jobs of the future. Robots will replace more manufacturing workers than nuclear physicists, because the latter perform less automatable work and are better equipped to take on new responsibilities. It will be hard for someone who never finished high school and works at a factory to reinvent himself as a data analyst, while an engineer or physicist won't have much trouble making the transition to another job that requires creativity and abstract reasoning.

As robots and other intelligent machines replace more

manual workers, salespersons, receptionists, and administrative assistants performing routine tasks, there will be a widening social gap between people with higher education degrees and those who never finished high school. Education is, and will increasingly be, the secret to survival and success in the labor market. Society will be divided into three general groups. The first will be members of the elites, who will be able to adapt to the ever-changing technological landscape and who will earn the most money, followed by a second group made up primarily of those who provide personalized services to the elite, including personal trainers, Zumba class instructors, meditation gurus, piano teachers, and personal chefs, and finally a third group of those who will be mostly unemployed and may be receiving a universal basic income as compensation for being the victims of technological unemployment. Historian and futurist Yuval Noah Harari has referred to this third category as "the useless class."

Not only will there be higher unemployment, there will be lower wages for those who don't have access to the upper stratum. A 2018 working document from the International Monetary Fund—which does not reflect the official view of the IMF, but is influential among the institution's policy makers—concluded that "automation is very good for growth, and very bad for equality." Frey, the Oxford economist, told me in an interview that most of the jobs of the future will be in the personal services sector, which depend largely on consumer preferences and are more difficult to automate. He added that he's not so much forecasting a jobless future, but "a future of continued polarization, where we see a few new jobs emerging in technology industries and we see a lot of demand for more personal services than are typically lower paid."

So, are we headed for a society in which those who don't write algorithms will end up as Zumba instructors? I asked him. Frey responded that—while it would be an exaggeration to say that a big chunk of the workforce will be made up of Zumba instructors—"when we examined which jobs had been the fastest-growing over the past five years, Zumba instructor was one of them . . . And I think that most new jobs are indeed going to be associated with categories that relate to this type of personal services."

WILL COMPUTERS TAKE OVER?

After my visit to the Oxford Martin School at the University of Oxford, I headed to the Future of Humanity Institute, a nearby think tank that has drawn international attention for its ominous predictions about the potential superpowers of computers. Nick Bostrom, the institute's founding director, had become famous for his recent book on artificial intelligence titled *Superintelligence: Paths, Dangers, Strategies.* Bostrom and his team studied the possible long-term effects of artificial intelligence, and reached a conclusion that seems to come straight out of a science fiction movie: that superintelligent machines will soon have the ability to think for themselves. According to Bostrom, mankind must take precautions starting now—as it did in the twentieth century when scientists produced the first atomic weapons—to prevent its own destruction at the hands of this new source of intelligent life. Bostrom had gained notoriety in academic and business circles after Bill Gates and Elon Musk publicly recommended reading *Superintelligence,* and his book became a *New York Times* bestseller.

After a ten-minute walk through the streets of Oxford, which are lined with tiny shops and restaurants packed with students, I reached the Future of Humanity Institute. I was somewhat skeptical about what I would find there. I must confess, the name of the institution sounded a bit pretentious. I had read on its web page that it was an interdisciplinary research center affiliated with Oxford's Faculty of Philosophy, and I found myself wondering if Bostrom and his research team had real knowledge of mathematics and robotics, or if they were simply a bunch of philosophers speculating about the future.

My concerns increased when I arrived at the center—an architecturally modern building on one of the side streets in the downtown area—and read the office directory in the lobby. In the same building with the Future of Humanity Institute were other similar institutions such as the Centre for Effective Altruism and the Oxford Uehiro Centre for Practical Ethics. Clearly this was the epicenter of Oxford's idealists. But were they anchored in reality, or were they a group of well-intentioned though somewhat naive philosophers and poets? I asked myself.

But as soon as I entered the institute, it became clear to me that it wasn't a den of dreamers. Along with professors of robotics and artificial intelligence, I found researchers with Ph.D.s in cybernetic neurosciences, computational biochemistry, parabolic geometry, and several other related disciplines I had never heard of before. The institute is specifically aimed at studying the long-term impact—looking forward a hundred years or more—that new technologies could have on society and the environment, something that neither governments nor large corporations are doing.

Bostrom, who was in his midforties, is originally from Sweden. He studied philosophy, mathematics, logic, and artificial intelligence at the University of Gothenburg before earning master's degrees in philosophy, physics, and computational neuroscience at Stockholm University and King's College in London and a Ph.D. in philosophy from the London School of Economics. But his primary interest over the past several years has been artificial intelligence.

Bostrom contends that in the same manner as the United States and other nations engaged in an arms race in the twentieth century that resulted in the creation of atomic weapons, we are now in a new competition between countries or companies looking to create an artificial intelligence that exceeds that of humans. Just as past governments and scientific elites argued that if they didn't create an atomic bomb, their enemies would, the same is happening today with artificial intelligence. We are creating superintelligent machines that in the beginning will follow specific orders from a person or group of people, but eventually they will reach a point where they will make decisions on their own, which could affect the interests and even the safety of all of humanity, he says. So in order to avoid this potential catastrophe, Bostrom believes we must establish international safeguards and codes of conduct for artificial intelligence researchers and programmers.

WHAT HAPPENED TO HORSES COULD HAPPEN TO *HOMO SAPIENS*

When I asked him about the future of work, Bostrom told me he considers it very possible that people will become superfluous, just as horses did after the invention of cars. While Bostrom is much less pessimistic about the future of jobs than many of his colleagues, he does say that the horse analogy is perfect to illustrate what could happen to humans. Before the invention of the automobile, horses hauled carriages and plows, which helped to significantly increase productivity, he says. But then carriages were replaced by cars and plows by tractors, reducing the need for horses and leading to a collapse in the world horse population.

Horses were left without the jobs they needed to survive. Could the same thing happen to humans once robots start doing almost all of the world's work? Bostrom asks. The number of horses in the United States plummeted from 26 million in 1915 to just 2 million in 1950. Today, a few horses are used by police officers patrolling parks, but the vast majority of them are used for sporting or leisure activities.

With robots doing more of today's work and greatly increasing productivity, human labor will become less important, Bostrom predicts. We could be headed toward an incredibly wealthy world in which people will have no need to work and where most of those with jobs will be in the arts, humanities, athletics, meditation, or other activities designed to make life more enjoyable. So as Bostrom sees it, the automation of work by robots could ultimately lead either to a gloomy future, like that of horses, or to a blissful world where nobody will have to work at an undesirable job against his or her will.

A WORLD FULL OF UNEMPLOYED PEOPLE COULD BE WONDERFUL

I asked Bostrom if he wasn't worried about the possibility of a world without work. "Not necessarily," he responded. In fact, it could be something great, he added. It is quite possible that over time, as a greater percentage of the population stops working, people's perception of unemployment will change, and having a job will no longer be seen as something positive or indispensable. "My main fear, actually, is not joblessness. In a way, I see unemployment as something that should be our goal, to get machines to do all the things that currently only humans can do so that we don't have to work anymore."

When I looked at him with a mixture of surprise and skepticism and suggested that work isn't just a source of income but also a source of self-esteem, Bostrom disagreed. A world where the unemployed are viewed in a positive light wouldn't be anything new, he said. In previous centuries, aristocrats considered work as something dirty that only the common folk would engage in, he argued. Aristocrats devoted themselves to socializing, reading poetry, and listening to music, and yet they enjoyed the highest social status and felt that they were leading very meaningful lives, he said.

The idea that work is something that gives meaning to our lives is relatively new, and it might well be a fleeting idea, Bostrom said. A superproductive economy thanks to automation could potentially subsidize all human beings, and the concept of work itself would change forever. Seeing that I wasn't entirely convinced, Bostrom went on to point out that even today, there are large sections of society that don't have conventional jobs—students, for example—but who nevertheless lead purposeful lives and enjoy high levels of social approval. And there are entire nations, like Saudi Arabia, where a large percentage of the population doesn't work and has a guaranteed income, and yet these countries are still well regarded.

"Historically, if you look at who were regarded as high-status individuals, the aristocrats were the people who *didn't* have to work in order to live," Bostrom said. "Working was a sign of lower-class status. The more desirable way to spend your time was playing music, going on a hunt, drinking with your friends, tending your garden, traveling, and doing things because you wanted to do them rather than being forced to work. The current era is atypical in the sense that now the highest-status people are CEOs, doctors, lawyers, politicians—people who work hard all day. But that, I think, hasn't been the norm throughout history."

COULD WE BE HAPPY WITHOUT WORK?

But, going back to the example of Saudi Arabia, are people in that country happy not to be working? I asked. "No," he replied. "There seems to be a lot of evidence that there's a fair bit of discontent because they want to work and don't have the ability to change their society. But this is kind of a cultural thing, it's about how the society is set up. So with the right culture, I think a jobless society could be great, but with the wrong culture, it could be hell."

To reach the goal of a society of happily unemployed people, we would have to solve two basic problems: the technological challenge of making sure that intelligent machines do what we want them to do and the economic challenge of guaranteeing that all workers who lose their jobs to automation have an income, he said. "Fortunately, if machines really do gain great human capabilities, that would be a great boost to the economy. You would have massive economic growth because you would have the ability to automate everything. So the resources would be there. It would then be a political question as to how those resources would be distributed."

Bostrom described it as being like a return to the days of the great mammoth hunts, but with much more comfort. According to some anthropologists, prehistoric humans were a relatively workless society and had a lot of free time. When a hunting party of forty men killed a mammoth, there would be enough food to feed the entire community for a couple of months. "They wouldn't squabble over how big to slice everyone's steak," he said. "So if the artificial intelligence revolution happens in a similar sort of way, it would be like having a giant mammoth for all of humanity. Instead of squabbling over how exactly to carve it up, even if some people get slightly more, there could still be more than enough for everybody to get something in that type of scenario."

SOME JOBS WILL DISAPPEAR, BUT MOST WILL BE TRANSFORMED

Bostrom isn't completely convinced by his Oxford colleagues Frey and Osborne's study conclusion that 47 percent of jobs are in danger of being replaced by automation. As he explained to me, "the methodology is really a good idea, but you shouldn't trust any particular number too much . . . The 47 percent figure can be debated." He added that it will be very difficult in the near future to automate jobs that require creativity, social skills, or common sense, because it takes a long time for artificial intelligence to become as effective as humans in those fields.

For example, one of the most automatable jobs mentioned in the Frey report is that of insurance underwriter. In theory, these people collect and process data: in other words, it's routine work that could be done more simply and more quickly by an algorithm. "However," Bostrom says, "when I talk to real-life underwriters, they need to have business relationships with other people. They need to negotiate a fair bit. A lot of it is thinking about what's good for the company in the long run, doing quite complex evaluations. And then selling stuff to other people, convincing them, playing golf with them, which is quite an important skill when it comes to social relations."

Bostrom went on to say that there are some jobs that might seem routine at first glance, but require a lot of common sense. It's very hard to automate common sense. You need that human skill, for instance, to detect if the blueprint for a skyscraper mistakenly calls for it to be built out of wood because someone entered the wrong data into a computer. For now, he explained, artificial intelligence just can't emulate human common sense.

WHAT WOULD HAPPEN IF ROBOTS GO CRAZY?

Without detracting from Bostrom's concern that artificial superintelligence could end up having a mind of its own and destroying humanity, I have a much simpler fear: that the robots and algorithms that we are already using may suddenly go crazy. In 2018, there were many stories in the media about people who got a big fright when their Alexa, Amazon's virtual assistant, unexpectedly let out an eerie laugh. The company later admitted that the machine was mistakenly hearing the command "Alexa, laugh" when other words were spoken and said it was working to fix the problem. I've been even more concerned about the robots going crazy after I had my own personal scary experience with the Alexa that my son had given me as a birthday present.

My Alexa personal assistant lives in a small cylindrical speaker with a light at the top. The speaker turns on when she hears the word *Alexa,* and you can ask her whatever you want, whether it's play a song, check the weather forecast, or read the latest headlines. You can also ask her to order a pizza or buy a book off Amazon's website. According to the company, Alexa is already in more than twenty million American homes.

In our house, we mostly use her to check the weather and listen to the latest National Public Radio (NPR) news broadcasts. More than anything, she's been a good conversation piece, especially when we have visitors from other countries where Alexa still isn't available. But the particular incident I had with her makes me wonder what will happen as we increasingly allow our daily life to be assisted—if not directed—by virtual assistants in our homes, GPS navigators in our cars, medical diagnostic robots in our hospitals, and other intelligent machines everywhere.

I was working one morning in my home office when suddenly I heard a male voice coming from my living room. It never crossed my mind that it could be Alexa, who sits on a small end table next to a sofa, because nobody had asked her to turn on. I was alone, my wife was traveling, and we have no pets. There was nobody around who could have woken her up by calling her name.

At once frightened and frustrated that I didn't have any solid object to grab and use to face a possible robber, I slowly walked into the living room. My heart was pounding. But nobody was there: just Alexa, who had somehow managed to turn herself on and was now broadcasting the latest news on NPR.

I called Amazon's customer service department, and a representative told me that what had happened was quite unusual and could have been caused by a "technical glitch." I called Amazon's media department and was told that the NPR program could have been on pause and that Alexa might have "thought" she heard the word *resume.* Another possibility was that some radio or television elsewhere in the house had uttered the word *Alexa* followed by *NPR,* thus triggering the device. But none of these potential explanations satisfied me because Alexa had been off for days, if not weeks, and there were no other devices in the house that were turned on at the time.

I wrote a column in the *Miami Herald* about what had happened to me, and afterward I was flooded with comments from readers who had experienced similar situations with that and other smart machines. Many recounted the mishaps they suffered because their GPS system had led them to the wrong place. Who can't identify with that? Another reader complained that the sensor in his car was constantly warning him of low pressure in one of the tires, and yet a quick stop at a gas station confirmed that it was properly inflated. These trips to the air pump quickly became as wearisome as they were worthless, so he stopped paying attention to the indicator light on his dashboard altogether, he said. Someone else offered his sympathy, saying that he felt similarly lost when his refrigerator warned him that the ice machine had broken when in fact it was running quite smoothly.

What will happen when, thanks to the Internet of Things, the refrigerator takes it upon itself to call a repair service based on a "technical glitch"? Or in an even more dangerous scenario, what would happen when a robot makes a mistake during open-heart surgery or during a cancer diagnosis? Or when the automated machine guns in South Korea's northern border fail to listen to their human operator because of a "technical failure" and open fire on North Korea? The techno-optimists will argue that the chances of these things happening will be infinitely fewer than mistakes due to human error. But regardless, it's a subject that requires much greater attention. Before we worry about intelligent machines becoming so smart that they can rule the world, we should be worrying about a much more basic threat: that they may simply go crazy.

THERE IS HOPE FOR THE FUTURE, BUT THE TRANSITION WILL BE HARSH

So what are my conclusions after interviewing some of the world's leading futurologists? One of the main ones—in addition to others that I'll address in the final chapter—is that, yes, some jobs will cease to exist, but the vast majority won't disappear. Instead, they'll be transformed. Much of what we are doing today will be done by intelligent machines, and that will require us to constantly update our skills. In many cases, we will have to reinvent ourselves. There's no doubt about it: many of us will lose our jobs. The big question for each of us, and for society in general, is how traumatic the transition to an automated world will be.

I am a techno-optimist, at least in the long term. Automating the labor force will bring about a tremendous increase in productivity, drive down costs, and grow the economy to the benefit of all. But when it comes to the short term, until the increased productivity is translated into massive national revenues, and until we are able to agree on how to distribute these revenues, many workers will be unemployed and marginalized. As much as the techno-optimists are correct in saying that new technologies will create many indirect jobs, there is one incontrovertible fact: the manufacturing companies of the past employed many more people than the data companies of today, and they offered many more social benefits than current service jobs do. And it will take us quite some time to change our current culture that glorifies work, as Bostrom proposes, so those who lose their jobs don't also lose their self-esteem and sense of purpose. Can we really be happy if we're unemployed or if we are all shining one another's shoes? Not at the moment.

Transitioning into a more automated world will be harsh, and it will create even more social turbulence than what we have recently seen in many industrialized countries. The new populist, nationalist, and sometimes racist movements that won elections in the United States and Europe erroneously blame job losses and wage depreciation on immigration. But these are false claims: jobs aren't being threatened by immigrants, but by automation. In fact, illegal immigration in the United States has fallen dramatically in recent years. Apprehensions of undocumented immigrants along the Mexico border totaled 310,000 in 2017, down from 1.7 million in 2000, according to U.S. Border Patrol statistics. As professors Daron Acemoglu of MIT and Pascual Restrepo of Boston University have shown, President Trump won the 2016 presidential election thanks in no small part to the growing sense of discontent with automation in some northern states. "The swing to Republicans between 2008 and 2016 is quite a bit stronger in commuting zones most affected by industrial robots," Acemoglu noted.

We will have to come up with educational and social solutions as soon as possible to prevent short-term technological unemployment from becoming a long-term social disaster. If we don't, we will see a growing backlash against automation, and against technology in general, that will adversely affect our economies. Just as we saw an anti-globalization movement in the 1990s and 2000s, we are likely to see an anti-robotization movement in the 2020s and 2030s. The protests against Uber by taxi drivers in some of the world's big capitals, or against Facebook by Americans concerned about what they see as the company's failure to protect their privacy, are just a prologue of what we may see happening in coming decades.

We will have to place the social impact of technology at the center of our political agenda, and we will have to be prepared to adapt as quickly as possible to the coming transformations, lest they catch us by surprise. And we will have to find new solutions, such as a universal basic income in exchange for community work, in order to avoid massive social conflicts. In the chapters that follow, we will look at some of the changes that will take place in a number of different occupations—ranging from law to medicine, finance, commerce, manufacturing, cultural industries, and journalism—and discuss how we can adapt to, and perhaps even improve our lives in, an increasingly automated world.

2

THEY'RE COMING FOR JOURNALISTS!

THE FUTURE OF THE MEDIA

MIAMI, FLORIDA

Journalism is far from being one of the industries that employs the most workers, but I'm going to start with it because it's among those that are being most affected by automation, and it also happens to be the one I know best. The birth of the Internet, when people began to read the news online for free, struck journalism like a tsunami and wiped away tens of thousands of jobs. In the United States alone, according to the Department of Labor, the number of reporters, correspondents, and editors across the print, radio, and television platforms has fallen by 38 percent in the last decade, from 66,000 to 41,000 employees. In other words, 25,000 journalists have lost their jobs in the past ten years.

But what's even more worrisome is that, during this same period, the increase in jobs among exclusively digital journalists wasn't even close to offsetting the loss of jobs in print magazines and newspapers. According to a study published by the *Columbia Journalism Review* based on data from the U.S. Bureau of Labor Statistics' Occupational Employment Statistics program, "in 2005, for every one digital-only journalist, there were 20 newspaper journalists. In 2015, for every one digital-only journalist, there were four newspaper journalists."

Exclusively digital media outlets had their boom in the early 2000s, when many venture capitalists bet large sums of money on Internet news websites. But most of these websites failed to find a business model for making money off their massive audiences. In addition to growing competition from platforms such as Twitter, Facebook, and other social media networks that were increasingly monopolizing both readers' attention and advertisers' dollars, digital newspapers and magazines were faced with the challenge that a good number of their readers were spread not only across the country but across the globe. Traditional advertisers didn't care about these websites' far-flung readers. Retail stores, supermarkets, and car dealerships, for example, were only interested in reaching the local market. A grocery store in Brooklyn didn't care if a news website had readers in South Korea: it wanted to reach Brooklyn residents, or—even better—people living within a few blocks from its location. After the novelty wore off, many exclusively online websites went bankrupt.

And in 2018, when newspapers and magazines were once again beginning to balance their books by spreading the news through Facebook to that social network's 2 billion people, they woke up to several new, completely unexpected blows. Facebook cofounder and chairman and CEO Mark Zuckerberg had announced that the company's new algorithm would be giving higher priority to messages between family and friends about childbirths, marriages, and other family events than to news. Headlines and video footage from journalistic sources would be relegated to a second-tier category. In other words, Facebook was getting back to its roots: a social network devoted to exchanging messages between friends and family members. The company had most likely noticed that young people were increasingly switching to other social networks that didn't bombard them with what could be seen as boring news, or perhaps headlines didn't keep them on the site as long as conversations with friends about more trivial topics.

Zuckerberg may have decided to downgrade the flow of news on Facebook because of the widespread criticism of his company after U.S. intelligence agencies disclosed that Russian hackers linked to the Kremlin had used the social network to spread fake news and help Trump win the 2016 presidential elections. There was also speculation that Facebook's new strategy was part of the company's attempt to enter China, a key market that Zuckerberg's company had not yet been able to approach because of China's censorship laws. Whatever the reason, the fact is that Facebook's decision shook the journalistic world to the core because many media outlets were relying on that platform for nearly 40 percent of their readership. As *The New York Times* noted, "The algorithm changes will almost certainly affect ad-supported media companies like BuzzFeed and Bustle, which depend in part on Facebook for eyeballs." In addition, it said, both *The New York Times* and *The Washington Post* "will also have to confront likely declines in traffic." The entire media industry was hit hard by the change in the Facebook algorithm, and all projections seemed to indicate that jobs in journalism would continue to fall.

THE DISAPPEARANCE OF DESIGNERS, EDITORS, AND TRANSLATORS

I've witnessed with my own eyes the shrinkage of American newsrooms, as many of my colleagues' jobs were terminated in recent years. Google's search engine eliminated most of the library researchers who previously helped reporters find or double-check their data. Electronic pagination has replaced most newspaper layout artists, who used to be an ever-present feature in newsrooms with their large drawing tables and T-squares where they used to design each page. The spell-check programs we all have on our computers have done away with many copy editors. And lately, Google Translate has begun to eliminate the jobs of translators, who occupy many seats on the international desks of newsrooms.

The accuracy of automated translations has improved dramatically, to the point that machine translation programs can now translate documents in less than a second and require relatively little human editing. For decades, at the *Miami Herald,* I used to use several outside translators. I would write my columns in English, send them out to be translated into Spanish, and would then check the Spanish version before publication. But one day in late 2016, something unexpected happened that led me to discover the new automated translation programs: the translators weren't available—they were on vacation or too busy with other assignments—so a colleague in the newsroom told me she would run my column through Google Translate. My first reaction was to laugh; I had tried Google Translate in the past, and it was a disaster. But when I received the text this time, I was amazed by how good it had become. While it had some mistakes, the translation was fairly well done, and editing it took me roughly the same time it used to take me to edit a human translator.

When I asked what had happened, a Google engineer told me that they had actually just started using artificial intelligence for its automated translations between English and Spanish, French, German, Chinese, Japanese, Korean, and Turkish, with spectacular results. She added that the program had improved more in recent weeks than it had since its beginnings more than a decade earlier. And, she assured me, thanks to artificial intelligence, which allows the program to constantly learn from its mistakes, the translations would rapidly become increasingly better.

A few weeks later, *The New York Times* ran an extensive story on the remarkable improvements made by machine translation programs thanks to artificial intelligence. "The A.I. system had demonstrated overnight improvements roughly equal to the total gains the old one had accrued over its entire lifetime," the article read. Shortly thereafter, I found myself using Google Translate rather than outside freelance translators. I had mixed emotions about it. On the one hand, I was amazed by the technological advance, which made my life easier. I no longer had to wait long hours for a human translator to get my columns and return them to me in Spanish. Now it could be done in a matter of seconds. But on the other hand, what was the human cost of this new technological marvel? What had happened to the person or people who used to translate my columns?

THE INTERVIEWS IN THIS BOOK WERE TRANSCRIBED BY A MACHINE

Several other parts of my job have been automated as well over the past two years. When I started doing research for this book five years ago, I did things the same way I'd been doing them for decades. I'd record my interviews and then transcribe them myself. This process was extremely tedious and often lasted for hours on end, but it was faster, more effective, and cheaper than hiring a freelancer to transcribe the tapes or digital recordings. But in 2016 I discovered online transcription services like Rev.com—which primarily use a combination of automated programs and freelance editors from around the world—and I started using them. At first they charged between eighty cents and a dollar per minute of audio, but they simplified my life immensely.

Since then, I haven't transcribed a single recorded interview. In 2017, I started using Trint.com, an automated transcription service that worked even faster: it could have a transcript back to me in less than an hour, at a cost of just twenty cents per minute of audio, though not quite as precise as those edited by humans. A year later, Temi.com offered transcriptions "in five minutes" at a cost of only ten cents per minute. These programs are often cheaper because instead of using human editors, they place the burden of correcting and polishing the text on you yourself. Many of them allow you to mark with your cursor the words or phrases that don't seem correct, and listen to that precise part of the original audio, which makes the process of correction relatively simple.

Now, whenever I do a face-to-face or a telephone interview, I record it on my smartphone and email it directly to a transcription service. Then I'll go to the gym or the supermarket, and when I get home two hours later, the transcription is waiting for me in my inbox, ready to be used. This leaves me much more free time and mental energy for doing further research, conducting other interviews, or just running errands. But on the other hand, this new technology undoubtedly has a human cost. What will become of the transcriptionists who do this work for a living? Much like many translators, they may find themselves looking for a new line of work.

"COMPUTER KEYBOARDS WILL DISAPPEAR WITHIN THE NEXT FIVE TO TEN YEARS"

Journalists and almost everyone else will be using new automated writing programs going forward. The very act of writing itself will become automated as people begin using speech-to-text conversion programs instead of typing on a keyboard as we do now. I admit that I don't see myself dictating my books or articles into a machine any time soon, but if you look at any American child under the age of thirteen, you'll realize the direction in which things are going: they have spent their entire lives asking questions orally of virtual assistants like Siri or Alexa, as opposed to typing them into Google's search engine.

Technology companies are already anticipating that writing, as it's done today, will soon be considered old-fashioned. As Claudio Muruzábal, president for SAP Latin America and the Caribbean, told me, "computer keyboards will disappear within the next five to ten years." He added, "Just like you are now used to asking Alexa to play a song, you will get used to dictating your articles and emails."

When I told him that while I don't see myself giving up my keyboard any time soon, I was already using automated services to transcribe my interviews, he explained that very soon the whole process of what I'm doing will become much easier. "The different systems will be more integrated," he said. "Now you interview someone, you record it, you email it from your phone to your computer, and from there you send it to a transcription service. After you get the text back, you send it to another website to translate it, and maybe to another one to edit it. The real revolution is going to be when you can do all of this at once, in one place, with one single piece of integrated software." In other words, soon enough I'll be able to conduct an interview, hit a button on my cell phone, and say, "Transcribe, translate, and edit this." "The entire process is going to be much friendlier," Muruzábal told me. "You won't need to jump from one system to another. The phone will do it all by itself."

Technology buffs say this whole process of automation will

substantially improve the quality of journalism because—just as today's word processors suggest synonyms—soon-to-appear software programs will be able to offer ideas for enriching our articles. For example, they'll be suggesting historical references, comparisons with other people and countries, and even sources. If I'm writing an article about the future of computer keyboards, the software itself will take note and a list of experts I may want to interview will pop up on the screen, along with their respective contact information. A number of technology companies are already working on augmentation journalism, which will give more tools to journalists to do their job. Much like programs for transcription, translation, editing, and synonym search engines before it, the new augmentation journalism software programs will undoubtedly allow reporters to devote more time to research and analysis. But the question remains: What will happen when ever more intelligent computers start doing investigative reporting and write opinion pieces as well?

WHO SAID THAT POLITICAL AND ECONOMIC ANALYSTS ARE SAFE?

Although tech company spokespeople claim that intelligent machines will never replace opinion writers or investigative reporters because those jobs require a sixth sense that computers lack, there are important voices that are beginning to contradict that assertion. Andrew McAfee and Erik Brynjolfsson, the MIT professors who coauthored *The Second Machine Age*, have concluded that the so-called experts—whether prominent journalists, economists, or politicians—are much more prone to mistakes than computers. "We need to rely less on expert judgments and predictions," they wrote, adding that a well-designed, tried-and-true computer program "tends to perform as well, or better than, human experts making similar decisions. Too often, we continue to rely on human judgment when machines can do better."

The authors give a number of examples of algorithms that are proving to be more accurate—and more judicious—than human beings, including the case of the Israeli traffic court judges discussed in the previous chapter. Unlike those judges, they point out, algorithms don't get upset when they're hungry or get more punitive as the day goes on. A similar study, conducted in the United States, showed that judges who graduated from a well-known state university issue far more severe sentences the morning after their football team suffered an unexpected loss.

And when it comes to economic forecasts, the authors cite a study conducted by sociologist Chris Snijders, who "used 5,200 computer equipment purchases by Dutch companies to build a mathematical model predicting adherence to budget, timeliness of delivery, and buyer satisfaction with each transaction. He then used this model to predict these outcomes for a different set of transactions taking place across several different industries, and also asked a group of purchasing managers in these sectors to do the same. Snijders's model beat the managers, even the above-average ones."

Even politicians could be overtaken by algorithms. The online news site Politico.com recently published a story with the provocative title "Could a Robot Be President?" The article noted that, after the many blunders committed by President Trump, "a small group of scientists and thinkers believes there could be an alternative, a way to save the president—and the rest of us—from him or herself." It also added that "unlike a human, a robot could take into account vast amounts of data about the possible outcomes of a particular policy. It could foresee pitfalls that would escape a human mind and weigh the options more reliably than any person could—without individual impulses or biases coming into play." Furthermore, robots can't be bribed, and they can't be influenced by lobbyists. The article also suggested that, since robots are programmed by humans, elections wouldn't be about deciding the presidency, but about deciding who would program the robot-president.

All this may seem like science fiction, and I myself am quite skeptical about the benefits of giving computers so much power. After all, machines are programmed by humans, and they can make very dangerous decisions if their programmers make a mistake. But it is important to note that growing numbers of scientists are saying that artificial intelligence–powered robots will be able to make much more judicious decisions than humans and that a growing number of those humans are beginning to believe them. If this quasi-religious faith in data continues gaining ground, how long will it be before algorithms break into the fields of investigative journalism, economic predictions, and political decision-making?

AT *THE WASHINGTON POST,* BOTS ARE ALREADY WRITING POLITICAL ARTICLES

Very few people realized it at the time, but *The Washington Post* reached a technological milestone in November 2016 when it reported that Republican congressman Darrell Issa had won the highly contested race in California's 49th congressional district. At first glance, the story seemed much like any other that the paper's reporters had written that day: it stated that "Republicans retained control of the House and lost only a handful of seats from their commanding majority" and put the facts in context by noting the results were "a stunning reversal of fortune after many GOP leaders feared double-digit losses." The article went on to report that votes had been counted in 433 congressional districts and that Republicans had won 239 of them to the Democrats' 194. Some time after the article appeared, the tech magazine *Wired* published an article noting that election dispatches such as this "came with the clarity and verve for which *Post* reporters are known, with one key difference: It was generated by Heliograf, a bot that made its debut on the *Post*'s website last year and marked the most sophisticated use of artificial intelligence in journalism to date."

Indeed, the story didn't carry any reporter's byline. Instead, the byline read "From staff and wire reports, powered by Heliograf, the *Post*'s artificial intelligence system." That line, in fine print at the end of the story, went all but unnoticed. Amid the aftershocks of the political earthquake of Trump's unexpected election victory—against the predictions of nearly every poll—almost nobody noticed the fact that one of the world's leading newspapers was now publishing political stories written by robots.

Up to that point, it was no secret that certain sports and financial stories that consisted largely of citing data—like football game results or companies' quarterly earnings—were being generated by bots. *The Washington Post* itself had been experimenting with automated journalism during the Rio Olympics a few months earlier. And the Associated Press had been using the software known as Automated Insights for writing sports and financial articles for years. But when Amazon founder Jeff Bezos bought *The Washington Post* in 2013, the paper started experimenting with computer programs that could create more analytical articles. So during the 2016 elections, the *Post* began running—in plain sight, but without much fanfare—its first political pieces written by an intelligent machine.

Thanks to this new technology, *The Washington Post* was able to cover the results of roughly five hundred local elections that year, which otherwise would have required an army of journalists and cost a fortune in travel expenses. By publishing articles written by Heliograf, the paper was betting on increasing its readership by reaching new communities across the country. Instead of just trying to win over a large audience through a few high-impact national stories written by people who needed a lot of time to report them, Heliograf allowed the *Post* to target a number of geographically diverse audiences through a massive amount of automated stories on specific local races. Few New Yorkers would care about the results of an election in California's 49th congressional district, but millions of readers around the country were interested in the outcomes of elections in their own districts. Heliograf could get that specialized information to all of them in a matter of seconds, and it could automatically update the data in real time.

THE NEWS THAT WRITES ITSELF

Jeremy Gilbert, the director of strategic initiatives at *The Washington Post* who oversees the paper's usage of Heliograf, told me in an interview that the main goal of automating the news is to free up more reporters' time for substantial stories and to increase circulation by creating local or superspecific stories that can't be covered by humans, because it would be too expensive to do that. For example, it would be impossible for any newspaper to cover the roughly five hundred legislative races across the country in any sort of detail, he explained. Before Heliograf, the *Post* was only able to cover elections in the most important districts. But today, it can offer readers stories on every contest around the country, reaching new readers who previously didn't have access to detailed reports about the races in their own districts. Plus, each article is constantly updated as the vote count trickles in. In other words, as Gilbert said, the news constantly rewrites itself.

According to Gilbert, who was hired by the *Post* shortly after Bezos had purchased the paper, "the purpose of Heliograf is pretty straightforward: we want to take rogue and mundane tasks from our reporters and allow them to focus on much more interesting and sophisticated stories. For example, for the 2012 elections, we had human reporters and editors who wrote about 15 percent of all the stories related to congressional races, most of which we had no more information than was available through the Associated Press's vote totals. So in that case, that's not a good use of human time to read through a data stream and write fairly similar stories every time. So instead, what we did in 2016 was to build a system that could write those fairly template-driven stories and instead allow our humans to work on much more interesting stories for our audiences that still give us scale and reach."

How did they do this? It was really very simple. Before the 2016 elections, journalists wrote a number of templates, which are basically prototypes of articles that describe various possible outcomes, along with several analytical paragraphs giving the voting history of each specific district and detailing how each particular outcome would influence the general election. On the night of the election, an editor fed Heliograf with the results of each contest as they came in via the Associated Press, inserted them into the templates, selecting the analytical and historical context based on who was ahead, and updating—or, in some cases, changing—the story as new information flowed in. If the Democratic candidate won, the computer automatically added his biography, his stance on various political topics, and the impact that election would have on the balance of power in Congress. If the Republican candidate won, the computer would do the same thing with the corresponding information.

But were these stories written by the editor or by the computer? I asked. "By the computer," Gilbert replied. "But at the end of the day, it was *Washington Post* editors who were creating the different types of narratives and structures that the computer was combining to make up the story. So ultimately it's all human powered, but the computer is determining how to assemble the story based on the different options that are available to it and as it reads the data coming in. So on election night, when we say what happened in California's 49th congressional district, that was all determined by the computer, but the options the computer had were originally coming from journalists."

"FOR 2020, WE'RE GOING TO BE TELLING MUCH MORE SOPHISTICATED AUTOMATED STORIES"

For the 2018 midterm elections, *The Washington Post* was planning on using Heliograf to not only to write every article about the outcome of the roughly 500 local contests, as it had done in 2016, but also to write stories about the campaign contributions to each congressional candidate. For instance, Heliograf was scheduled to write stories on how much candidates and incumbents had received in donations from powerful lobbying groups such as the National Rifle Association. And Heliograf was programmed to turn out more articles based on opinion polls focusing on specific issues that could affect the elections or the fate of bills in Congress.

"Just to give you a sense, we have about sixty political writers, and on [the 2016] election night we probably had eighty or ninety people, including video coverage and the live blog," Gilbert explained. "For the most part, what we try to do with our human reporters was not have them do simple, tallying-type stories. They were free to look at broader trends, to focus on individuals, to do deeper reporting. We just didn't have them write stories that said, 'Here's who won in which district.' For 2020, we're going to be telling much more sophisticated automated stories. I absolutely believe that. I absolutely believe that it will allow us to focus even more of our human journalists on telling really unique, really human types of stories."

Gilbert isn't a technocrat spitting out the supposed benefits of Heliograf from the company's public relations manual. He seemed to be sincere. His background is in journalism, not technology. He had started his career as a reporter and art director at *The News-Press* in Fort Myers, Florida, before moving on to become a professor of journalism at Northwestern University, teaching artificial intelligence and machine-generated content, and to serve as a consultant for newspapers that were trying to adapt to digital journalism. After a few years of teaching and consulting, he was hired to be the *National Geographic*'s web page deputy editor, before settling down at *The Washington Post* in 2014. He considered himself primarily a journalist, or at least an advocate of good journalism. He told me, "My goal is to put as many reporters out in the field as possible. People interviewing people, writing analysis, helping the reader understand not just *what* happened but *why* it happened. That's what we should do with our humans. The machine is very good at telling you what happened, but it's not as great at understanding why that thing happened."

COMPUTERS WILL COVER FOOTBALL GAMES

When I interviewed him in 2017, Gilbert was about to launch his latest automated journalism project: articles generated by Heliograf about football and baseball games from hundreds of high schools in and around the Washington, D.C., area. "Right now, our reporters cover probably five or six high school games every Friday night," he explained. "Those are the most interesting games, which is great, but it doesn't allow us to cover all the other teams in schools in our area that might want coverage. Now, we could hire or relocate a bunch of journalists to cover those games, but instead, we can create a template-driven and algorithm-data-feed-driven approach with Heliograf that allows us to cover hundreds of high school games in a single night fairly instantaneously. That way, if your child goes to that school, and we don't happen to be covering that game with a human reporter, we can give them some type of story. So in that case, it's very much about scale."

The mechanics of automating high school football results would be similar to those used for local elections, Gilbert said. The scores and stats will be sent in to Heliograf by coaches from each team, and a newspaper editor will verify the data before it gets published to prevent anyone from cheating. Then in a matter of seconds, Heliograf will churn out a story on each game.

Gilbert is also preparing to publish automated Heliograf articles for the *Post*'s book section. "We are going to create short little narratives to accompany the titles on our bestseller list," he told me. "They will tell you what books are new to the list, who the new authors are, and we will be able to tell you how these books fare against historical data of other books we have in our database."

ARTICLES WILL BE TAILORED TO INDIVIDUAL READERS

One of the most interesting—or maybe disturbing, depending on how you look at it—things that Gilbert told me was that the automated articles produced by *The Washington Post,* and eventually just about every other paper, will be tailored to each individual reader's needs and interests. Using the data and preferences of everyone who subscribes to the paper's digital edition, Heliograf will create articles taking into account not only the city and neighborhood in which each subscriber lives but also his or her knowledge of the subject. If someone has already read hundreds of articles about Russian president Vladimir Putin over the past year, Heliograf will assume that this person is already an expert on Russia and won't bore him with information on the Russian leader's background. But if, on the other hand, someone is reading an online story about Putin for the first time, Heliograf will automatically tell the reader that the Russian president is a former KGB officer and give him several other details about his life and work.

"I think Jeff Bezos has pushed us very hard to think about the consumer first," Gilbert said. "In that light, there's a lot we could do with personalization around locations or reading habits. Meaning, if you've read everything there is to know, or everything at least that the *Post* has published, about the situation in Syria and there's a development today, a potential cease-fire, then we should tell you the thing that's new as opposed to telling you who the main characters are, what nations are involved, because you already know all of that," he explained. But if the reader hasn't read anything about Syria other than that there is a potential cease-fire, Gilbert explained, then the paper will give the whole backstory leading to this latest development.

Does that mean that *The Washington Post*'s intelligent machines will track people's reading habits and know exactly what each reader wants or needs to know? I asked him. "We'll have some very educated guesses," Gilbert said. "We'll certainly know how much they used our coverage. We're not tracking everything you read online, but if you're a subscriber to the *Post*—if you read a lot of the online content—then we'll know if you read any articles on Syria in the past week, or if you've read any of them at all."

So how far are we from getting personalized news? I asked. "I think we're talking a year or two," Gilbert replied. "For example, we're already starting to look at what kind of media each subscriber is consuming, whether you watch videos or not, so we can make videos a bigger or smaller part of the news you're getting. It's all about saving the reader's time. If you're not into watching videos, we'd much rather jump you into the story than force you to watch a video. If you're never going to interact with our informational graphics, then we shouldn't slow you down by putting that at the top of your story."

I was tempted to ask Gilbert about the political risks of this new technology. If the technology for tailor-made news expands, as it certainly will, won't criminal organizations, unscrupulous politicians, or governments use it to manipulate the news we get? Wasn't the 2018 scandal over the Cambridge Analytica technology firm's mining of Facebook users' data to compile psychological profiles only a prelude of what is coming? How long before news organizations and governments scour the entire Internet even more so than now, scooping up as much data as possible on what we're reading and watching so they can pump us full of whatever information reinforces or disputes our beliefs? I didn't ask because the answer was all too obvious: every new technological advance comes with potential dangers. Gilbert would surely tell me that if mankind had stopped developing nuclear energy for fear of atomic weapons, some of us would literally be in the dark. However, tailor-made news will have a huge political impact, one whose consequences still aren't clear to anybody. It's something that's already happening—as we've seen with the Russian disinformation campaign that helped Trump win the 2016 elections—and it won't be slowing down anytime soon.

WHAT THE NEWSROOMS OF THE FUTURE WILL LOOK LIKE

According to Gilbert, newsrooms will be much more automated five or ten years down the road, but it will be a gradual process. The most surprising thing for many veteran reporters will be the growing use of virtual reality headsets, the proliferation of augmented reality apps on smartphones, and the phasing out of computer keyboards. Much of our work will be done orally, thanks to advances in speech recognition software. According to Gilbert, instead of having keyboards, computers may simply have built-in speech recognition devices, and we'll edit our articles by speaking to them. "Judging by the number of people I see just talking to their cell phones to dictate text messages and emails, and the number of people who feel quite comfortable using virtual assistants like Echo and Alexa, I think this technology is moving much faster than, for example, virtual reality," he said. "I'd be surprised if most cars don't allow you to talk with them, or if most homes don't have some sort of voice-activated device, in the next two or three years." And the very same thing will happen with the machines used by many journalists, he added.

When it comes to the way news is written, Gilbert confirmed that—just as journalists have been using spell checkers and grammar correction software for some time now—a number of new tools will come into play in the coming years to help us do our jobs. "More stories will be hybrids of humans and automation," he said. "Software systems will be able to suggest different sources. They'll be able to write and rewrite background and contextual information that reporters would otherwise be doing. They'll be able to help identify tips for new stories. I also think that growing numbers of reporters will find themselves looking at their beats and finding ways they can expand the coverage they provide by using automation. So it'll be the reporters who will be driving what stories we automate instead of editors or technologists, which is the way things are done right now at the *Post.* I already have a lot of people in the newsroom coming to me and asking, 'Can't you just automate this part of my job so I can do this other thing that I really want to do?'"

Most data-centered sports and financial news will be automated, Gilbert continued. "If all you're doing is looking at the data coming in on a corporate earnings report and writing about that, that's not a particularly interesting story for anyone. It's a story that a machine can do faster and better. On the other hand, if you're seeing some unusual patterns in a corporate earnings report and you want to investigate what's happening, that's something a human can do much better than a machine." And there are other kinds of stories, like obituaries, that are always going to need a human touch. A computer can look up a dead person's résumé, draw up the facts of his or her death, and list the different positions that person held, but it won't be interesting without a journalist to interview the relatives and tell stories that don't appear in any official records, he explained.

I asked Gilbert whether journalists at the *Post*'s newsroom see him as the enemy who sooner or later will automate all of their jobs and leave them unemployed. "I don't think so," he said. "I've been very happily surprised by the reaction to the automation tools, especially. There are lots of more people who are interested in how automation can help them than there are people actually working on automation projects right now. We've been lining up a whole host of potential users, and that's a good thing. I mean, it suggests to me that the newsroom is much less afraid than they are eager to save themselves time so they can go and do other things. We ask a lot of our reporters and editors. We ask them to be active on social media, we ask them to help with the production of their stories, we ask them to be very active on television and to be quoted by other media organizations. If they can save a little bit of time, if they can identify stories that nobody else has, that's definitely to their benefit."

THE WASHINGTON POST GOT A NEW LIFE THANKS TO TECHNOLOGY—OR THANKS TO TRUMP?

Perhaps because it was bought by the megabillionaire founder of Amazon, *The Washington Post* has been one of the few newspapers in which automation has not resulted in massive layoffs. On the contrary, the paper—which like most papers in the country was increasingly losing circulation and advertising back in 2013, and had just laid off fifty-four administrative employees—was reborn that year after being bought by the Silicon Valley tech mogul. The *Post* doubled its staff of technologists, bet everything on its digital edition, and soon enough began to see a serious increase in readership. In 2017, it announced plans to hire as many as sixty new journalists, something unheard of in an industry that was in rapid decline. According to the *Post*'s executives, technology wasn't destroying jobs, it was creating new ones.

"We're adding dozens of journalists," said Fred Ryan, the *Post*'s publisher and CEO, in late 2016. Thanks mainly to technological advances, the paper has seen a 75 percent increase in new subscribers, and it has doubled digital subscription revenue over that same year, he said. It's also getting ready to boost its mobile video output, send out stories via email, and promote investigative journalism. "Investigative reporting is central to our DNA," Ryan said. "Readers expect it."

According to Politico.com, Bezos, the *Post*'s new owner, invested up to $50 million in the paper, mostly in technology improvements. Now there are roughly eighty technologists in the newsroom, along with over seven hundred journalists. "This is the face of a modern newsroom," *Politico* wrote, "in which software development engineers, digital designers, production managers, mobile developers and video engineering produce content in real time." And the investment is paying off.

But to what extent was it technology—and not the barrage of news and scandals coming from Trump and his chaotic administration—that revived the *Post* in 2016 and 2017? Clearly, Bezos's investment has allowed the *Post* to introduce new technologies and increase its readership by giving people news about local elections and high school football scores. But it's also true that Trump's unexpected rise in the polls during the campaign and his subsequent—and controversial—electoral victory have produced a hunger for news that has rarely been seen in recent U.S. history. And *The Washington Post,* like *The New York Times,* was well positioned to take advantage of that hunger for investigative journalism.

THE DANGERS OF MICROTARGETING NEWS

After interviewing some of the top technology gurus in the newspaper business, I have no doubt that the news will become increasingly personalized and microtargeted. Just as algorithms for Amazon and Google are already tracking our personal interests and bombarding us with ads tailored specifically to us, the same thing will happen with the news. Many people are afraid—and rightly so—that the widespread use of microtargeted news based on the economic status of the neighborhoods in which we live and our online reading habits will turn us into an increasingly fragmented society. We will be living—even more than we already are—in information bubbles. Theoretically, the news we get will depend on who we are and what we want. But that can lend itself to dangerous distortions.

One of the media analysts I talked to who is most concerned about the dangers of personalized news is John Bracken, then the director of media innovation at the John S. and James L. Knight Foundation, which researches and finances new technologies for the newspaper industry. According to Bracken, "In the twentieth century, the notion of journalism and newspapers was the forum for an entire community. But what we've begun to see in the last twenty or twenty-five years is the disintegration of the mass media and a growing tendency toward microtargeted news." What we're seeing now is "the loss of a common public culture" and the formation of a "5,000-channel universe," he added.

The individualization of the news can leave us open to being politically manipulated, because the algorithms used by platforms like Google and Facebook are designed to satisfy the consumer, rather than fulfilling a public service, Bracken said. So what they do—as we saw with the 2016 U.S. presidential election—is to reinforce the political preferences of their audiences instead of giving them news from different angles so they can form their own opinions. In other words, Bracken said, the danger is that these technologies are encouraging extremist views.

"If I'm Facebook, my mission isn't to strengthen democracy. My mission is to keep you on my site and engaged," Bracken told me. The Facebook algorithm knows our preferences by having studied our reading habits, and based on that knowledge it will try to please us by giving us information that keeps us happy and plugged into its platform. If it sees that you tended to read articles favorable to either Hillary Clinton or Donald Trump during the campaign, it's going to give you more news that are in line with what you've read before. It's not going to put any effort into offering you opposing views that will upset you and drive you off the platform, he explained.

"I've seen a lot of attempts to build alternative networks, but people aren't going to them," he continued. "The reason Mark Zuckerberg is one of the richest men in the world, if not *the* richest man in the world, is because people like his platform and the way the algorithm works. It feeds people's neurons." Bracken concluded, "People, especially online, rarely say, 'Okay, I need to act civically now and get really good, reliable news and information.' When there's so much cotton candy out there, people go after the cotton candy."

FACEBOOK AND GOOGLE: ON THE DEFENSIVE

After Trump's victory, and the revelations by the CIA and the FBI that Russia had tipped the scales in Trump's favor by planting fake news on Facebook in key parts of the country, Zuckerberg's first reaction was to reject the backlash and say his company didn't generate news content but was simply a platform through which flowed all sorts of news. But when faced with a flood of criticism that Facebook's algorithms were allowing—if not actively fueling—the spreading of fake news, Zuckerberg was forced to admit that something wasn't working.

In a public posting to his own page on November 19, 2016, he wrote: "A lot of you have asked what we're doing about misinformation" and that "we take misinformation seriously. . . . We've made significant progress, but there is more work to be done." Zuckerberg promised to launch new ways of eliminating fake news, which included new algorithms for detecting made-up stories and tools so readers themselves can put up flags when they see false information being spread.

Facebook also looked for help from external, nongovernmental groups when it comes to verifying stories and instituted new programs for preventing algorithms from promoting ads for fake news sites.

But in 2018, Zuckerberg found himself in deeper trouble, after it was revealed that Facebook had failed to prevent Cambridge Analytica—a data-mining firm that had worked for the Trump campaign—from getting private information on 50 million Americans before the 2016 elections. Facebook's stock plummeted, and Zuckerberg was summoned to testify before Congress. His renewed apologies did not convince many critics. Whether it was because of privacy violations, distribution of fake news, or growing complaints that they were intentionally creating "social media addicts," Facebook and other social media firms were increasingly the object of a backlash against big tech, which is likely to increase if the trend toward personalized news continues.

THE REINVENTION OF *THE NEW YORK TIMES*

Not long after I spoke with Jeremy Gilbert, the director of strategic initiatives at *The Washington Post,* I interviewed Kinsey Wilson, who oversaw innovation and strategy at *The New York Times.* Wilson was promoted to executive vice president for product and technology in 2015. Under his tutelage, the paper began focusing its resources on the online edition and putting a great emphasis on the immediate publication of stories, promoting them on social media and increasing their visual content.

In recent years, the *Times* had reduced its workforce because of the drop in advertising that affected all print media. In 2014, the paper had cut one hundred newsroom positions, and in

2017 it announced a new round of buyouts, mainly in editing and supervision jobs. "Our goal is to significantly shift the balance of editors to reporters at The Times, giving us more on-the-ground journalists developing original work than ever before," the paper's senior editors wrote in an internal memo. But at the same time, the online edition was growing by leaps and bounds, reaching 2.2 million digital subscribers and reviving the company's hopes. The newspaper was being reinvented before our very eyes.

Wilson told me that the *Times,* like *The Washington Post,* was experimenting with sending personalized news to readers according to their geographic location, and it was also successfully using artificial intelligence to manage comments from readers in its online edition. Due to the large number of insulting, racist, and poorly written comments, along with automated message chains sent by political parties or public relations agencies, monitoring readers' comments had become a very labor-intensive task. Online "moderators" or human editors had to check the comments and then confirm whether they were authentic or sent by bots. This got to be so much work that many papers shut down their online Letters to the Editor sections in recent years. Instead, the *Times* made a deal with Google whereby the Silicon Valley–based giant started to handle the paper's readers' comments. The *Times* gave Google its entire archive of readers' comments that had been fact-checked and edited by human journalists, and Google then used the data to create an algorithm that learned from the editors' decisions and automated the process going forward.

According to Wilson, the automated system has been working quite well. Thanks to the archive of the *Times*' edited reader comments, the algorithm "did a very, very good job of predicting which comments were likely to be approved and which ones were likely to be rejected," he said. As a result of that, the

Times was able to increase its number of online stories with readers' comments from 10 percent to about 80 percent. "In essence, it allowed us to substantially scale up the community engagement on our pages," Wilson told me.

THE MEDIA OF THE FUTURE: INTEGRATING TEXT, AUDIO, VIDEO, AND IMAGES

When I asked Wilson how he imagines the future of journalism, he told me it will involve using interactive graphics, text, audio, and video to tell stories in an integrated way. Until recently, each of the media had its own way of conveying the news: print media did it through text, radio through audio, and television through video. But now there will be a new way of delivering the news, which will use all these communication forms and will drive us to use all our senses at the same time.

We will be able to combine all those different elements into more powerful forms of storytelling, Wilson told me. "We're moving from an era when television, newspapers, and radio were very distinct entities to one where you're seeing a much more profound integration of all those different forms, resulting in the very best kind of storytelling that's being done today. That, I think, is one of the trends we'll certainly be seeing more of." As an example, Wilson cited the Snapchat Discover application, where people can see videos combined with text, images, and even animations, in a very creative new way of presenting the news. Augmented reality will certainly be part of the media mix: *The New York Times* and *The Washington Post* have already used augmented reality to illustrate their coverage of the 2018 Olympic Winter Games in Pyeongchang, South Korea. Readers could type a code in the newspapers' Olympic stories on their smartphones, and see close-up details of what they were reading, such as a nearly microscopic view of U.S. speed skater J. R. Celski's gloves with plastic caps on his fingertips to protect his hands during turns.

Wilson is also predicting that virtual assistants like Alexa or Google Home will become "one of the most significant consumer product developments since the introduction of the iPhone." These voice-activated devices are already in our homes, and soon enough we'll be using them to open doors, turn on lights, control our screens, and also deliver the news in a smart way, so we aren't forced to read or listen to the same stories time and again.

"You're increasingly going to expect these devices to be smart enough to know what you've already read or seen or heard on the news," he said. "At the end of the day, these devices are going to be smart enough to know what your cadence is, what your rhythm is, and they'll be presenting the most relevant things they can to you."

RADIO WILL CONTINUE TO BE VERY IMPORTANT

When I asked the *New York Times*' innovation chief if radio has a future as an autonomous news delivery channel, I was surprised to hear him respond with a resounding yes. Wilson argues that radio has survived in a world dominated by television and has taken a long time to be influenced by the Internet because "it's the only medium that's at least partially passive. In other words, I can do other activities while I'm listening to radio. Television and print require 100 percent of my attention, or close to it, but with radio, I can easily move back and forth between full engagement and 50 percent engagement, depending on what other activities I'm doing. That's why radio is so popular in the car. I can focus my attention on driving and be listening to the radio at the same time."

But won't all of that change in coming years, I asked, when self-driving cars become popular? "Yes, but not exactly," Wilson replied. "Driverless cars will present a challenge for listeners, but I don't think radio will be going away. It all depends on the quality of the production, the kind of experience you're looking for. In many ways, nothing is more powerful than the spoken word in terms of getting inside people's heads and invoking a certain sense of connection and emotional resonance. I think, in one form or another, radio will remain a very important, very durable thing."

Wilson added, "I do think, particularly with the introduction of smart speakers (such as Alexa or Google Home), we'll see something similar to what happened in the music space over the last fifteen years: radio news reporting will gravitate quickly to these devices." In other words, just as the Internet paved the way for the creation of Pandora, Spotify, and other platforms where we can listen to all sorts of music, more radio news broadcasts will be channeled through new platforms in our virtual assistants through the web. It won't technically be radio, but in practice it will be the same thing: orally delivered news.

THE END OF TELEVISION?

For several years now, television has been losing audiences due to the migration of young people to the Internet. According to the specialized website MarketingCharts.com, Americans between the ages of eighteen and twenty-four watched an average of twenty-four hours of broadcast and cable TV per week in 2011. But by 2016, that number had dropped to fifteen hours per week. The trend is clear: more and more young people are moving away from traditional television to Internet video platforms like YouTube, Netflix, Roku, Hulu, and HBO.

Cable TV consumers are now opting for streaming services, which are cheaper and allow them to watch what they want, when they want it.

Joi Ito, director of the MIT Media Lab, perhaps the world's best-known media research center, told me in an interview that "TV as a delivery channel, as a distribution method, is on the way out." But that doesn't mean that the people who produce television content are going to disappear, he said. Far from it, there are growing numbers of made-for-TV movies and series being produced for Netflix and other online platforms. At the same time, television channels like HBO are increasingly moving toward the Internet. And the big broadcast and cable television networks are also quickly expanding their presence in social media and the web, he added.

Like Wilson, Ito believes that the various news delivery forms are merging, and that the more trusted and accepted brands are the ones that will survive. "CNN is becoming stronger and stronger as a website," Ito said. "All of the newspaper companies are starting to do video . . . *The New York Times* has the number one podcast out there, and that's audio. I think, on the journalism side, radio, television, and print are really starting to converge. I don't think that stand-alone television is really a thing anymore."

FEWER CAMERAMEN, SOUND ENGINEERS, AND TELEPROMPTER OPERATORS

When I first started my TV talk show *Oppenheimer Presenta* around fifteen years ago, long before it moved to CNN en Español, I remember that we needed a crew of four cameramen, four camera assistants, several lighting technicians, a sound engineer, a teleprompter operator, and a number of other technicians to tape each show. The studio floor was flooded with people. Nowadays, like many TV anchors in the United States, I'm virtually alone on the studio floor. The cameras are robotic. They are handled remotely by a director who tells me, through my earpiece, which of the three cameras I should look at. The cameras move from left to right, and up and down, completely on their own, with no human being behind them. When the director tells me to start the show looking at camera one, I turn to camera one. When he tells me we're cutting to camera two, I turn to camera two, and so on.

In most U.S. TV studios, you'll find no cameramen, no lighting technicians, no sound engineers, no floor managers. Often, there aren't even teleprompter operators. For several years now, we television hosts have handled the teleprompter ourselves with a pedal on the floor: viewers can't see it, but we press it with the tip of our foot, scrolling the text at the speed we want. Almost all the technical work has now been automated, and with the ever-growing audience for the homemade videos made by YouTubers, I expect this trend to increase.

YOUTUBERS: THE NEW STARS OF THE SMALL SCREEN

If I hadn't seen it with my own eyes, I never would have believed in the popularity of the so-called YouTubers. Until 2014, when I was on a book tour of Latin America to promote my book *Innovate or Die!,* I had never paid attention to YouTube shows. I didn't have the faintest idea about how popular they were. All I'd ever seen on YouTube was an interview or maybe a video of a kitten playing the piano. So when I got the schedule for interviews my publisher had set up with major television stations and newspapers across the continent, I asked the Penguin Random House publicist to please cancel a particular interview with a Mexican news commentator/comedian who was listed as "Chumel Torres, YouTuber." The schedule was too grinding that day, and I was already exhausted, I argued.

The publicist looked at me, completely stunned. "Are you crazy?" she said. "This guy has more followers than anyone. Everyone watches his show, it's the best!" she assured me. I asked some of my Mexican friends, and they confirmed that yes, Chumel Torres was indeed an Internet sensation in Mexico, especially among young people. I reluctantly agreed to do the interview. To my big surprise, not only had Torres read the book from cover to cover—something that many professional journalists who had interviewed me hadn't done—but he turned out to be an excellent interviewer, coming up with some of the best questions I got on the tour. He is a young engineer who quit his job with a multinational company to team up with two friends—also young professionals—to start a fun, satirical political Trevor Noah–style show on YouTube. It soon became a hit. My publicist had been right all along. While the interviews in which I promoted my book with some of Mexico's best-known TV journalists had gotten 4,000 or 5,000 hits on YouTube, the one with Chumel Torres reached nearly 400,000.

PEWDIEPIE HAS 61.8 MILLION FOLLOWERS AND EARNED $15 MILLION IN ONE YEAR

Shortly after that, at a gala for advertisers, YouTube president Susan Wojcicki made a bold announcement. "Today, I'm happy to announce that on mobile alone YouTube now reaches more eighteen- to forty-nine-year-olds than any network—broadcast or cable," she boasted. "In fact, we reach more eighteen- to forty-nine-year-olds during primetime than the top ten TV shows combined."

Wojcicki's figures were debatable because she was not specifying whether any YouTube program could reach the same audience as a network TV program and was not saying whether she was comparing puppy video audiences with those of the top ten TV shows. Still, YouTubers are drawing amazing crowds. The most successful YouTube star at the time of this writing is a Swede who goes by the name PewDiePie. He has over 61.8 million followers and earns around $15 million a year, according to *Business Insider.* Next on the list is Chile's Germán Garmendia, who has 33.5 million followers and has annual earnings of $5.5 million, followed by Spain's Rubén Doblas Gundersen, better known as ElRubiusOMG, with 28.4 million followers.

JOURNALISM WILL BECOME A MORE COLLABORATIVE ART

What will be the future of journalists? I asked the innovation chiefs of both *The Washington Post* and *The New York Times.* What advice would they give to young people thinking of entering the profession? Gilbert and Wilson agreed that there will always be a need for journalists—regardless of the media they use to reach their audience. Journalists will continue to investigate, interpret, and express their opinions about the news of the day. And specialists will also continue to be needed, to explain complex issues in easy-to-understand language. What will change is the way that we'll be delivering that information.

"The practice of journalism is increasingly becoming a highly collaborative art," Wilson told me, "because technology is changing, because the tools we have at our disposal are changing, because the ways in which people consume information are changing. It will require both an extraordinary level of curiosity and [much] versatility on the part of journalists. It's no longer the kind of solo act that it used to be. It requires a kind of flexibility and an understanding of how to respond to new storytelling techniques and tools, and to immerse yourself in that. It will require constant learning over the course of your career." Increasingly, print, radio, and television journalists will be working together in order to see what's the most efficient way to present each individual story. Some stories will require more written content, others will need more audio, and others more visual effects. But most, if not all, will be the result of teamwork.

When I asked Gilbert for his advice for young journalists who are starting their careers, he told me that—in addition to being curious, persistent, and flexible, and learning how to tell a story using different media—reporters will require a basic understanding of data analysis, statistics, and math.

"A lot of the skills are still the same: I think you need to be a dogged reporter. Our best journalists are those who can get to someone and sort of read the situation and ask the follow-up question that's both critical and unexpected. Those kinds of skills are absolutely essential," Gilbert told me. "But on the other hand, data analysis is something that absolutely needs to be taught. I don't think it should be taught *instead* of writing, but I think it's pretty foolish to train someone as a reporter who doesn't have any aspect of data analysis to their job. Virtually every beat I can think of, whether you're talking about covering fashion or architecture or investigative journalism, politics, business, financial, or technology—all of those things should probably have some element of data analysis, and certainly the ability to understand and work with numbers. You can't say, 'I'm a reporter because I don't like math,' or 'I went to journalism school because I didn't want to study math.' We all need to do math, whether we're journalists or just citizens. It's critical."

Data-driven journalism is already a reality in every corner

of the profession, and it's changing the face of U.S. newsrooms. At the *Miami Herald,* there is a giant screen in the middle of the newsroom showing real-time results of Chartbeat, the program that shows a ranking of the newspaper's most visited stories on the web that day. In addition, all the paper's reporters get a weekly chart with their respective stories' click numbers, and are expected to increase their figures by about 10 percent a year. We get regular coaching sessions on headline writing and search engine optimization. We are expected to pay attention to our audience. "Listening to your readers doesn't mean that you lose your journalism values," says the *Herald*'s executive editor, Mindy Marques.

AFTER THE PANAMA PAPERS: A.I.-DRIVEN JOURNALISM

The Panama Papers investigation may go down in history as the first example of journalism assisted by artificial intelligence and directed by journalists who specialized in data analysis. The investigation, which earned a Pulitzer Prize for the *Miami Herald,* began in late 2014 when the German newspaper *Süddeutsche Zeitung* obtained from an anonymous source nearly 13 million files from the database of the world's fourth biggest offshore law firm, Panama's Mossack Fonseca. The German paper contacted the International Consortium of Investigative Journalists (ICIJ) for help in determining whether the leaked documents included instances of massive money laundering. The ICIJ then assembled a team of nearly six hundred journalists from roughly a hundred media outlets around the world to review the documents.

Matthew Caruana Galizia, a software engineer and data journalist from Malta who set up the database for the Panama Papers investigation, told me that his team created a database with a search engine that allowed journalists to search for the names they were interested in among the nearly 13 million files. Without having that search system in its closed platform, he explained, it would have been impossible for reporters around the world to do the research because there was no human way to peruse and cross-check 13 million documents.

Now that ICIJ has created this platform, the next time there's a massive data leak, reporters will be able to use artificial intelligence not only to search for people but also to make connections between those people and other personalities or organizations, he told me. The ICIJ is expecting to have its new platform up and running by 2019, he said.

"This is going to revolutionize the industry," said Caruana Galizia, who studied journalism at City University of London. "Those applications are going to free up journalists from the boring and expensive task of research, which means spending entire days in the archives, searching manually and aimlessly for patterns. It won't replace a journalist's job, but it will make it more efficient."

THE COMPUTER WILL INCREASE JOURNALISTS' CAPACITY, BUT IT WON'T REPLACE THEM

A comprehensive report issued by the Associated Press, titled "The Future of Augmented Journalism: A Guide for Newsrooms in the Age of Smart Machines," concluded that while artificial intelligence will have a tremendous impact on the media industry, "technology changes, journalism doesn't." According to the study, "AI is not a silver bullet. Artificial intelligence can't solve every problem. As the technology evolves, it will certainly allow for more precise analysis, but there will always be challenges the technology can't overcome."

For example, "AI is susceptible to the same biases and errors as humans. Artificial intelligence is designed by humans, and humans make mistakes. Therefore, AI can make mistakes. Furthermore, an AI system is only as good as the data that goes into it." The study offers a hypothetical example in which journalists could create an algorithm to find out in what parts of the world oil drilling has caused deforestation. But if because of an oversight the journalists feed the algorithm only with images of deforestation in mountain ranges caused by oil drilling, the intelligent machine would mistakenly conclude that oil companies cause deforestation only in mountainous regions. According to the study, artificial intelligence will be crucial when it comes to processing data and analyzing millions of documents in a matter of seconds, but there will always be a need for human journalists to check the conclusions of the intelligent machines. The study concludes that "artificial intelligence can help augment journalism, but it will never replace journalism. AI might aid in the reporting process, but journalists will always need to put the pieces together and construct a digestible, creative narrative."

I agree, though artificial intelligence is likely to cause many journalists to lose their jobs along the way. The next time there is a Panama Papers–type investigation, it may no longer require nearly 600 reporters across the world. The industry will no longer hire mostly liberal arts graduates, but will increasingly recruit data analysts and engineers. And reporters will have to be versed in print, audio, and visual media in order to tell their stories. The way the news is presented and analyzed will be very different, though the essence of journalism won't change. For many of us, hopefully, it will continue to be the most wonderful job on earth.

3

THEY'RE COMING FOR SERVICE WORKERS!

THE FUTURE OF RESTAURANTS, SUPERMARKETS, AND RETAIL STORES

TOKYO, JAPAN

While in Japan, I saw the future of restaurants with my own eyes. Besides staying in a hotel run by robots, I ate at sushi restaurants where the hostesses, servers, and even the chefs were robots. In one of them, Hamazushi, in the Shinagawa shopping center in southern Tokyo, I was welcomed by a humanoid robot named Pepper, who spread his arms and bowed slightly while saying in Japanese, "Welcome, I am the host." Then he asked us, "For how many people would you like a table?" Luckily I was there with my wife and some Japanese friends from Miami—Masami and his wife, Mihoko—who could interpret what Pepper was saying for us. The robot pointed to a screen on its chest where we could indicate, from one to ten, the number of people in our party.

"Would you like a table or would you prefer to sit at the bar?" the robot then asked, spreading its arms and showing its palms. When we said that we'd like a table, Pepper replied, "I'll have one for you right away." He then issued a ticket with the number 449 printed on it, and a few minutes later, a TV screen on the wall informed us that our group, 449, could take our seats at table 24.

It was easy enough to find it because the tables were arranged like train cars around a conveyor belt carrying the dishes, each of which carried a small sign with a number matching a corresponding table. Once we settled ourselves at the table, we began placing our orders using an electronic tablet located there. The table was already stocked with everything we would need for our meal, from chopsticks to a box of tea bags and a tap for hot water. Soon enough, our orders came rolling down the line to our table. Much to my surprise, the sushi was pretty good, or at least it seemed fresh!

THE MYSTERY OF THE ROBOTIC SUSHI CHEF

I was curious to find out whether the sushi itself was prepared by a chef or a robot, so I asked Masami to ask a young woman busing tables—the only flesh-and-blood worker in sight—if we could see the kitchen. In Japanese, Masami explained to her that I was a curious tourist visiting from the United States. The young woman stared at us bewildered before stammering that she'd have to check with the manager. A few minutes later, she returned to say that because of company policy, it wouldn't be possible for us to visit the kitchen. We asked if we could speak with the manager to see if he might reconsider, and soon enough, a man roughly forty years old wearing a light blue uniform and a chef's hat showed up. He was wearing a name tag on his chest that read *Araki*. Politely yet quite firmly Araki informed us that he could not allow customers into the kitchen without authorization from corporate headquarters. But through our friend Masami, I pressed him to tell me if the sushi was prepared by a chef or a robot. The manager started off by claiming that this was a company secret, but—

after much insistence and a lot of back-and-forth—he ended up admitting that the sushi "is prepared automatically."

I had more questions. How many people work at this particular restaurant? I asked. Again, Araki replied that this was also a company secret, but after a prolonged discussion in Japanese—of which I wasn't able to understand a word—Masami told me what he had been able to uncover. Apparently, each restaurant in the Hamazushi chain employs about ten people, spread across several shifts, and most of them are part-timers. Once Araki had left with a polite, respectful bow, we did our math. There were sixty-six tables, each of which could seat from four to six people, meaning that the restaurant had a capacity of 250 customers. And there probably were only four human employees working per shift: one at the register, who was there just in case someone wanted to pay with cash instead of using a credit card at one of the table tablets; two whose job was to clean the tables; and one who managed the place.

Our friend Masami, a scientist who had worked with the University of Miami, did a quick Google search on his phone and learned that the Hamazushi chain has 454 restaurants with a full-time staff of 466 workers, plus another 21,600 who work part-time. Since most Japanese companies don't pay part-timers medical insurance or a pension, we concluded that Araki, the manager, was probably the only full-time employee there at the restaurant. The rest were most likely students or housewives who were working part-time to make ends meet.

"It's a great business model," Masami said. The company was most likely turning a massive profit, thanks to its savings on labor costs. And customers were happy to pay less for the food, benefiting from that same savings. Whatever way you slice it, the four of us enjoyed a delicious meal, had a few beers, and paid a grand total of fifty-five dollars, which was pretty cheap by Japanese standards.

MANY JAPANESE CHEFS HAVE ALREADY BEEN REPLACED BY ROBOTS

Hamazushi is just one of several restaurant chains in Japan that is using conveyor belts instead of servers. One of them, Kura, with more than 350 locations, has already started automating the quality control of its sushi dishes. It uses sensors to track how long each plate has been on the conveyor belt and removes the ones that have been out for too long. Many of these restaurants refuse to say whether the chefs who prepare the sushi are humans or robots, but—after having seen them firsthand—I'm convinced that if they aren't already fully automated, they will be soon. Over the past few years, a growing number of restaurants are saying sayonara to their chefs.

But it's not only in Japan: the automated sushi chefs have already landed on American shores. Sushi Station, which opened in the United States in 2016, employs two robots to fill and slice their rolls. Each robot, designed by the Autec company, costs $19,000 and "it does wonders," according to Aki Noda, president of Sushi Station, which is based in Elgin, Illinois. In 2018, four recent MIT graduates opened a restaurant in downtown Boston called Spyce, the entire kitchen of which is staffed by robots. It offers half a dozen bowls of Asian, Latin, and Mediterranean dishes for as little as $7.50 a bowl, thanks to its savings in human labor costs. In the future, there will still be chefs who invent new dishes and constantly renew their restaurants' menus, but the task of preparing the food—especially in fast-food restaurants—will be increasingly handled by robots.

THE ROBOT THAT MAKES 400 HAMBURGERS AN HOUR

Several U.S. companies are already producing robots that can grill hamburgers. Flippy, which looks more like an assembly line box on wheels than a robot, made its debut at the Cali-Burger chain of restaurants in California in 2017. Its creator, Miso Robotics, which describes Flippy as a "kitchen assistant," takes the raw hamburgers from a rack, slaps them on the grill, monitors the cooking time and temperature of each patty, and then places the finished burger on a tray. Then a human assistant places the burger on a bun, adds lettuce and tomato, and voilà, the dish is ready to serve. While reading about this, I found myself wondering about how much longer the human assistant will have a job before the robotic arm takes over his duties as well.

Since 2009, another company, Momentum Machines, has been developing a robot that not only grills the hamburgers but also lays them on buns and adds all the toppings. Not only can this robot turn out 400 burgers an hour, but—according to the company—it can also produce higher-quality food because restaurants can use what they save on labor costs to buy better ingredients, resulting in gourmet quality at more affordable prices. According to the Momentum Machines website, "Our first device makes gourmet burgers from scratch with no human interaction. These burgers are fresh-ground and grilled to order and accented by an infinitely personalizable variety of produce, seasonings, and sauces. Serving a burger this great at such affordable prices would be impossible without culinary automation."

"Our device isn't meant to make employees more efficient," says Momentum Machines' cofounder, Alexandros Vardakostas. "It's meant to completely obviate them." He isn't worried in the least about overtly contradicting the public relations line of most, if not all, robotics companies: that machines won't replace workers. On the contrary, Vardakostas has given technological unemployment a positive twist, turning it into a promotional tool. I wouldn't be surprised if other entrepreneurs soon copy his line, arguing that their products can use better materials thanks to their savings in labor costs.

Momentum Machines openly admits that its robots will eliminate some of the 3.6 million fast-food jobs across the United States. But the company also says that "we want to help the people who may transition to a new job as a result of our technology the best way we know how: education." And to do so, Momentum Machines says it will be "partnering with vocational schools to offer discounted technical training for anyone displaced by [our] robot."

ROBOT-MADE PIZZAS

In California, the Zume Pizza chain is replacing its cooks with robots and thereby cutting its labor expenses in half. "What we are doing is leveraging the power of this evolution of automation, these intelligent robots, to put better food on people's tables," says company cofounder Julia Collins. She adds that "there are humans and robots collaborating to make better food, to make more fulfilling jobs and to make a more stable working environment for the folks that are working with us." The most tedious and repetitive tasks, like having to slide a pizza into a 400-degree oven hundreds of times a day, no longer have to be done by humans, she says.

Zume Pizza, whose factory is barely two minutes from the Google headquarters in Mountain View, is basically a pizza distribution service whose delivery trucks are more like kitchens on wheels. Each truck is operated by a single employee and includes fifty-six ovens that switch on automatically roughly ten minutes before the pizza is delivered to each home. Back at headquarters, two robots prepare the pizzas and—for now—several human employees load them onto the trucks. Each mechanical pizza maker costs between $25,000 and $30,000, but the company gets a return on its investment almost immediately with the savings in wages and social benefits.

Looking ahead, if the cost of pizza-making robots keeps falling, what will happen when these automated cooks cost a mere $2,000 or $3,000, work 24/7, and don't ever take vacations? How could a restaurant with human chefs earning $40,000 annually ever compete with that? Chances are that we're going to be seeing lots more restaurants like Zume Pizza. Gourmet restaurants with human chefs will always exist as an option for those of us who are willing to pay a little bit more, but the trend toward robot cooks will be hard to stop.

TABLETS ARE ALREADY REPLACING SERVERS

But the great revolution in restaurants will not be the automation of chefs, but the automation of waiters and cashiers. Just as I saw at Panera in Miami, every major fast-food chain in the United States is rapidly automating its service personnel. Most of them, like McDonald's, Wendy's, Pizza Hut, Hardee's, Chili's, and Olive Garden, are now using tablets with which guests can place their orders and pay their checks. The trend started back in 2013 when Applebee's announced it would be putting 100,000 tablets in its 1,900 locations across the country, and it has been growing ever since.

"Whether people like it or not, automation is coming," says Andy Puzder, the former CEO of Carl's Jr. and Hardee's. The major reason is consumer preference, Puzder says. "Research shows that many appreciate the speed, order accuracy, and convenience of touch screens. This is particularly so among millennials, who already do so much on smartphones and tablets. I've watched people—young and old—waiting in line to use the touch screens while employees stand idle at the counter. The other reason is costs. While the technology is becoming much cheaper, government mandates have been making labor much more expensive," he says.

HOT-FOOD VENDING MACHINES

Hot-food vending machines, like the one that sold me the ready-to-eat noodles at the Henn na Hotel in Tokyo, are also spreading like wildfire. They already are a $7.5 billion industry in the United States, according to the IBISWorld industry market research firm. One of the pioneering brands is Burritobox, which sells a variety of Tex-Mex foods, and which first appeared at a West Hollywood gas station in 2014. For $4.95, they deliver a hot plate in ninety seconds and entertain the customer with a music video while the food is cooking.

"This is not a vending machine, it's an automated restaurant," says Denis Koci, the thirtysomething cofounder of the company. "There are real humans making the burritos. Everything is handmade." The food is prepared in restaurant supply kitchens, frozen, and delivered to the machines, where it is defrosted upon order. An inspector visits each location daily to make sure the food is fresh, Koci says.

Many people, including me, after my experience with reheated noodles in Tokyo, don't look forward to a dish spat out of a vending machine and find the whole idea quite unappealing. But many others are always in a hurry and find it more convenient. "Millennials, accustomed to apps and online services such as Uber, Amazon.com, and GrubHub, increasingly don't want to interact with other humans when ordering dinner," says a Bloomberg.com article on the automation of restaurants.

And if Japan is a preview of what's to come, it will be increasingly difficult to stop hot-food vending machines from spreading. In Japan, you can find them on nearly every corner. Japan has the highest vending machine density on earth—5 million of these machines, or one for every twenty-three humans. Altogether, they generate annual sales of over $60 billion, according to the Japan Vending Machine Manufacturers Association. If they've already reached Japan's affluent suburbs, will anyone stop them from spreading across the globe?

MY VISIT TO AN AUTOMATED RESTAURANT IN SAN FRANCISCO

Shortly after my trip to Japan, I visited Eatsa, one of the first automated restaurants in the United States. It's in downtown San Francisco, and its motto—splashed across a giant screen—is "Better, faster food." It's part of a vegan and organic chain catering to those who want to eat on the go, but healthily at the same time. Inside, the restaurant has a futuristic feel not unlike an Apple store, with white walls and minimalist furniture. Near the entrance, there are several kiosks topped with tablets for customers to place their orders. I walked up to one, and after swiping my credit card, I was greeted by my name. Then the screen lit up with several culinary options, including vegan, gluten free, or dishes with "no restrictions."

When I tapped the vegan option, I was presented with images of a number of different quinoa dishes, along with their respective prices. When I finished placing my order, the tablet told me to wait until my first name and initial appeared on a large video screen on the wall. Indeed, my name was flashed across the screen shortly thereafter, indicating that I could pick up my meal in box number 19. It was one of many illuminated glass boxes that resembled microwaves on one of the walls, where my dish was waiting for me. A projection on the box's door—I have no idea where it came from—told me to tap twice to open, which I did, and there was my dish, ready to be taken to one of the tables.

There were no servers in sight. The only visible employee was a young man in jeans and a black T-shirt standing by the door with a name tag that simply read *Host.* Curious, I asked the young man what his job there was, and he replied that he was there to answer any of the customers' questions and address any potential problems with the machines. Not only were there no servers, he explained, there were no cashiers or managers. But behind the wall of glass boxes, there were actual humans placing the dishes. The food itself was prepared in a kitchen on the other side of the city that supplied all the other Eatsa restaurants in San Francisco, he explained.

And how is the company doing? I asked. The host assured me that they were doing great. The first Eatsa location opened in San Francisco in 2015, and new branches were opening in New York, Chicago, and Washington, D.C., he said. The restaurant was unpretentious—it was open until five o'clock in the afternoon, mainly serving breakfast and lunch to office workers—but the young clientele seemed to be enjoying the experience. While eating my dessert of chia and strawberries—which, I must admit, wasn't the tastiest thing I've ever eaten—I didn't see anyone over the age of forty. Most customers appeared to be in their twenties or early thirties.

THE EATSA MODEL WILL SPREAD QUICKLY

Some food industry analysts doubt that the Eatsa model will gain much traction because humans are social animals. Since ancient times, we have gone to restaurants and taverns to eat alongside other human beings and connect with them. Even when we eat out by ourselves, don't we all exchange a joke or a smile with a server and sometimes even know them by name? they argue.* But Andrew McAfee, coauthor of the book *The Second Machine Age,* argues that automated restaurants will become increasingly successful because people want to interact with their friends, not with their waiters.

Although McAfee acknowledges that we are a deeply social species, he maintains that when we go to eat out at a restaurant with friends, our main priority is not to interact with waiters, but to have a good time with our tablemates. "Listening to a recitation of the specials, getting the paper bill and handing off a credit card . . . are distractions from my restaurant experience, not additions to it," he argues.

THE OTHER FACTOR DRIVING AUTOMATION: WAGES

Puzder, the former chief executive officer of CKE Restaurants—and who briefly acquired national fame in 2017 when Trump nominated him to be secretary of labor, an offer he was forced to decline after a wave of criticism because of his stance against the minimum wage, among other things—is

* In fact, in October 2017, Eatsa announced that it was closing five of its seven locations across the country, leaving only the original two in San Francisco. The company acknowledged that it had been a bit too hasty in its decision to expand into other markets.

one of many industry executives predicting that restaurants will become increasingly automated because they won't be able to meet the growing pressure for higher wages. According to him, it's no surprise that an automated restaurant such as Eatsa cropped up in San Francisco, a city with one of the highest minimum wages and some of the most restrictive labor regulations in the country.

Puzder, who launched an industry campaign against a labor union's demand to raise the minimum wage to $15 per hour nationwide, warned that "the low-labor Eatsa concept may be a harbinger of the future. If consumers prefer it, or if government-mandated labor-cost increases drive prices too high, the traditional full-service restaurant model, like those old gas stations with the employees swarming over your car, could well become a thing of the past." Puzder obviously had a personal agenda when he wrote that, which was to convince the government not to raise the minimum wage. Nevertheless, it's very likely that the fast-food industry will become nearly fully automated in the not-too-distant future, and that restaurants that serve the public with human cooks and waiters will be more of a luxury reserved for special occasions.

RESTAURANTS WILL BE HIRING ENGINEERS AND DATA ANALYSTS

I asked several industry experts about what will happen to the servers. Some replied that they'll remain only at fine dining establishments and might otherwise be replaced by "culinary advisers" or nutritionists, who will make the rounds of the dining room, offering guests information on the calories, the nutritional value, and the particular properties of each dish. But most waiters are doomed to disappear, they said.

Instead, restaurants will be needing engineers, data analysts, and social media experts. Engineers will manage and maintain the robots, while data analysts and social network experts will be in charge of attracting and retaining customers.

By mining data from Facebook, Twitter, and mobile reservation apps, many restaurants are already creating profiles for each and every one of their clients—their birthdays, their culinary preferences, their favorite drinks, their food allergies, and even their favorite tables—in order to be able to create personalized promotional campaigns. Are your friends wishing you a happy birthday on social media? Well, a local restaurant might be sending you an email to congratulate you, and also to take the opportunity to offer you a discount if you have your birthday dinner there with your friends. Haven't been back to the same restaurant in a couple of months? A computer program will send you a personalized message offering a special promotion of your favorite dish to win you back.

A growing number of restaurants are hiring data managers to create customer profiles based on information culled from social media postings, Google searches, and dishes that customers have ordered in previous visits. Did you order chicken with a truffle sauce on two of your last three visits to one particular restaurant? The next time you go there, the server might greet you by name and might recommend new dishes featuring that same sauce that you liked the last time. Did you pay for your meal with a credit card linked to an airline's travel rewards program? Well, your server might strike up a conversation about travel destinations just to make you feel more at home.

And that congratulatory email you get for your birthday, job promotion, or some other special event? It will also tell you about new menu items with truffle sauce that you shouldn't miss. Fig & Olive, a restaurant chain in New York, has a database of over 500,000 customers and claims to have significantly increased sales thanks to personalized email campaigns.

A recent one of these, aimed at clients who hadn't been back for a meal within thirty days, began with three simple words: "We miss you!"

WRITERS, PHOTOGRAPHERS, AND VIDEOGRAPHERS TO MAKE DISHES MORE APPETIZING

Will there be any room for spontaneity and innovation in restaurants? Yes, of course, according to what a number of industry futurologists told me. Human chefs in fine dining establishments will continue to be—as they always have been—true artists. They will always experiment with new combinations, new presentations, and new taste sensations. And to make their signature creations known, they will increasingly need photographers, videographers, virtual reality device operators, social network administrators, and website designers.

Customers used to go to the restaurant, but now the restaurant will go to the customer. And in order to do so, each restaurant will need an army of professionals, including writers. Each dish will have a story, or maybe even more than one, that will need to be told so that people can read it on their cell phones while they're waiting for their food. In addition to the number of calories and the opinions health experts might have about the nutritional qualities of that particular dish, restaurant writers will also tell us how and when a dish originated, where it is most popular, and what challenges it had to overcome before reaching your plate. The writer may even include the commercial and political conflicts that might have been involved . . . if the restaurant's data manager determines that you're interested in these sorts of things, of course.

THE CRISIS OF RETAIL STORES

In 2017, Macy's—one of the most iconic department stores in America—announced that 10,100 workers would be laid off and sixty-eight locations would be closing across the country. This news made headlines, but it only confirmed an ongoing trend: retail outlets around the world were closing in record numbers because they could not compete with e-commerce. Besides Macy's, in just the first few months of that same year, closings were announced for 552 Radio Shack stores, 400 Payless locations, 250 of The Limited, 138 JCPenneys, 108 Kmarts, and 42 Sears. A study conducted by Credit Suisse projected that as many as 8,600 brick-and-mortar stores would close by the end of 2017 alone, more than the 6,163 that had closed during the great recession of 2008, despite the fact that the U.S. economy had recovered significantly since that time.

And while physical stores still account for over 80 percent of total retail sales, there is a "retail apocalypse" going on, and there's no end in sight, according to *Business Insider.* Even Ralph Lauren, the iconic clothing label, announced the shuttering of its famous store on Fifth Avenue in Manhattan as part of its cost reduction plan. It was increasingly difficult for brick-and-mortar stores to compete with Amazon and other e-commerce companies, who among other things don't have to pay rent or pass on the labor costs of salespeople to the public.

Amazon has rocked the retail landscape like an earthquake. Tired of having to deal with traffic to travel to physical retail stores and wasting their time searching shelves to find what they want to buy, people are increasingly gravitating to online shopping. More stores are following Radio Shack into bankruptcy proceedings, and many suburban shopping centers are starting to look like ghost towns filled with empty buildings. And this trend may accelerate when virtual reality becomes more commonplace and people can browse store shelves from the comfort of their living rooms.

It won't be easy for brick-and-mortar stores to escape the current retail crisis: many stores that are trying to convert to full-blown online retailers are realizing that they are coming from far behind and have a lot of ground to make up. Amazon is enjoying a huge advantage, accounting for 53 percent of all online commerce, according to the eMarketer market research firm. The rest of the retail industry has to scramble for a piece of the remaining 47 percent of e-commerce sales.

AMAZON IS WIPING OUT PHYSICAL STORES

"Millions of retail jobs are threatened as Amazon's share of online purchases keeps climbing," read a recent headline on MarketWatch.com. The same article included a graph showing how Amazon's annual revenue had grown from $20 billion in 2008 to nearly $170 billion in 2017. That's over 20 percent a year. According to Rex Nutting, who wrote the article, Amazon could have annual revenue in excess of $500 billion in just five years, and most brick-and-mortar stores will be a thing of the past. It's no coincidence that Jeff Bezos, Amazon's founder, overtook Bill Gates in *Forbes* magazine's ranking of the richest people in the world. Amazon's plans to create 100,000 jobs should not be cause for celebration because what the company is not telling us—Nutting argues—is that "every job created at Amazon destroys one or two or three others" at Macy's, Sears, Kmart, or other brick-and-mortar retail stores.

So what's the big deal? some could ask. Can't workers who lost their jobs at big physical stores just go find a job at Amazon or other online retailers? Not really, says Nutting, because Amazon needs many fewer workers than Macy's or similar physical department stores that have salespeople, cashiers, guards, and other employees. Amazon, on the other hand, has mainly workers who pull the product and load it onto trucks: workers who are increasingly being replaced by robots.

In the United States alone, around 12 million retail sales jobs are currently threatened by Amazon, Nutting said. Especially endangered are the 6.2 million people who work for companies that have outlets at shopping centers, like furniture stores, accessories, electronics, clothing, sporting goods, and general merchandise stores. And now Amazon is entering new business sectors, including supermarkets and the delivery of packages with drones that, according to a company announcement, will soon be able to make home deliveries straight to your front door. How many of the 600,000 U.S. Postal Service jobs will be terminated when Amazon's drones take to the air? Nutting wonders.

NOT EVEN GROCERY STORES ARE SAFE FROM AMAZON

In 2018, amid great public fanfare, Amazon opened its first fully automated supermarket in Seattle, Washington. A commercial that aired on YouTube in 2016, titled "Introducing Amazon Go," had already hit 11 million views by the time of the store's opening. The video shows several thirtysomethings shopping happily, selecting their items with the company's new app. "No lines. No checkout. You just grab and go!" says the video.

It's true: in this new automated supermarket, there are no cashiers, so there's no need to wait in line before you leave. You just download the app on your smartphone, walk in, and start shopping. Every time you grab an item off the shelf, it's automatically added to your virtual cart. The customer doesn't have to do anything. "It's that simple," the commercial says. It then shows a young woman putting a cupcake back on the shelf: "If you change your mind about that cupcake," it continues, "just put it back." Once you've finished shopping, just walk out: your purchases will automatically be charged to your Amazon account. According to press reports, the company planned to open twenty fully automated physical stores within the next two years, and two thousand in the next ten.

Wasn't Amazon afraid that a grocery store without cashiers or salespeople would stir up criticism? Wouldn't there be protests from the 3.5 million cashiers working in the United States? Amazon has said that these workers won't be fired but rather reassigned to other positions like helping customers who have technical difficulties or who are having trouble finding the items they want in the store. Apparently, the company made a calculated bet that more people would be more excited by the novelty of a store with no checkout lines than upset by the possibility of cashiers losing their jobs. And apparently they were right. When I last checked in to watch the "Introducing Amazon Go" commercial on YouTube, 87,000 had given it the thumbs-up of approval while a mere 8,400 had given it a thumbs-down. In other words, those who approved of the automated supermarket outweighed the naysayers nine to one. And on January 22, 2018, when the Seattle store first opened its doors, there was a big crowd waiting to enter. Ironically, a line of people had formed outside a supermarket whose main attraction was supposed to be eliminating lines.

THE ROBOTS ARE ALREADY BEHIND THE COUNTER

How long before Pepper, Nao, and other robots I saw in Japanese banks and stores aren't simply standing at the entrance to greet customers but are also behind the counter replacing the salesclerks? On a recent visit to Silicon Valley, I was able to see robot "sales assistants" at Lowe's, one of the largest home-improvement chains in the country. When I entered the giant store, one of these robots was walking—actually it was rolling, because it had wheels—down the main entrance area. It was a white tower about five feet tall with electronic tablets embedded in its chest and back, cameras on its sides, and a dome-shaped sensor on its head.

According to executives of Fellow Robots, the company that created them, the robots weren't built with arms and legs because "we were afraid that people would get scared if they turned down an aisle and suddenly found themselves face-to-face with a human-looking robot." So, to avoid potential heart attacks, the company designed the robots as rolling towers with a tablet on the front to interact with customers and one on the back to advertise current sales.

When I walked up to the device, it told me in a female voice, "Hi, I'm a robot. Can I help you find something?" Without waiting for me to respond, she continued: "What are you looking for today?" When I said, just to test the machine, that I was looking for lightbulbs, she raised her tablet slightly and showed me a dozen or so different images of lightbulbs with their corresponding prices. I tapped to select one, and the robot said, "That item appears to be in aisle twelve. Would you like me to take you there?" I responded affirmatively, and the robot said, "Sure, follow me." With that, she made a 90-degree turn, shifted from side to side as if searching for the right path, and rolled off.

It wasn't exactly a straight shot, because the robot had to stop from time to time. The sensors seemed to be confused every time we passed another customer, and the robot had to reset itself before getting back on course. But eventually she led me to the shelf where the lightbulbs I had chosen were located. Like many of the robots I had met in Japan, this one was obviously still learning. But it was headed in the right direction and was likely to learn rapidly from her own experiences and those of her fellow robots. With time, she would no longer need to stop so often on her way to the lightbulb section.

THE LOWEBOT DOES TWO JOBS

According to Fellow Robots' CEO Marco Mascorro, his robots working at Lowe's stores—known as LoweBots—perform two different kinds of jobs: they assist customers, and they track store inventory. The latter function is important, because they can count and replace items in real time, as soon as products are pulled from the shelves, he told me. His LoweBots haven't eliminated any human jobs, he claimed. Instead, they have allowed human employees to skip the most annoying parts of their jobs, like taking inventory, and focus on what they like doing best.

"Before, employees had to spend hours walking the aisles and checking to see what was missing from the shelves," he told me. "And in a store with over fifty thousand items, that's a really hard job to do. Now the robots do that for us, and employees can spend their time doing what they really enjoy, which is using their experience to teach clients how to fix a leaky kitchen faucet or replace an old pipe." I gave Mascorro half a nod, as if saying "maybe, maybe not." When I left the store, I found myself wondering whether the next stage in LoweBot development would be doing what employees supposedly liked best: instructing customers how to make basic home repairs. I wouldn't be surprised if that starts happening in a very short time.

WE'LL BE HOUSE HUNTING WITH VIRTUAL REALITY HEADSETS

As if e-commerce and robots weren't enough of a threat, human salespeople will see their jobs cut back by the growing use of virtual reality headsets, with which buyers will be able to see products in full-size 3-D images from the comfort of their own homes. On one of my visits to Google headquarters in Mountain View, California, I was given a demonstration of virtual reality shopping that left me speechless, although—as with any technology that's growing exponentially—what I saw that day may be old news by the time you read these lines.

I was sitting in a Google conference room with Sophie Miller, a business development manager for Daydream, the Google division that produces the company's augmented reality and virtual reality devices.* As she explained, augmenting reality with smartphone apps already allows us to virtually "test" different pieces of furniture in our living rooms so we can decide what best matches the color of our walls. In much the same way, we can "try on" different styles of clothes so we can virtually see how they look on us.

Miller took a Google device similar to a smartphone but specifically programmed in augmented reality, pointed it at one of the walls of the conference room, and showed me an image of the very same room without any furniture. On the screen, the place had literally and instantly been emptied. Then she used the device to search the Internet for a furniture store and began adding a number of different tables, chairs, and desks

* While many people use the terms *virtual reality* and *augmented reality* interchangeably, experts use virtual reality to refer to virtual images that imitate the real world, whereas augmented reality is a mixture of both real and virtual content achieved by adding digitized text, sounds, and images to actual physical spaces.

to the empty virtual room so we could choose the styles and colors that we liked the most.

"Visualization is a big part of sales," she said. "If a customer can see a product, they are three times more likely to buy it. Before, that wasn't always possible, because stores might not have every style of a chair in every possible color in inventory. But with augmented reality, you can see every possible combination in the actual room where you want to put them."

Augmented reality means businesses won't need the square footage they once did, because they won't need to have so many products on the sales floor, Miller continued. "Retail companies are always asking how we can do more with less space. Well, augmented reality goes a long way to solving that problem." Several BMW dealerships already have headsets to help their customers order the car they want. With these devices, customers can visualize different colors for the body and the seats, and see how the automobile would look with different sets of accessories, she added.

VIRTUAL REALITY: THE NEW TECHNOLOGICAL REVOLUTION

Using augmented reality devices will help both customers and stores avoid a number of headaches, such as returning items, Miller said. "When you're buying an oven or a refrigerator, one of the biggest problems is whether it will fit in your kitchen," she explained. "Returning them costs the stores a lot of money in terms of time and transportation costs, and for customers it means taking another day off work to wait at home for another unit to be delivered. But with augmented reality, you can set a full-size 3-D oven or fridge in your virtual kitchen and see how it fits before ordering it." This wasn't possible when we were able to shop online in only two dimensions, but it is now, she added. Outlets might not disappear completely, but 3-D augmented reality will make them much less necessary.

But was Miller biased by the fact that Google has its own augmented reality device to promote? According to a study by Bank of America and Merrill Lynch aimed at advising their clients about potential investments, virtual technology and augmented reality represent a new "technological revolution" similar to the one we experienced with the emergence of the Internet and smartphones. According to their study, virtual reality goggles and headsets could become "the one device to disrupt and rule the world of technology." The study went on to predict that virtual reality "will ultimately impact every sector and company by transforming how they communicate, design, manufacture, and sell products."

As with smartphones, which had been around for some time but became a global phenomenon only in 2007, virtual reality has been used for decades—by pilot simulators at flight schools, for instance—but really took off when the Pokémon Go game soared to record sales in 2016. The study predicted that the price of virtual reality devices would reach an "inflection point" in early 2020, when they would become objects of mass consumption. Among other signs that virtual reality will revolutionize the world of technology in coming years is the fact that there are already many "unicorns"—start-ups that have more than $100 million in investment—in this field. One of them, Oculus, was bought by Facebook for $2 billion.

What's more, with advances in the sensors, battery power, and memory of cell phones, we will soon be able to have virtual reality experiences with our smartphones without the need for visors or goggles, the study predicts. It's hard to imagine that people won't prefer to do their shopping from their cell phones with virtual reality. Not only will they save time and energy, but it will enable them to instantly see comparable products and their respective prices as well. How can brick-and-mortar stores compete with that?

TECHNO-OPTIMISTS CLAIM THERE WILL BE MORE SALES JOBS

While the most pressing challenge for physical stores is e-commerce, which has already left tens of thousands of salespeople out in the rain, techno-optimists like Bret Swanson argue that online retail companies end up creating more jobs than they destroy. Amazon, he points out, went from having just 32,000 employees worldwide in 2012 to 341,000 in 2017.

According to a study titled "The Coming Productivity Boom" by coauthors Swanson and Michael Mandel, e-commerce created 355,000 U.S. jobs between 2007 and 2017, while brick-and-mortar retailers—including department stores, jewelry stores, electronics stores, and bookstores—lost 51,000 jobs during that same period.

Swanson and Mandel acknowledge that e-commerce does end up killing some jobs, but they argue that the same thing happened several decades ago when shopping malls put small, family-owned operations out of business. Mandel also disputes the argument that e-commerce jobs don't pay as well as physical commerce does. "Production and non-supervisory workers in the e-commerce sector, including fulfillment centers, earn an average of $17.41 per hour," he says, "compared to $13.83 in general retail—a 26% premium." Skeptics, however, question the methodology of these studies, which were sponsored by tech firms. They add that the exponential increase in e-commerce sales will make job losses much more severe as time goes by.

APPLE'S EXAMPLE PROVES THAT PHYSICAL STORES AREN'T DEAD

Besides the statistics—which each side spins in the way that suits it best—the other big argument put forth by optimists is that physical stores won't disappear, though they will surely be reduced in number. Instead, they'll evolve into showrooms for products that can be ordered online, and they will attract customers with experiences not necessarily related to the store, such as concerts or artificial snow skiing slopes.

"Look at the way the Apple store has surprised everybody," Swanson told me, citing the example of tech firms that have opened physical stores to showcase their products and educate the public about them. "When they started, nobody thought they would work, because most people would order online. Today, they employ 40,000 in retail locations. The experience has been widely successful." And this approach is likely to be copied by other kinds of companies, he predicted. "As some retail jobs go away, other retail jobs go up. Maybe people won't be checking out your product at the register, but they will be more helpful in letting you know how to use what it is that you're buying."

And Apple isn't the only tech firm opening physical stores. Amazon and other e-commerce companies are doing the same. Not only has Amazon opened its automated supermarket in Seattle, but it is opening some brick-and-mortar bookstores for people who enjoy that sort of experience. In much the same way, Bonobos, an online men's clothing store, has opened more than thirty physical locations so its clients can try on suits before buying them. These stores don't actually sell the product: if customers like what they see, they buy it online and have it shipped to their house.

The Bonobos store on Fifth Avenue in New York doesn't

have suits of all shapes and sizes; instead it has just a few samples. People get fitted and order the final product online. That way, the physical store doesn't have to spend a fortune to stock a ton of merchandise in one of the most expensive locations in the city. Instead, you can just keep a floor model of each product on hand while keeping the rest of the inventory in a warehouse outside the city, where the rent is much cheaper. Paul Evans shoes, Warby Parker eyewear, and Zalora clothes in Singapore, Malaysia, Hong Kong, and other Asian locations are doing the same.

SHOPPING CENTERS WILL OFFER "MEMORABLE EXPERIENCES"

The shopping malls that will survive through 2025 will be the ones that offer "memorable experiences" to their customers. For some time now, massive malls in Minnesota, Dubai, Bangkok, and other cities have offered indoor ski slopes and scuba diving tanks as extra incentives to draw in shoppers. These added attractions will be expanding to include all sorts of activities, including soccer fields, tennis courts, concert halls, conference centers, yoga classes, and cooking classes.

They won't be able to rely simply on retail stores to bring in the shoppers, because customers will have the more convenient option of buying whatever they want online or with virtual reality devices. Malls will have to go the extra mile to make people say, "Wow!" and want to visit them. They'll have to have public spaces with dynamic, ever-changing content and host events that will constantly surprise their visitors. Shopping centers will sell experiences, and they will charge stores for the privilege of having showrooms.

Not surprisingly, when Canada's Triple Five Group announced in 2018 that it would build a $4 billion mall in

Miami, Florida, that would be the largest in the United States, the company's president, Don Ghermezian, said, "We're not building a mega-mall. We're not in the mall business." While most of the planned American Dream Miami mall's space would be used for shops, developers referred to the project as a "theme park." It will have an indoor ski slope, a lake with submarine rides, a roller coaster, an aquarium, and a permanent Cirque du Soleil show, they said. Malls will not simply be distribution channels, but places to lure potential clients, promote goods, and provide information to customers. Rather than just selling goods, they will be aimed at engaging people and allowing them to make informed decisions so that they can buy their products either physically or online.

SALESPEOPLE WILL BECOME CONSULTANTS

What will happen to the millions of salespeople at brick-and-mortar stores around the world? Swanson, like many other optimists, believes they'll evolve into sales consultants: specialists who are much more knowledgeable than their customers about the products they sell, and who will serve mainly as a source of expert advice. This is exactly what employees at Apple's physical stores do, and why—according to official company policy—they are referred to not as salespeople but "geniuses."

As anyone who's entered one of the more than five hundred brick-and-mortar Apple stores around the world has probably noticed, as soon as you step inside there's a young person dressed in black who says, "Wait just a minute, one of our geniuses will be with you shortly." What was initially a cute term is now an official title for these salespeople, who are first and foremost technical consultants and advisers. Interestingly enough, Apple's founder, Steve Jobs, was initially opposed to the idea of having "geniuses" in his company's stores. Ron Johnson, Apple's former retail head, says he will never forget the day when he suggested hiring them to serve their customers. "He said, 'Ron, you might have the right idea, but here's the big gap: I've never met someone who knows technology who knows how to connect with people. They're all geeks! You can call it the Geek Bar,'" he recalls. But Johnson managed to convince Jobs that all the "geniuses" would be young folks in their twenties, and they would be a tremendous help to people having issues with their smartphones. The idea, of course, turned out to be a home run.

CONSULTANTS SHOULD KNOW MORE THAN SALESPEOPLE

The notion of turning salespeople into expert advisers isn't anything new. Richard Branson, the billionaire founder of Virgin Records whom I had interviewed and quoted in *Innovate or Die!,* built his business empire thanks in part to this very idea. As a young man, Branson had created a company called Virgin Mail Order. The Virgin name was based on the fact that neither he nor his company's cofounders knew anything about the recording business. When it came to that, they were total virgins. All they knew was that they liked music, and that the record shops in London didn't know anything about the artists young people were listening to. Traditional record stores were selling music, but they might as well have been selling shoes.

So Branson and his partners decided to rent a space and use hippies who loved rock music as their salespeople. Decked out in jeans and sandals, they welcomed customers as if they were old friends. People would go inside—their eyes often bloodshot from smoking a joint or two—relax on a couch, and listen to whatever the Virgin staffers recommended. It was a totally new experience for the shoppers, and it turned out to be a huge success. Within a matter of months, Branson had opened a total of fourteen record shops all over England.

What Virgin and later Apple did—serving the public with experts rather than nonspecialized salespeople—is one of the things that brick-and-mortar stores will have to do to survive. Another thing they will have to do is offer free technical advice to potential customers, wherever they are. Companies like Best Buy have already started pulling employees off the sales floor and sending them directly into people's homes. In 2018, the company had three hundred former in-store sales associates working as in-home consultants to meet with customers and offer suggestions about which entertainment equipment to buy and how to best install it. It's a free service for the customer, in the sense that there's no obligation to buy anything, and—according to the company—it's neutral. The consultants aren't instructed to recommend products by any particular company over another, and instead tailor their advice to the individual needs of each customer. The secret is to connect the public with experts and specialists who can help make informed decisions. And for that to take place, the consultants have to be knowledgeable, educated enough to interact with an increasingly sophisticated public, and able to provide answers to questions that people can't find online. Sales advisers will have to gain people's trust in order to make their sales.

STORES WILL NEED SOCIAL MEDIA ANALYSTS

In addition to sales consultants, physical stores that want to survive in the era of e-commerce will need to hire data analysts to find out what their customers want, so as to make personalized offers to them. These analysts will mine people's data from their accounts on Facebook, Twitter, and other social media and use them to anticipate their preferences. Armed with this information—and with new biometric recognition technology and GPS systems that allow stores to identify customers as soon as they enter their premises—sales consultants will be able to approach customers already knowing their favorite tastes, brands, and colors. They will use this information, for instance, to lead the customers to the section of the store that would interest them the most. As soon as you step in the door, a consultant—knowing that you are a frequent buyer of ties—may say to you, "Hi there, did you know we have a special deal going on in the men's department today? There's a 30 percent discount on blue ties." And you will open your eyes in astonishment, as if you had blindly stumbled upon a hidden treasure, and go directly to the men's department.

Stores can even do this via email or text message, notifying us through our smartphones as soon as we enter a store that there's a special sale on blue ties. If I've just bought a watch, the store may send me a quick text message to say, "Thanks for buying your watch, Andrés," followed by another saying, "Be sure to take advantage of this limited-time special on watch batteries! They're in aisle D, thirty feet ahead of you, on your left-hand side." If it's raining outside, another message may tell me, "Andrés, the National Weather Service expects this storm to last for two hours. If you need an umbrella, we have them on sale in aisle G."

Since 2013, an increasing number of stores have been using technologies such as iBeacon to identify the exact location of each and every customer in a store. Apple has been using such apps for years. In exchange for downloading these apps, customers get special discounts, a digital map of the store indicating where they can find the products they're looking for, and reviews other customers have written about those same products. Many other stores, from pharmacies to supermarkets, are now using these hyperlocation technologies to maximize their sales.

Why are so many people willing to download apps that constantly track where they are located? Because the allure of getting a discount is much more powerful than the fear of giving up a little bit of privacy or being bombarded with ads. And all of this will lead stores to hire more data engineers and programmers who might not be out there on the sales floor but—according to the techno-optimists—will do jobs that didn't exist before.

But will there be enough openings for social media analysts and data engineers to offset the huge number of sales jobs that will be lost to automation? We'll analyze that in greater detail later in this book, but for now, let me tell you that—as you might already suspect—I think that in the short run it will be extremely difficult to replace the millions of salespeople, waiters, and other customer service employees who will be forced out of their jobs by robots and e-commerce. Countries will have to begin looking as soon as possible for new ways to reinsert some of these people into the workforce and to find new means of giving economic support and a sense of dignity to those who aren't able to reinvent themselves. Otherwise, we'll end up living in a world with growing unemployment and rising anger and resentment.

4

THEY'RE COMING FOR BANKERS!

THE FUTURE OF BANKING

TOKYO, NEW YORK

When I walked into the branch of Mizuho Bank, one of the largest in Japan, located on elegant Chuo-ku Street in the center of Ginza, Tokyo, I was greeted with a broad smile and open arms by the same sort of humanoid robot I had seen serving folks at a number of restaurants around the city. This machine, about four feet tall with a tablet on its chest for providing information and interacting with customers, fixed its electronic eyes on me as soon as I entered—a sensor on its forehead allowed him to detect the motion of someone entering the bank branch—and said with an intentionally robotic yet rather warm voice, "Welcome, I'm Pepper."

The robot then asked me to take a number, and—according to my Japanese interpreter, because this Pepper in particular wasn't multilingual—said, "Please choose what you want from the following menu." Pepper offered me a number of options via the tablet, including a quiz game to guess my personality type and other puzzles apparently aimed at helping me kill time while I was waiting to see a human teller. But another option Pepper offered caught my attention: Was I interested in car insurance, home insurance, life insurance, or any of the bank's other insurance policies? When I tapped "life insurance," the robot asked me a number of more specific questions and then offered me its opinion, always looking me in the eye and accompanying his words with hand gestures. "Hmm, I understand," Pepper said. "Now I'll tell you what kind of life insurance is best suited to you." After raising its eyes, as if it was thinking hard, Pepper announced its decision: "The insurance policy that best suits you is Kaigo Hoken. Please go to the last desk at the end of the room and tell the agent that you're interested in learning more about Kaigo Hoken."

Pepper had just done part of the work of both a receptionist and an insurance salesperson, leaving the bank's staff to close the deal. And, as I later learned, that particular Pepper was one of the more limited versions of the bank's robots. At other branches, the humanoid robots could speak multiple languages—the customers start the conversation by choosing the language in which they'd like to communicate—and act as fully automated receptionists, able to answer any questions, direct clients to the appropriate bank department, or clear up any questions about the various types of personal and commercial loans, mortgages, savings accounts, and investments.

According to a press release from SoftBank, the Japanese electronics giant that created Pepper, this was the first robot in the world that could detect human emotions and respond accordingly while simultaneously providing information in a fun and useful manner. "He is kind, endearing and surprising," the company website says. In other words, the perfect bank clerk.

BANK BRANCHES AND EMPLOYEES WILL BE CUT BY 50 PERCENT

But the greatest threat to banking jobs aren't robotic receptionists like Pepper. It's the closing of entire branches because of the increasing use of online banking, the gradual disappearance of cash, and the replacement of many traditional banks with virtual financial institutions that operate exclusively in cyberspace.

In the developed world, growing numbers of people are using their cell phones, tablets, personal computers, and ATMs for all their banking needs. As such, the need to interact with an actual human teller is in decline. According to a 2015 survey conducted by the consulting company Accenture, an average client in the United States interacts with his or her bank about seventeen times per month, while "nonhuman contact," such as Internet and mobile banking, ATMs, and social media accounts for all but two of those interactions. Today, some clients still go to physical branches if they need to open a new account—that's one of the main reasons these branches still exist—or because they prefer to deal with a human being when it comes to making important, complicated decisions. But for your average day-to-day transactions, like making payments or transferring money from one account to another, visiting a branch is simply a waste of time.

Antony Jenkins, the former CEO of Barclays who predicted that up to half of all bank branches and employees in the industrialized world would disappear in the next ten years, may have been right all along. According to *The Economist* magazine, in the United States alone, over 10,000 branches—more than 10 percent of the total in existence—closed between the 2008 financial crisis and 2017. And in 2015 alone, the largest banks in both the United States and Europe laid off nearly 100,000 employees. A study by Citi Global Perspectives & Solutions (GPS) predicts that American and European banks will be laying off around 1.8 million employees over the next ten years.

There are now entire towns, like Windsor, population 6,200, in upstate New York, where there are no brick-and-mortar banks anymore: the last one, First Niagara Bank, shut its doors in 2017. There are around 1,100 towns across America that have done away with banks, and "that figure could easily double if small community banks continue to close," says *The Economist*. In the Netherlands, the number of bank branches per 100,000 people has already fallen by 56 percent from 2004 to 2014, and the decline is showing no signs of bottoming out. In Denmark, the decline over that same period was 44 percent, and in the United Kingdom, it was 13 percent. The trend is clear.

BRANCHES WILL DISAPPEAR MORE SLOWLY IN LATIN AMERICA AND INDIA

The decline in physical bank branches won't be taking place at the same rate in all countries. According to Citi's "Digital Disruption" report, while the number of banks and bank employees will continue to fall in developed countries like the United States, Japan, Germany, and South Korea, that won't happen in emerging nations, where a large part of the population still remains outside the banking system. "We agree with Antony Jenkins' comment that the number of branches could well halve over the next decade—however, while we believe that this will be the case in some European markets, it would be overly simplistic to assume a reduction of branches globally at the same rate because of regional differences in customer digital acceptance and demographic mix," the report says. "In an emerging market where retail banking penetration is low, branches will continue to grow—for example, in India."

The report also shows that, while the number of bank employees fell in both the United States and Europe, the number in Latin America is actually up: between 2009 and 2014, it increased from 690,000 to 1 million. But it won't be long before the penetration rate of Latin American banks reaches the levels of more developed countries, and there will be no need to add more physical branches. In the next decade—and perhaps even before that—the number of Latin Americans with a bank account will soar, as will the percentage of those who will interact with their banks online. It's inevitable, and it's already happening in some of the region's more developed countries. In late 2017, Banco Falabella of Chile opened its first digital financial center—or virtual branch—in Santiago, the Chilean capital. The branch has only one human assistant to teach clients how to manage their accounts online or from the convenience of their smartphone or home computer. The experiment worked so well that the bank's CEO, Gastón Bottazzini, said he was planning to open seven more virtual branches by the end of 2018.

Bank branches probably won't disappear altogether, but they will transition into financial advice centers, with many fewer employees. Physically they'll look more like living rooms, with works of art on the walls and comfortable sofas where customers can sit and have a coffee with a consultant instead of standing in line to wait for their turn with a teller at the counter. Or they may be just kiosks, in supermarkets or other stores, where people can withdraw cash, deposit checks, or speak with an adviser by video conference. Banks will no longer need to handle transactions and accounting work in house, because all of these sorts of things will be automated.

"Roughly 60 to 70 percent of retail banking employees are

doing manual processing driven jobs," says Jonathan Larsen, Citi's former global head of retail and mortgages. "If all the current manual processing can be replaced by automation, these jobs can disappear or evolve." Banks will have to shrink because "branches and associated staff costs make up about 65 percent of the total retail cost base of a larger bank and a lot of these costs can be removed via automation," he says. Processing jobs will be cut not only because virtually all transactions will be carried out electronically, but also because physical money, checks, and credit cards will increasingly be replaced by new forms of virtual payment. In fact, most of Europe's Nordic countries have already become cash-free societies.

THE END OF CASH

In Sweden, checks have disappeared since about a decade ago, having been almost entirely replaced by electronic payment systems. Ask a Swede to write you a check, and he will stare at you in bewilderment. Bills and coins now represent just 2 percent of all money exchanging hands in Sweden, compared with 7.7 percent in the United States and an average of 10 percent across all of Europe. Most Swedish kids have never even seen a check, because they have grown up buying things with debit cards and—increasingly—with their cell phones. There is so little cash that even the homeless now have cell phone apps to accept money on the streets.

And what's even stranger is the fact that more than half of all major bank branches in Sweden no longer accept cash deposits, because the overall amounts are so small that it's just not worth for them to pay for security services. Many are also eliminating ATMs, which are attracting more dust than customers. This same trend is taking place across Denmark, Norway, and the Netherlands, which are rapidly becoming cashless societies.

In 2015, the government of Denmark proposed allowing restaurants, clothing stores, and other retail establishments to stop accepting cash payments as part of a package of measures designed to help small businesses cut their monitoring and processing fees and to allow for better tax accountability. The proposal, which called for eliminating cash completely by 2030, was not passed by the Danish Parliament because of domestic political disputes. But the banks are supporting it to save processing costs, and experts believe it will eventually become law.

Anette Broløs, the president of the Fintech Innovation and Research Centre in Copenhagen, told me she expects cash to completely vanish from her country in the next ten years. When I asked her about the advantages of a society's being cashless, she replied that it would save a lot of money. "Cash isn't necessarily expensive for the individual consumer, but it is for society as a whole. It's expensive to print, to redesign, and to transport, and moving it every day from one place to another produces a lot of toxic gas emissions," she told me. Why incur all these costs if fewer people are using it than ever? she asked.

IN DENMARK, BANK ROBBERS ARE LEAVING EMPTY-HANDED

Banks in Denmark now handle so little cash that even criminals have lost interest in robbing them. The Danish Bankers Association issued a press release in February 2016 stating that "for the fifth year in a row, banks have experienced a fall in the number of bank robberies. The number has fallen from 21 bank robberies in 2014 to 14 bank robberies in 2015." The statement added, a bit pompously, that "the Danish Bankers Association is very pleased with this development."

Intrigued by this news, I called up Michael Busk-Jepsen, executive director of the Danish Bankers Association, and asked him why bank robberies are on the decline. He confirmed that thieves no longer bother robbing banks because banks no longer have much cash. "We've had cases where the robbers found so little cash that they basically left empty-handed," he told me matter-of-factly. "Business has really fallen off for back robbers these days." Supporters of gradually eliminating cash also point out that it would also be a great idea for developing nations because it would help them put an end to tax evasion, corruption, and the underground economy. Indeed, in a cashless society, it will be much more difficult to bribe an elected official or to do business off the books. The question in emerging economies, for the time being, will be how to eliminate cash without further marginalizing large numbers of poor people who don't have smartphones or access to online banking.

THE NEW VIRTUAL BANKS

In the United States, virtual banks like Schwab.com, Betterment.com, Nutmeg.com, Wealthfront.com, and Robinhood.com are capturing deposits from growing numbers of young people who don't want to pay the relatively high administration fees charged by traditional banks, which have to pay for rents and customer service employees. Most virtual banks have practically no overhead—they operate with only a few managers supported by algorithms—and can afford to manage investments charging a commission of only 0.25 percent per year, which is considerably less than the average 1 percent charged by brick-and-mortar banks. And they boast of having algorithms that are as sophisticated as, if not more sophisticated than, physical banks. By 2016, virtual banks and their robo-advisers were already managing around $20 billion in assets. That's still just a fraction of the market when compared with the trillions of dollars managed by traditional banks, but with the growing popularity of online banking among young adults, it seems likely to grow rapidly. According to McKinsey, they could be handling as much as $13.5 trillion in assets within just a few years.

Will robo-advisers make human financial advisers obsolete? According to Citi's analysis, the need for financial analysts will decrease in the coming years but won't disappear entirely. While artificial intelligence will make financial advice much cheaper, there will be more people out there wanting to receive it and able to afford it. Millions of people who didn't have access to investment banks will now have such access, while upscale customers will continue to get more specialized advice from humans, Citi says.

"We see the advent of robo-advice as an example of automation improving the productivity of traditional investment advisers, and not a situation where there is significant risk of job substitution," the study says. It estimates that while the number of personal financial advisers doubled in the United States between 2000 and 2010, it is expected to increase by only 27 percent from 2012 to 2022. "Higher net worth or more sophisticated investors will, in our view, always demand face-to-face advice. However, we believe the services offered by advisers have the potential to be augmented by virtual and robo-advice tools, increasing individual adviser productivity, and ability to service more clients, or in more user-friendly and/or sophisticated ways," it concludes. But, as we will see, this bank's predictions may be overly optimistic.

THE AUTOMATION OF BIG BANKS

In response to the threat posed by online banking—and the expected entry of giant nonbank players, such as Amazon, into the banking industry—large investment banks like Goldman

Sachs and JPMorgan Chase are stealing from their rivals' playbook and offering increasingly more of their services online. As Jamie Dimon, CEO of JPMorgan, has noted, "Silicon Valley is coming. There are hundreds of start-ups with a lot of brains and money working on various alternatives to traditional banking." To confront this challenge, JPMorgan Chase and other banks began buying up financial technology companies and using their algorithms to increasingly replace human analysts. So much so that Goldman Sachs CEO Lloyd Blankfein, talking about the future of his firm, calls Goldman Sachs "a tech company."

Instead of hiring more young people with economics or finance degrees, Goldman Sachs began looking for engineers and programmers. In 2015, the company had roughly 33,000 employees, of whom 9,000 were engineers and programmers. Ironically, Goldman Sachs already had more engineers and programmers than either Facebook or Twitter. Goldman Sachs had acquired in 2014 part of a firm called Kensho Technologies, whose algorithms could in a matter of seconds make financial calculations and projections that previously took hundreds of human analysts hours—if not days—to compile.

Before becoming Kensho's largest investor, Goldman Sachs's human analysts used to eagerly wait for the U.S. Bureau of Labor Statistics to release its monthly employment report. It is one of the primary tools for measuring the state of the economy both in the United States and around the world, and it's released on the first Friday of every month at 8:30 A.M. As soon as the statistics were released, an army of analysts calculated their impact on the economy, and based on those numbers, they made their recommendations to investors. But now Kensho's algorithm can run those same numbers in minutes. By 8:32 that same morning, Kensho has already analyzed the information, produced a brief synopsis, and offered thirteen forecasts on how the new statistics would affect various types of investments, based on how the market had behaved in the past under similar conditions. And by 8:35 in the morning, after cross-checking the information with dozens of other databases, Kensho has placed its recommendations up on the computer screens of Goldman Sachs analysts so they can be immediately passed along to their clients. Overnight, the robots have become major players on Wall Street.

ALGORITHMS THAT REPLACE BANKERS

Kensho's founder, thirty-two-year-old Daniel Nadler, came up with the name for his company after a trip to Japan one summer while working on his Ph.D. in economics at Harvard. He dabbled in meditation and learned the word *kensho,* which is the term for one of the first states of awareness in the Zen Buddhist progression. Less than two years after selling his tech company to Goldman Sachs, Nadler was already openly admitting fears that his algorithms would put an end to a number of Wall Street banking jobs.

In an interview with *The New York Times,* Nadler predicted that within the next decade, between a third and a half of financial sector workers would lose their jobs because of Kensho and other algorithms. It will be part of a continuing trend, he said. First to go were the administrative assistants, who became redundant when stock tickers and trading tickets became automated, Nadler explained. Then came the financial researchers and analysts, forced out by software that could process much more data in much less time. In the coming few years, many of the bankers who deal directly with clients will be gone because more sophisticated and customer-friendly websites will allow clients to do most of their investing online. "I'm assuming that the majority of those people over a five- to ten-year horizon are not going to be replaced by other people," Nadler predicts.

"THE NET-NET TO SOCIETY . . . IS A NET LOSS"

"We've created, on paper at least, more than a dozen millionaires," the young multimillionaire, who counts a number of other large investment banks besides Goldman Sachs among his clients, says. "That might help people sleep better at night, but we are creating a very small number of high-paying jobs in return for destroying a very large number of fairly high-paying jobs, and the net-net to society, absent some sort of policy intervention or new industry that no one's thought of yet to employ all those people, is a net loss."

Not only are robo-analysts more efficient than humans when it comes to processing data like the Department of Labor's monthly employment statistics, but they can analyze policy trends and make economic forecasts with much greater precision, Nadler explains. In the past, when the civil war in Syria was in the news, many clients called their bankers to ask whether they should be investing in oil companies, or to find out how the latest events would affect their portfolios. When faced with questions like that, investment bankers would huddle with their analysts to find out how the markets had reacted to similar situations in the past and then make their recommendations based on the consensus of their experts. The problem with this approach was that it took time, and when the bank was finally ready to make a recommendation, circumstances on the ground had often changed and the opportunity to invest was gone.

Now all a banker has to do is fire up his Kensho program, type in *Syria* along with other search terms like *oil prices* and the name of an oil company, and he or she will get an answer in much the same way a Google search operates. But whereas a general Google search engine gives us all possible results that contain the search keywords, Kensho automatically classifies the results based on how they will affect certain stocks. After doing a search with the terms *escalation in the Syrian civil war,* a trader can get recommendations—based on similar events in the past—on whether to invest in a particular oil company or on how events will impact the market in Germany or affect the value of the peso in Mexico. Doing the same analysis without automation "would have taken days, probably forty man-hours, from people who were making an average of $350,000 to $500,000 a year," Nadler says.

FINANCIAL ADVISERS WILL BE A LUXURY FOR THE ULTRARICH

Increasingly, people will be getting financial advice primarily from algorithms, but there will still be some jobs for human financial advisers. According to the EY consulting firm, formerly known as Ernst & Young, "while the data-crunching can be automated, the role (of a financial adviser) itself requires a degree of human interaction and—critically—judgment that cannot be effectively marshaled by machines." As Karl Meekings, one of the primary authors of this study and the strategic analyst of global banking and capital markets of EY, explained to me, "algorithms will become increasingly efficient at making financial forecasts, but they don't work as well when something unexpected happens, so a human presence will always be needed to deal with unanticipated events." When I asked him specifically which kinds of financial advisers will survive, Meekings responded that it will be those who can coach clients through very complex business or tax structures, who can break down the algorithms' recommendations in a personalized way, or who specialize in nontraditional investments like fine art, wines, or other collectibles.

John Garvey, the global financial services leader at PwC and one of the lead authors of his company's study on the future of banking, explained to me that human financial advisers work better than algorithms when there isn't much information available to the public about a particular potential investment. "For example," he said, "when it comes to investing in real estate, or wine, or film projects, where there isn't much public information available, a real-life financial adviser can do a better job making some phone calls, going to look at the actual building, or consulting with wine specialists. The less public information there is, the more need there will be for a personal financial adviser."

HUMANS WILL BE NEEDED TO ANSWER THE UNSCRIPTED QUESTIONS

The increasing popularity of online banking will require more qualified people to personally answer clients' questions. Who among us hasn't been annoyed when we call a bank and get an automated response, or an employee who can do no more than read off canned responses from a list that doesn't address our particular question? To solve this problem, banks will need versatile people who can answer questions about their financial services in a clear and understandable way. Communication skills will be as necessary as, or more necessary than, financial knowledge. "Call centers" will be rebranded as "specialized advisory centers," and will need more highly educated workers, with better communication skills.

"There's always the chance that a client will ask an unscripted question, and well-trained employees will be needed to handle such questions," Meekings told me. "For example, a robot can tell you that in order to open a shared bank account with another person, you'll have to go to the nearest branch and sign some forms. But what if you can't make it to the bank branch because you just got sick and you're bedridden? If you ask the bank to make an exception and open your new account via email, considering that the bank already has your signature on file, that sort of thing might not be in the robot's script. The robot may not know how to answer you. That's why robots will always need someone to assist them."

ALGORITHMS HAVE FEWER CONFLICTS OF INTEREST

Betterment.com, one of the best-known virtual banks in America, began operating in 2010. Its founder, Jon Stein, was only thirty years old at the time. He had a bachelor's degree in economics from Harvard and a master's in business administration from Columbia. Stein says he always wanted to do something important, like launching his own company. He was passionate about the idea of offering automated financial services right from the start because he saw the banking industry as a whole to be totally outdated and thought that banks were often charging clients too much for their services.

"I got into this business because I was frustrated personally." Stein was quoted as saying by Techonomy.com. He also believed that there were too many conflicts of interest in the financial services world. "You know, your broker might have a bad day, might have an interest in some stock that they're promoting, might have a financial interest in selling you one thing over another." By comparison, when you trust software to make these decisions, there are fewer conflicts of interest, and the system is more efficient and reliable, he argued.

Unlike Kensho's founder, Nadler, Stein is optimistic that financial algorithms won't produce massive layoffs in the banking industry. Financial advisers will be able to serve more customers than ever, he said. "Ultimately, this technology is going to be used by everyone, whether you're investing on your own directly or you have an adviser, because it's just that much better than not using technology," he added.

Just eight years after starting up, Betterment.com already had served more than 270,000 customers and managed more than $10 billion in assets, according to the company's website. It has made a bigger bang than most new companies that are shaking up Wall Street. Others, like Robinhood.com, another virtual bank founded by young people sporting jeans and flip-flops, are making even bolder moves, like offering automated financial investments without charging commission. Much like Internet music platforms that offer free music and charge for optional extra channels, Robinhood.com charges only those customers who want premium services.

ANOTHER THREAT TO BANKS: PEER-TO-PEER LENDING

Another form of virtual banking that is undercutting the industry's foundations are interpersonal loans, also known as peer-to-peer lending. As Uber does with people who need a lift, peer-to-peer lending platforms directly connect people who need a loan with those who can offer it, bypassing banks altogether. This allows both parties to save the commissions banks charge for their operating costs. Peer-to-peer lending platforms like LendingClub.com or Prosper.com accounted for $65 billion in global transactions in 2015 and are projected to skyrocket to $1 trillion by 2025. And in China, where traditional banks are more bureaucratic than in most other countries, the switch to peer-to-peer lending platforms like Ant Financial and Lufax has been massive: by 2016, these and other similar platforms had already surpassed traditional banks as the country's largest source of personal loans.

The first major online platform for interpersonal loans was Zopa, which was created in the United Kingdom in 2005. It was followed a year later by LendingClub.com and Prosper.com in San Francisco. These companies typically offer loans in the range of $1,000 to $40,000 to cover credit card debts, to pay for medical expenses, or to help small businesses grow. Many people carrying large amounts of credit card debt—and thus paying high monthly interest rates—would rather borrow from a peer-to-peer lending platform, cancel out their debt, and pay back the loan at a much lower interest rate than banks would charge. In 2016, LendingClub.com, which claims to be the largest virtual lending company in the United States, boasted on its website that it had given out over $21 billion in loans since its inception in 2006.

But what protection do online lenders have? How do they know that debtors will pay them back? Companies like LendingClub.com run a credit check, just as any traditional bank would do, and in some cases ask for guarantees or collateral. And often the ones making the loans aren't just individuals but are pension funds and other institutional investors looking for better profit margins than what they could get from buying stocks or bonds on the open market. These investors don't typically lend money to just one person at a time, but to many at once. For example, LendingClub.com allows investors to buy "notes" at $50 apiece, so instead of investing $5,000 in a loan to a single person, they can diversify their investment and lend that same amount to a hundred people. If one of them doesn't repay the debt, the investor has lost only $50.

LendingClub.com handles collections every month, takes its commission, and sends the rest back to investors. According to the company, its rate of return for investors has averaged 6.2 percent, which is higher than most other investments. But the company was shaken by a financial scandal in 2016 when it was reported that its founder and CEO, Renaud Laplanche, had been fired by the board for alleged wrongdoing, and the company was being investigated by the Department of Justice.

The news sent shockwaves through the industry, and many investors were scared off. A short while thereafter, Prosper.com announced that it was laying off over a quarter of its workforce. During the ensuing months, criticism began to grow amid concerns that online lending platforms weren't being properly regulated. Opinions were divided between those who said that LendingClub.com and Prosper.com would end up being bought out by the big banks, eager to take advantage of their technological know-how, and those who saw this as simply a stumbling block, and believed that the online platforms would eventually demolish the brick-and-mortar banks.

THE CROWDFUNDING PHENOMENON

Another source of nonbank lending that is expanding rapidly is crowdfunding, or the process whereby many individual people lend money for a particular project. Just as Uber is a platform that connects people who need a ride with those who are willing to use their cars as private taxis, crowdfunding platforms like Kickstarter.com, Indiegogo.com, or CircleUp.com connect people who want to raise money for a creative project with others who are willing to invest in their venture. It's an increasingly popular fund-raising mechanism among people who need loans to produce movies or other artistic and cultural projects, but it is also being used by business start-ups that either couldn't get traditional bank loans or didn't want to pay the high interest rates associated with them.

In my book *Innovate or Die!* I cited the case of Rafael Atijas, a New York University student and music lover who invented a three-stringed guitar to teach children how to play the instrument without going through the pains of having to learn it with a six-stringed instrument. Atijas built his first guitar in Uruguay and promoted it on Kickstarter.com in 2011, telling potential buyers in his sales pitch that he needed to raise $15,000 in one month to produce his guitars. That way, parents interested in buying his guitar for their children could use their credit card with the understanding that if Atijas didn't reach his goal and the project didn't take off, their purchase would be canceled and their money returned. Atijas raised $65,000—four times what he was hoping for—from roughly four hundred investors, so he built six hundred guitars in China and started selling them on his website, loogguitars.com, for $150 each. Soon enough, he was selling thousands of children's guitars in thirty different nations, all without borrowing a penny from any bank.

Since Atijas started his guitar project on Kickstarter.com back in 2011, more than three hundred crowdfunding websites have popped up in the United States alone. These platforms are being used not only to raise funds for books, film projects, and other artistic works, but also to sponsor investigative journalism, geographical explorations, and a wide variety of altruistic causes. Globally, crowdfunding sites have increased from a dozen or so in 2009 to over 1,200 in 2015, according to a study by the Massolution consulting firm. And while it will be a long time before the total amount of crowdfunding loans equals that of traditional banks, their market share is growing.

BLOCKCHAIN WILL CHANGE THE BANKING INDUSTRY

In the medium term, starting a decade from now, blockchain is likely to be the most disruptive factor in the banking industry. It even has the potential to end banks as we know them. Blockchain is a digital record of encrypted financial transactions made outside the traditional banking system that works with virtual currencies like Bitcoin. When you make a transaction like buying a cup of coffee in blockchain, you enter a personal code known as a key, and the information is broadcast over the Internet to all the computers, or nodes, in the system. If the system validates the operation, the transaction is completed and registered in what is known as a block. So unlike with banks, the blockchain database is not stored in any single location, and the records are easily accessible and verifiable.

So what are blockchain's advantages? When it comes to legitimate transactions, the platform cuts out intermediaries—the banks. In doing so, according to supporters, it makes for a much safer and cheaper transaction. While a hacker can penetrate a bank, the blockchain is a decentralized system, which means that a hacker would have to penetrate thousands or even millions of nodes in order to break into the system. And as Alec Ross writes in his book *The Industries of the Future,* "The blockchain could provide a much lower-cost solution for transactions that require a third-party intermediary as a guarantor, such as legal documents, brokerage fees, and ticket purchases."

Many economists, including a number of Nobel Prize winners, believe that digital currencies like Bitcoin are a bubble that is being used primarily by criminals—because transactions can be handled with pseudonyms—and that it will end up hurting many innocent people. Nobel Prize–winning economist and *New York Times* columnist Paul Krugman, for example, has equated this crypto-currency with barbarism. His fellow Nobel laureate Joseph Stiglitz has described Bitcoin as a currency that has become popular only as a means of skirting government regulations, and that therefore it should be banned. And famed New York University economist Nouriel Roubini, who predicted the 2008 financial crisis, has gone so far as to reject the idea that Bitcoin is a currency. He tweeted that Bitcoin is "a Ponzi game and a conduit for criminal/illegal activities."

But others passionately defend Bitcoin. Salim Ismail, one of the founders of Singularity University, told me that Bitcoin and the blockchain "will undoubtedly be the most important innovation in the banking industry. They will completely change the way we deal with money, and I wouldn't be surprised if Bitcoin becomes not the world's backup currency, but its primary one." Ismail offered bank transfers as an example. Today we make these transfers through banks, which charge us a percentage for authentication services and protection from hackers. But with the blockchain, there's no need for a bank's authentication, because there are countless encrypted copies of each transaction. And it allows for a completely transparent record of all activity without the possibility of fraud, loss of data, or cyber piracy, he assured me.

"Consumer banking as we know it will disappear in a decade or so," he added. "Banks are going through the same thing that the recording industry did. A few years ago there were eight big music labels, but thanks to digital platforms like Pandora and Spotify, people started getting music for free, and the record companies went bankrupt!"

What would you recommend that today's young bankers do? I asked Ismail. He said, "First, I would recommend them to understand how blockchain and Bitcoin work. And then I would recommend them to try to convince their bosses to start moving toward blockchain and—if that doesn't work—to look for a job at a company that is already doing that."

After the rush on Bitcoin—whose value skyrocketed from $900 to nearly $20,000 per unit in 2017, only to drop to around $6,000 by early 2018—many other leading economists joined Krugman, Stiglitz, and Roubini in concluding that Bitcoin is a bubble. But even they were much more optimistic about blockchain: they saw it as a promising technology for virtual currency platforms other than Bitcoin, as well as for medical records or any other sort of data.

BANKERS OF THE FUTURE WILL BE DATA ANALYSTS

Ismail's forecast about the end of banks may be a bit out there, but the fact is that traditional banks are rapidly losing their monopoly on taking deposits, offering loans, and making payments. Their future lies not in conducting transactions, but in doing data analysis and offering personalized economic advice to the super-rich. Banks will have to focus more on customers and less on products. Current bank departments—such as their credit card, loans, and mortgage divisions—will become rapidly outdated, since intelligent machines will be doing most of that. The main job of human bankers will be to find customers wherever they are. They will be mostly data analysts whose job will be to explore people's social media and online shopping habits to identify potential clients and offer them their algorithms' specialized services. The banks' data analysts will notice, for instance, when somebody writes on her Facebook page that she recently got a promotion, and then reach out to her to offer a new line of credit. Or they'll see on Twitter that a company is getting harsh reviews from its customers for one of its leading products, and anticipate declining sales long before the next quarterly report is available, allowing the banks to freeze their line of credit or propose a new business model.

Banks will be using data analysis "to understand a customer's need and be present at the time of the need with a relevant offer. For example, spotting that a current bank customer is walking into a car showroom, and sending a message that the customer has been pre-authorized for financing (based upon analysis of existing accounts and spending behaviors)," says the PwC consulting firm. Not surprisingly, when PwC surveyed 560 bank executives across seventeen countries on what will be the "areas of significant effort" in the industry in 2020, two of the most common responses were "enhancing customer data collection" and "allowing for increased customer choice in configuring product features, including pricing."

TECHNOLOGY WILL GROW THE CLIENT BASE

As the number of virtual banks grows, along with the number of traditional banks that are becoming increasingly automated, more and more engineers and programmers will be needed to maintain and improve the performance of the robots, as well as to make them more intelligent. According to EY's Meekings, "The technological areas of the banking industry will undoubtedly be the ones with the highest growth in terms of jobs. This will become more and more important."

The good news for bankers, especially those in developing countries, is that technology will allow them to vastly increase their client base. It has been estimated that by 2040, as many as 1.8 billion people will be moving from rural areas into cities worldwide and that over half of those people currently do not have bank accounts. According to PwC, "Banking the unbanked (urban and rural) will become a primary policy objective in both developed and emerging markets."

The banks' clientele will also grow because the global middle class is expected to expand by 180 percent over the next two decades, creating new needs that will require new services. For example, the gradual aging of the population in most countries means that more people will be planning for their retirement and looking for more long-term investment opportunities. As PwC's Garvey told me, thanks to technology, "we will see a democratization of investment advisory services. Nowadays, rich people get better advice on their investments. You need to have a sizable enough balance for the large investment firms to take you on as a client. But with the automation of many financial services, it will be much easier for more people like teachers, for example, to get solid advice on how to invest their long-term savings for retirement."

BANKERS ON BIKES

In the short term, many bankers will survive by reinventing themselves and finding underserved niches where they can offer their services. One of the most interesting examples of innovation in the world of traditional banking that I came across while doing research for this book was Tucán, a subsidiary of Banco de Costa Rica, which started attracting new clients in rural areas by using local grocers as de facto bank branches and by sending bankers out on motorcycles to reach the more remote locations in the countryside. Tucán teamed up with small grocery stores, convenience stores, and hardware stores in rural areas and in effect turned them into bank branches. Why build a new branch when a local shopkeeper already has a storefront and can offer the same banking services in exchange for a commission? By 2017, Tucán had more than 620 of these branches in markets, bodegas, restaurants, and general stores across the country.

The bank also offers "express services," where bankers on motorcycles ride out into the countryside to meet with farmers, usually at dawn, before the workday begins, to offer them financial services. Instead of waiting for customers to come to the bank, the bank is going to the customers. Why aren't these kinds of innovations seen more often in other countries? One reason is that banks have long prided themselves on being "traditional" and have shied away from sharing their services with nonbank actors. But another reason is that big banks have often been overprotected by regulations that prevent other industries from providing banking services. With no need to compete with other industries, banks could just rest on their laurels. But the technological onslaught will force them to change, to be more creative, and to look for new ways to bring in clients.

THE WOMEN'S BANK OF COSTA RICA

Another example of banks finding new niche markets that I found in Costa Rica is Banco Kristal, also a subsidiary of the Banco de Costa Rica. It's a bank run by women, staffed by women, and exclusively for women. Banco Kristal first opened in December 2015, and within a year it had six branch locations and plans to open a total of sixty by 2020. It was established on the premise that women are a key segment of the population that has been traditionally neglected by the banking industry. Women not only account for half the population but also often manage their families' savings. Plus, there is a growing population of single or divorced mothers, who are in charge of providing for their children's health and education.

To build a new base of female clients, Banco Kristal hit the market with a chain of stores—yes, they call them stores instead of branches—that don't resemble traditional banks in the slightest. Instead of traditional tellers and loan officers, Banco Kristal simply has advisers. And instead of having their employees standing behind counters or sitting in cubicles, Banco Kristal has several small tables where the advisers can sit down and talk with their clients. In the corner of each location is a space with games where children can play and have fun while their mothers discuss matters with the bankers. While children are tolerated, if not particularly welcome, in traditional banks, Banco Kristal's advisers are trained to go out of their way to make sure that the kids have a good time.

As soon as a woman enters a branch with her child, an adviser welcomes her and asks the child if he or she would like to go play in the game area. The adviser is expected not to sit down and begin talking business with the mother until the child is safely settled in. As simple as it may seem, paying extra attention to the children has been a tremendous success, according to Banco Kristal's executives.

In addition, the Banco Kristal stores offer their clients all sorts of products tailored specifically for them, like special lines of credit for cosmetic surgery, at lower interest rates than other banks. And their websites offer a very simple system of electronic "envelopes" into which clients can deposit their savings: just as their grandmothers once labeled paper envelopes according to what the cash inside was being saved for—for example, *expenses, college tuition,* or *vacation*—Banco Kristal clients can do the same sort of thing online.

While it's too early to tell whether Banco Kristal's experiment will be successful in the long-term, the early results seem quite positive. During its first year of operation, the bank managed to bring in 55,000 new clients, doubling what it had hoped for when it first opened for business, and the average account balance was $170 per client, which is well above the $60 average for traditional brick-and-mortar banks across Costa Rica, its top executives told me.

MOST BANKERS WILL BE WOMEN

What will the typical banker of the future look like? It won't be a serious-looking gentleman dressed in a suit and tie, as it has been in the past. According to the EY study, "the banker of the future is more likely to be a young female technologist." The same study also found that "banking lags behind a number of other industries in gender and ethnic diversity." In order to survive, banks will have to connect with a new generation of clients, especially women, young people, and those who change jobs every couple of years or work flexible schedules from homes, like those who manage their own small businesses, it says.

An unprecedented number of women already serve as heads of their households. In the United States, women control about half of all private wealth and are the main source of income in 40 percent of families. Globally, women control 65 percent of discretionary consumer spending, and that figure will be growing in the years to come. Meanwhile, the study also shows that 73 percent of women say they're dissatisfied with the banking industry: among other things, they cite that they receive less attention than male customers from bank employees.

To capture the expanding world of potential female clients, banks will increasingly need executives and employees who better reflect the demographic landscape of their communities. According to the EY study, "there is a positive correlation between greater gender balance on boards, higher share price and better financial performance. From 2005 to 2014, boards with a higher-than-average percentage of women outperformed those with a lower than average percentage by 36%."

In short, building upon the seemingly oversimplified forecast that the bankers of the future will be "young female technologists," we can anticipate that bankers will be young people—women and men—whose jobs will focus on analyzing data, creating algorithms, offering personalized financial advice, caring for and maintaining robots, and providing smart customer service. They will be expected to go where the clients are—whether in remote corners of the Internet or in rural areas accessible only by motorcycle—and not expect the clients to come to them.

Bank employees who perform administrative tasks like filing papers or filling out loan application forms are likely to lose their jobs. These employees, who often don't have a college degree and currently make up about 30 percent of the workforce at most retail banks, will gradually be replaced by more skilled college graduates. "But those lost jobs won't be replaced by an equal percentage of new positions," PwC's Garvey told me. "A more likely figure is that twenty administrative employees whose jobs are automated will be replaced by a single data analyst." In other words, there will still be bankers, but they will be very different from those of the past, and there will be fewer of them.

5

THEY'RE COMING FOR LAWYERS!

THE FUTURE OF LAW, ACCOUNTING, AND INSURANCE FIRMS

NEW YORK, MIAMI

When BakerHostetler, one of the largest law firms in the country, announced in 2016 that it had just hired its first robot attorney, named Ross, both the company and the manufacturer were quick to say that no attorneys who currently worked for the firm would be losing their jobs. There was nothing to fear, the firm said. This new robotic lawyer would be just another member of the human team of fifty-odd people working in the firm's bankruptcy division, helping with routine case law research, which had previously been done by young associates fresh out of law school.

Ross, the robot, is powered by IBM's Watson, the famous supercomputer that won the *Jeopardy!* contest, the law firm explained. Unlike a Google search, which provides lawyers with numerous articles that they can read and evaluate, Watson searches hundreds of databases stored in its own memory, processes the information, and decides for itself which are the most relevant ones so it can deliver a specific response. In other words, it not only reads the articles but culls the most important information attorneys are looking for. "ROSS is not a way to replace our attorneys—it is a supplemental tool to help them move faster, learn faster, and continually improve," claimed BakerHostetler's chief information officer, Bob Craig.

But should we really believe Craig's reassuring assertion? Many attorneys took Craig's words with a grain of salt, fearing that their profession could soon become automated like so many others. In answering questions on *Jeopardy!,* for example, Watson consulted two hundred million pages of content, including the entire Wikipedia encyclopedia, without even being connected to the Internet. What lawyer could compete with that? For now, Ross is simply a service to which attorneys can subscribe online. But since it has an independent database, many in the industry are wondering when this new robot attorney will take on a human's job and sit at a desk in the firm's offices alongside his flesh-and-blood colleagues.

Andrew Arruda, chief executive of Ross Intelligence, the company that built the robot lawyer, has said that their "goal is to have ROSS on the legal team of every lawyer in the world." And professor Ryan Calo, an expert on the intersection of technology and law, has predicted that sooner or later "*not* using these systems will come to be viewed as antiquated and even irresponsible, like writing a brief on a typewriter."

HOW MANY LAWYERS WILL BE REPLACED BY ROBOTS?

How many human attorneys will be replaced by the new robot lawyers like Ross in the coming years? In some fields of law, the number could be substantial. Robots and online legal platforms like LegalZoom, RocketLawyer, and LawDepot are already offering many routine legal services that have traditionally been performed by human lawyers, such as wills, divorce proceedings, and rental agreements. In the future, a sizable part of legal consultations will be carried out online. Just as Uber has replaced many traditional taxi drivers, online platforms will replace many of the attorneys currently offering the most basic legal services.

These platforms are in general easy to use. They strike up a dialogue with potential clients, asking what sort of legal services they are looking for, and they offer a menu of options. Do you need a will, a prenup, a divorce settlement, or a partnership agreement? After clicking on the corresponding box, the client answers a few specific questions about the case, and the virtual attorney creates the requested legal document.

The combination of robot attorneys like Ross and virtual legal services platforms like LegalZoom is already rocking the legal profession. According to the *Financial Times,* in the United Kingdom alone, 31,000 law-related jobs—most of them paralegals and secretaries—have disappeared, and another 114,000 are expected to vanish over the next two decades. In the United States, some are making even more dire predictions. F. Daniel Siciliano, a professor at Stanford Law School who focuses on how technology impacts his profession, has said that in fifteen years, "two-thirds of lawyers won't practice law, at least not the way they practice now. Many won't be lawyers at all."

THE UBERIZATION OF LAW

Nowadays it's quite hard for a low-income person to hire a good attorney. In order to practice, lawyers in the United States—unlike in many other countries—must pass a very rigorous bar exam after their graduation from law school and are among the best-paid professionals out there. A young attorney working for a midsize or large firm can charge around three hundred dollars an hour, while more experienced lawyers can charge twice that, and the most renowned attorneys in their fields can command up to a thousand dollars an hour. It's no coincidence that cheaper online platforms have not only cropped up but are also growing by leaps and bounds.

LegalZoom.com, for example, charges a minimum of $29 to draw up a rental agreement, $69 for a basic will, and $299 for an uncontested divorce. Each of these tasks would take a human attorney several hours to prepare, at a minimum rate of $300 per hour, making it much more expensive. Therefore, millions of people are beginning to use virtual legal platforms not only to produce basic contracts but also to send threatening letters to delinquent debtors or neighbors who play the music too loud. In many cases, these platforms aren't even run by attorneys. Just as growing numbers of people use Uber and Lyft drivers who don't have taxi licenses, people are increasingly using legal services run by entrepreneurs who never had to pass a state bar exam.

At the time of this writing, RocketLawyer.com has already created 40 million legal documents, answered more than 500,000 legal questions, and registered 7 million businesses, according to the company's website. Just as Uber's defenders argue that it's not worth paying for a traditional taxi service if you can use a private one for less, supporters of these legal online platforms say it makes no sense to pay a human lawyer to draw up a routine contract or register a new company when an algorithm can do the same task easily and more cheaply.

Many attorneys at large firms, however, argue that these legal services websites are aimed at the poorest sectors of the population who normally wouldn't hire a lawyer. Besides, legal platforms perform only routine tasks and don't threaten the jobs of attorneys dealing with more complex cases. Abraham C. Reich, a partner and former cochair of Fox Rothschild, a national firm of around 800 attorneys based in Philadelphia, told me that "we really haven't been impacted by these websites because we represent clients with more sophisticated legal issues. Plus, you have to read the fine print on websites like LegalZoom.com. Even though they offer you some service for a hundred dollars, if there are ever any complications with the case, they refer you to a lawyer. I don't know what their income structure is, but I wouldn't be surprised if a good part of their income comes from getting you a low-cost lawyer."

DONOTPAY.COM IS ALREADY OFFERING FREE ONLINE LEGAL SERVICES

When twenty-year-old Stanford University student Joshua Browder was named by the British daily *Financial Times* as one of the most innovative lawyers in the United States in 2017, the young man could hardly believe it. He wasn't even a lawyer. Browder said that he was nevertheless honored by the distinction. He tweeted, "Despite not being a lawyer, nor a college graduate, and wanting to make the entire $200bn profession free!" Browder, born in the United Kingdom to an American father, was the founder of DoNotPay.com, a free website to help people fight traffic tickets in court. The young man had received numerous parking and traffic tickets as a teenager in London and had discovered that the appeals process was so routine that he could basically just send the same letter all the time.

So Browder created his website, DoNotPay.com, where people who felt they had been ticketed unfairly could answer a few basic questions about the incident—such as whether they had parked outside the lines because of a medical emergency or because a "No Parking" sign was blocked from their view—and the program would produce the legal paperwork for appealing the case. DoNotPay.com became an instant success. According to Browder, by the end of 2017, the platform had saved people $9.3 million by challenging 375,000 parking tickets.

It was so successful, in fact, that Browder soon expanded the scope of his website to include legal letters challenging other types of issues, from broken rental agreements to claims against airlines for delayed flights. When you first visit the website, you're greeted with a line asking, "What can I help you with?" You then type in the nature of your problem, answer a few basic questions, and receive an automated legal document to send to the party who committed the offense. After receiving $1.1 million in seed funding from a top venture capital firm, Browder said that his company will continue to offer free legal services. Like many other free websites, it will accept ads in the future in order to fund much more ambitious free legal services, he said.

"I am not doing this to make any money whatsoever," Browder said, adding that he has always resented the fact that many lawyers profit from poor people's troubles. "As part of the funding (and all future financings), I will take a $1/pound salary until the law is free for everyone in America/UK," he said. "Of course, we are a long way from that goal, but I hope that DoNotPay will ultimately give everyone the same legal power as the richest in society." For now, DoNotPay.com is a fairly bare-bones website, but its mission to offer free legal services to everybody could shake up at least part of the legal industry in the long run.

ALGORITHMS ARE ALSO LOOKING TO REPLACE JUDGES

Besides the robot lawyers, there are growing numbers of legal websites that offer to solve disputes, posing a threat to the jobs of judges and mediators. The best-known of these websites is Modria.com, cofounded in 2011 by Colin Rule, former director of online dispute resolution for eBay and PayPal. He claims to have successfully resolved some 400 million disputes between people who bought products online and those who sold them. There are already three times as many legal disputes between buyers and sellers on eBay that have been decided with "online dispute resolution" than all the lawsuits filed in the entire U.S. court system.

And the spread of these algorithms suggests that in the near future, computer programs will be able to resolve increasingly complex cases. If computer programs can already resolve disputes between buyers and sellers on eBay, why couldn't they do the same for disputes between husbands and wives, for example, or creditors and debtors? Unlike RocketLawyer.com, Modria .com doesn't work for individual clients, but is subcontracted by companies. In other words, companies hire Modria.com to resolve complaints from unhappy customers, instead of having their own in-house dispute-resolution departments. Typically, Modria.com resolves complaints from people who bought something online, whether it's a shirt that doesn't fit, a dress that arrived too late to wear to a wedding, or an electronic device that simply doesn't work. Its algorithms solve these disputes without any human intervention, the company says.

IN FIVE OR TEN YEARS, MODRIA WILL BE ABLE TO RESOLVE ANY DISPUTE

Let's say someone just paid $500 for a guitar on eBay, but when it arrived, it came with a crack. Angry, the customer doesn't want to waste time on hold waiting to speak with someone in customer service who might be on the other side of the globe, or with a robot, so he decides to file a complaint online. He visits the "resolve your problem" page on eBay's website, and eBay forwards the complaint to Modria.com. There the unhappy customer can choose from a menu of options such as "the product arrived late," "the product was damaged," or "the product was not as described."

Then Modria's algorithm finds out—using automated searches—whether the customer has filed previous complaints against the seller, whether the guitar was sent on time, and if the package was delayed at any point during the shipping process. Based on this information, Modria's algorithm automatically reaches a verdict. For instance, it may call for exchanging the damaged guitar for a new one, and possibly include a fifty-dollar credit for the inconvenience, in hopes of keeping the customer happy and willing to return to the same e-commerce site in the future.

If the customer still isn't satisfied with the algorithm's ruling, the same "resolve your problem" page on eBay's website offers an option to appeal, which is also automated. According to Modria.com president Scott Carr, 90 percent of the more than 60 million online disputes handled by Modria are resolved through these first two stages. If the algorithm can't resolve the issue by this point, then one of Modria's human mediators will intervene, Carr explains on the company's website. But with advances in artificial intelligence, within the next five to ten years, the algorithm should be able to handle just about any dispute without the need to use a human arbitrator as a last resort, Carr added.

Benjamin Barton, a professor at the University of Tennessee's College of Law and author of *Glass Half Full,* a book about the future of lawyers, predicts that platforms like Modria.com will be replacing growing numbers of lawyers and judges, and not just because online services offer cheaper services. Barton points out that one of the major reasons is the fact that courts around the world simply can't handle the number of pending cases, and fewer companies and individuals are willing to wait months or years to have their disputes resolved. "Right now, Modria promises an elegant solution to a previously insoluble problem: how to deal with the mass of smaller disputes created by e-business," he writes. "Tomorrow, it may try to solve a different problem: how to deal with larger, more expensive disputes."

WILL YOU NEED A LAWYER TO BUY OR SELL YOUR HOME?

Blockchain, the network of encrypted financial transactions, could also end up replacing lawyers and notaries who do the legal paperwork in real estate transactions. Alec Ross, former senior adviser for innovation to Hillary Clinton while she was secretary of state, says that what struck him the most when he bought a home in 2014 was that the procedure had changed very little since his parents had bought their home fifty years earlier. "There were huge piles of paper with signatures and seals," he recalls in his book *The Industries of the Future.* "It took weeks to sort the records, and on the day of the sale, it took hours to get through all the paperwork. The process of verification was manual and ridiculously expensive. We paid thousands of dollars in legal closing costs to verify a transfer that could be done electronically for nearly nothing if some technology-based ingenuity were applied. . . . It is hard to think that a young lawyer today could count on 45 years of employment organizing legal documents for home buyers."

THE FLESH-AND-BLOOD LAWYERS STRIKE BACK

In some countries, lawyers are already publicly fighting back against what they see as a growing threat from robots. Just as taxi driver guilds rebelled against Uber and attacked their drivers in Paris, Buenos Aires, and other cities around the world, lawyers' associations are taking action against LegalZoom, RocketLawyer, and other legal services websites. These associations, much like those of taxi drivers, argue that state laws prohibit the practice of law by anyone who is unlicensed, in this case by people who have not graduated from law school and passed the bar. In a number of cases, lawyers' associations have gone to court looking to shut them down. But in the long run they are likely fighting a losing battle, just as the cabdrivers did.

Back in 1999, the Unauthorized Practice of Law Committee—a Texas committee formed to enforce that state's laws on the unauthorized practice of law—filed a suit against Parsons Technology, a software manufacturer whose product, Quicken Family Lawyer, or QFL, helped people create basic legal documents like wills, contracts, and rental agreements. A court initially ruled in favor of the committee, but as time went by, consumers filed an increasing number of challenges, demanding access to cheaper legal services.

As the popularity of online legal services platforms grew, and as traffic on websites like LegalZoom and RocketLawyer skyrocketed, judges across the country began dismissing lawsuits against them. In many cases, even when a court managed to shut down a website, the company behind it would simply begin operating out of England—where the law allows for many basic legal services to be offered by people without law degrees—or some other country across the globe.

In 2016, during the semiannual meeting of the American Bar Association, Pennsylvania state bar association president

William Pugh threatened to withdraw from the ABA if the association didn't deep-six a basic legal services program for small companies that it was developing jointly with RocketLawyer.com. Under pressure from Pugh and his colleagues, the ABA quickly announced that the program would be terminated, at least for the time being.

But few believe that Pugh's victory over the ABA will last. According to Josias "Joe" N. Dewey, a law professor at the University of Miami and the founder of LegalTechLabs, what we're seeing is "a struggle between the past and the future" in which Pugh and his supporters were "protecting an economic cartel" and "conspiring against the client's freedom to choose cheaper legal services." Traditional lawyers will not be able to withstand the offensive of low-cost legal technology, he says.

THE COMING POST-PROFESSIONAL SOCIETY

There is a growing consensus among scholars that as with other industries, attorneys will no longer enjoy an absolute monopoly on exercising their profession. One of the best-known supporters of this theory is University of Oxford professor Richard Susskind, president of Great Britain's Society for Computers and Law, a columnist for the *Times* of London, and author of the book *The End of Lawyers?*

According to Susskind, professions as they exist today are in danger of extinction because they offer outdated, expensive, and elitist services in which the knowledge of a few is accessible only to a small section of society. They are increasingly being replaced by online alternatives that are not only cheaper but often better. "In a 'technology-based Internet society,' we predict that increasingly capable machines, operating on their own or with non-specialist users, will take on many of the tasks that have been the historic preserve of the professions," he and Daniel Susskind write in *The Future of the Professions*. "We anticipate an 'incremental transformation' in the way that we produce and distribute expertise in society. This will lead eventually to a dismantling of the traditional professions."

Until now, lawyers, accountants, and other professionals were defined by their possession of a specialized knowledge, specific credentials such as university degrees or licenses to practice their trade, and the ability to perform highly regulated tasks. Only attorneys or notaries could draw up certain legal documents, just as doctors are the only ones who can prescribe certain medications. Through a tacit agreement with society, these professionals offer their specialized knowledge to the public in exchange for being able to enjoy a monopoly on their work. But that agreement is rapidly vanishing, because in the age of the Internet, professionals have ceased to be the absolute owners of their specialized knowledge, Susskind argues. Anyone with access to Google can retrieve a large part of this knowledge in a matter of seconds, and for free. Why should society force people to pay for what they can do by themselves?

LAWYERS IN ENGLAND HAVE ALREADY LOST THEIR MONOPOLY

Even if one believes that human attorneys will continue to be an indispensable part of the legal profession for years to come, at least part of their work—especially the simpler contracts and documents—will increasingly be offered through alternative sources like websites run by people without J.D.s or professional licenses, Susskind says. The Oxford professor, who has become a champion of what he calls the "modernization of professions," says that it's only a matter of time until social pressures break down the attorneys' monopoly on the legal profession in the United States and other countries, because there's no longer any justification for them to be the sole owners of legal knowledge and thus able to charge exorbitant fees.

In England and Australia, for example, the laws have already been relaxed to allow people without law degrees to offer legal services. The Co-operative Bank, with headquarters in Manchester, England, for example, has announced that it will be offering legal services at 350 of its branches, and many are predicting that large superstores like Walmart or Sears will soon be doing the same. To protect themselves from the growing threat of competition, large law firms are beginning to diversify their sources of income. Like traditional banks did when they started offering services online in order to be able to compete with virtual banks, many law firms are beginning to offer basic legal services online, such as the drafting of simple contracts. According to Susskind, these firms will soon be hiring paralegals—perhaps even from low-wage countries—to run their online service programs. In the near future, the big law firms won't resemble the ones we read about in John Grisham novels in the least. Instead, they'll be replaced by firms offering more affordable legal services that will be staffed by robot-assisted attorneys, by online law offices, or by accounting companies, banks, grocery stores, and other businesses that are already starting to do legal work.

WHAT PARTS OF A LAWYER'S JOB CAN BE AUTOMATED?

John O. McGinnis, a professor at Northwestern University's Pritzker School of Law, and Russell G. Pearce, a professor at Fordham University's School of Law, concluded in a study that the parts of a lawyer's job that are most likely to be automated in the near future will be reviewing documents, researching case history, and analyzing the chances of a case's success.

Before the introduction of Ross and other legal services robots, attorneys had to search records on specialized Internet sites like Lexis by using keywords, much like when one does a Google search. But that was a tricky thing, because there was always the possibility that a highly relevant document wouldn't show up because it didn't contain the specific keyword an attorney had typed in. The opposite was possible, too: that the search could produce documents containing the keyword but completely irrelevant to the matter at hand. Now, thanks to artificial intelligence, algorithms have perfected the art of deciding whether a particular document is relevant to a particular case or not. Artificial intelligence allows for searches using basic concepts expressed in simple language, as opposed to highly specific keywords, in order to find relevant materials.

The algorithms aren't perfect, of course, but the authors of the study argue that robots make far fewer mistakes. "Imperfection is the norm," they say, "even when lawyers perform document review, where fatigue, boredom, and other frailties—which do not affect machines—can substantially reduce the accuracy of document review." But now, they say, search engines for case histories and other legal matters will be incredibly more effective.

WILLS, PRENUPS, AND INCORPORATIONS

McGinnis and Pearce maintain that while lawyers have used boilerplate legal documents since the Middle Ages, artificial intelligence will revolutionize their use because it will be able to adapt them to meet individual situations in a split second. In this day and age, anyone can enter their personal data on LegalZoom.com or any other legal services website and draw up a will or incorporate a new company in the public registry. But with advances in artificial intelligence, more complex documents will be personalized and perfected to the point that they'll be much more than simple drafts.

"Of course, at first, lawyers will still be very involved in marking up the first drafts that machines create. But even at this stage, the savings can be very large," McGinnis and Pearce argue. "In the future, machine processing will be able to automate a form, tailor it according to the specific facts and legal arguments, and track its effect in future litigation. As hardware and software capacity improves, so too will the generated documents. We predict that within ten to fifteen years, computer-based services will routinely generate the first draft of most transactional documents."

THE ALGORITHMS THAT PREDICT WHO WILL WIN A CASE

Thanks to new developments in algorithms, the new field of predictive analysis is revolutionizing the legal world. Attorneys can now use real data to predict their chances of winning at trial. For now, when a lawyer advises a client about the advantages of going to trial or negotiating a settlement, the lawyer does so based on his personal experience or intuition. But this has obvious limitations. By comparison, "the advantage of predictive analytics is that it provides a mechanism both to access a vast amount of information and systematically mine that information to understand the likely outcome of the case at hand," McGinnis and Pearce write.

There already are Internet companies like LexMachina .com that have files on millions of patent cases, which they can use to detect trends and make predictions about whether a patent application might be approved before it's even submitted. And the LexMachina.com model is being applied to several other areas of the law, up to and including cases on their way to the U.S. Supreme Court. McGinnis and Pearce admit that predictive analyses on patent approval or Supreme Court decisions are easier to run than others because—especially in regard to the Supreme Court, which has only nine judges—there is a relatively limited number of cases and the voting habits of each justice's decisions are easier to foresee. But the authors predict that hurdle will also be overcome in the coming years as predictive studies will spread across just about every facet of the legal profession.

"To be sure, legal analytics will still leave a role for lawyers. A lawyer's judgment may still add some value to the predictions derived from machine intelligence, even if the machine prediction alone is better than the lawyer's prediction alone. Over time, however, legal analytics will reduce the value of a lawyer's assessment in at least some cases," McGinnis and Pearce write. Some investors are so confident in the legal predictions churned out by algorithms that they are willing to offer loans to people who are considered likely to win in court. The Silicon Valley website Legalist.com, for instance, offers "funding for your lawsuit." If you need some cash to get your lawsuit up and running, and the company's algorithm decides that your chances of winning are good, they'll give you a loan in exchange for a percentage of your eventual settlement. Could this be the start of a new industry? Will we bet money on other people's cases based on which algorithm we think will do the best job?

ROBOTS THAT PICK THE BEST LAWYER FOR YOU

Predictive data analysis is increasingly being used not only to evaluate the chances of a case's success but also to forecast which law firm or particular lawyer will be the best suited for your need. LexMachina.com, a division of LexisNexis, which was created by Stanford Law School, and Miami-based Premonition.com do just that. They help clients evaluate law firms before hiring them, and enable firms to assess themselves, so that they can promote their services more successfully if they rank high on a particular legal service.

LexMachina's "comparator apps" allow subscribers to compare up to four courts, judges, or firms in a matter of seconds. According to the announcement posted on the company's website when the product was first launched in 2016, the "comparator" ranks law firms by their success rate, their respective experience with specific types of cases, the amount of time it took to resolve each case, and the complaints filed against them by clients.

For example, if a company wants to hire a law firm to bring a case against someone who has violated one of its patents, it can quickly search for the top four firms specializing in that sort of case. Then the prospective client can enter these four names into a form on the website, establish his priorities—"the least expensive one," for instance—and voilà: LexMachina gives its recommendation on which would be the law firm best suited for the case.

The rankings aren't based solely on winning percentages and costs, but on several other needs that potential customers may have. There might, for example, be two firms that charge the same fees and have a similar success rate, but one of them could have much more experience in certain cases or resolve them much more quickly than the other. If a LexMachina client needs to close a case as soon as possible—because someone is infringing on a patent, costing the company many thousands or even millions of dollars, for example—the app will prioritize the firms that have the shortest turnaround times. And soon these apps are likely to offer comparisons of individual attorneys within a firm and determine who would be best suited to each particular case.

THE GOOD NEWS: ATTORNEYS WILL HAVE MORE CLIENTS

The good news for lawyers is that their client base will expand substantially. Currently, only higher-earning people tend to use an attorney for a prenup or commercial contract, but soon enough lawyers will be able to offer such services to the entire population at very low cost, because all they'll have to do is proofread—and occasionally slightly edit—the documents written by robots. Algorithms will be taking care of the most tedious parts of their jobs.

Plus, there are still aspects of the law where computers will have a hard time replacing human beings. It's hard to imagine, for example, a robot making a good opening or closing statement to a judge and jury. And while algorithms will affect their litigation indirectly—running predictive analyses will encourage parties to start a lawsuit or reach an agreement—it will still be quite some time before a robot actually argues a case, or at least does so with the eloquence of a human attorney.

There will also be a need for humans to both interpret new laws and to anticipate changes in the law. Smart machines operate on existing information, and they're more effective than people when it comes to predicting trends based on past cases, but they're not so good with present or future events, where there's less data to analyze. Algorithms are only as good as the data they're fed. And while artificial intelligence will grow its intuitive capacities with time, it's the human lawyers who gather for drinks with government officials, fellow lawyers, or other parties and hear the latest rumors about things that may not yet be public.

In areas in which regulations change constantly, like banking, attorneys who are more aware of which rules are being drafted will always be able to offer better advice to clients than computer programs that rely only on public materials. And lawyers will survive because of the personal relationships they develop not only with their sources but also with their clients.

"Lawyers do more than undertake legal analysis," McGinnis and Pearce write. "They bond with their clients, thereby fostering relationships of trust, which allow the lawyer to facilitate clients to see their long-term legal self-interest, even when clients' passions and confusions cloud that interest. Machines are unlikely to perform this bonding function and, thus, will be unlikely to substantially affect this important aspect of the lawyer-client relationship."

They add, "The overall effect of the machine invasion thus will be quite mixed for lawyers, but particularly difficult for nonspecialized lawyers of average or worse than average ability. For consumers at every level, the progress of machine intelligence is excellent news, offering lower prices and more transparency. It is especially good for the underserved middle class and even the poor who are more likely to access legal services at prices they can afford." There will always be legal superstars, or attorneys who continue providing services that cannot be Uberized: the ones who "practice in highly specialized areas of law subject to rapid change, appear in court, or provide services where human relationships are central to their quality," predict the two professors. "Otherwise, no effective barriers to the advance of machine lawyering in legal practices exist. . . . Ultimately, therefore, the disruptive effect of machine intelligence will trigger the end of lawyers' monopoly and provide a benefit to society and clients as legal services become more transparent and affordable to consumers, and access to justice thereby becomes more widely available," they conclude.

THE ACCOUNTANTS ARE COMING

Large accounting firms like Deloitte, EY, KPMG, and PwC—which are now referring to themselves as multidisciplinary professional services companies, or even more pompously, integrated global services for business solutions firms—are jumping rapidly into the legal field. While these companies are not yet authorized to offer legal services in the United States, they are already doing so in England, Australia, and Mexico, and to a lesser extent in China, Japan, Germany, France, Spain, Italy, and Canada.

"LAWYERS BEWARE: The Accountants Are Coming After Your Business" read a headline in the British magazine *The Economist.* According to the article, the four largest accounting firms have combined annual revenues of $120 billion, which easily exceeds the $89 billion generated by the hundred largest law firms in the world. Once upon a time, attorneys and accountants competed for advice on tax services, but not much else. Now, though, the area between the two professions is becoming increasingly gray.

The "Big Four"—as Deloitte, EY, KPMG, and PwC are known in the business world—are adding legal departments and even buying up law firms across the globe. PwC, for example, is now the tenth largest law firm on the planet based on the number of attorneys and paralegals. And in a three-year span, between 2013 and 2016, EY's legal arm expanded from twenty-three to sixty-four countries.

In the United States and other countries in which they can't act as attorneys, accounting firms are increasingly offering legal services that complement their primary business, such as drafting boilerplate business contracts or processing immigration papers for their foreign clients. It's only a matter of time, though, before they expand into other areas, such as litigation, that are currently exclusive to law firms. Eventually the accounting firms will go head-to-head with law firms.

THE ACCOUNTANTS' COMPETITIVE ADVANTAGE

Do accounting firms have a competitive advantage over law firms? In more than one way, they do. They can offer cheaper legal services to their corporate clients, since they don't bill by the hour as do most lawyers in America, Great Britain, and many other countries. These multidisciplinary accounting firms charge a fixed flat rate for the services they provide, including legal services. For clients who are tired of spending fortunes to pay their legal bills, that's a powerful incentive that isn't likely to go away anytime soon.

Faced with this onslaught from accountants, the lawyers are pushing back and expanding their own practice areas. Throughout the United States and Europe, law firms are buying up subsidiaries that can offer insurance, investment advice, public relations strategies, and consulting services of all kinds. For lawyers, "there's good news and bad news," Mark L. Silow, chair of the firm Fox Rothschild, told me. "The bad news is that there will be more competition for what lawyers have historically done, but there may also be more business opportunities for areas where lawyers have not been active. Right now, it's unclear whether the pluses or minuses will prevail."

THE RISE OF THE ROBO-ACCOUNTANTS

There is a powerful reason why accounting firms are diversifying their services and jumping into the legal field as fast as they can: they know that their traditional accounting business—preparing tax returns—will be nearly fully automated. According to Vasant Dhar, professor at the Stern School of Business and the Center for Data Science at New York University, websites that offer automated tax returns are putting the jobs of roughly two million accountants, bookkeepers, and auditors at risk in the United States alone.

The millions of people who watched the 2017 Super Bowl saw revealing commercials by two big accounting companies—H&R Block and TurboTax—that essentially conceded the victory of intelligent machines over human accountants. The two companies' ads boasted of having computers that were more efficient than humans to prepare tax returns. The ads heralded an inevitable automation of the accounting profession. "Robots Will Soon Do Your Taxes. Bye-Bye, Accounting Jobs," read a *Wired* magazine headline. The story said that, as is the case with lawyers, the accountants who will survive will be those who specialize in complex cases, or have clients with very particular needs, or who supervise the work of the intelligent machines that will do most of the traditional accountants' work.

No matter how good accountants may be, they will never have the knowledge acquired by a robot like IBM's Watson. As Bill Cobb, former CEO of H&R Block, explained, robots are able to absorb millions upon millions of bytes of data previously processed by the firm, which no human accountant could even begin to digest. With that massive amount of data, an intelligent machine can find tax deductions and loopholes that most human accountants would miss. "If you're a journalist in California, married, filing jointly, [IBM's Watson is] going to know what other journalists in California, filing jointly or not, have been able to find as deductions or credits," Cobb said. He added that "even the best tax pro can't know the ins and outs of how the tax code applies to every profession, but Watson can."

And it won't be too long before even robo-accounting firms will be in trouble, because the Internal Revenue Service will be sending you its automated tax bill directly, bypassing accountants altogether. The government tax agency's database will have all the information it will need about the payments you made and deductible expenditures you are entitled to, and will send you a letter or an email saying how much you owe. And you will call an accountant only if you believe there was a mistake and want to dispute that bill. Whether they belong to big automated private firms or to the government, robots are going to do your taxes.

INSURANCE AGENTS UNDERMINED BY ALGORITHMS

The same phenomenon that is affecting attorneys and accountants—the growing competition from automated platforms such as RocketLawyer.com and TurboTax.com—is also taking a toll on insurance brokers. A New York website called Lemonade.com is offering property insurance at a much lower rate than traditional insurance companies, and claims to have sold more than two thousand policies in its first three months. Lemonade.com can offer cheap insurance policies because it's almost completely automated—algorithms, rather than people, calculate insurance premiums—and competes with companies that have a huge overhead.

Lemonade.com promises you "90 seconds to get insured. 3 minutes to get paid," instead of having to negotiate for hours with a traditional insurance agent.

When a customer named Brandon filed a claim about a stolen coat, for instance, all he had to do was answer a few questions on his phone, and in three seconds he was reimbursed, the company said. That's a world record for the insurance industry, it said. According to Jim Hageman, Lemonade's chief claims officer, during those three seconds the company's algorithm "reviewed the claim, cross-checked it with the policy, ran 18 anti-fraud algorithms, approved it, sent payment instructions to the bank and informed Brandon." All that in just three seconds.

According to *The Economist,* "The industry is still astonishingly reliant on human labor. Underwriters look at data but plenty still rely on human judgment to evaluate risks and set premiums." Insurers got their first wake-up call when websites started offering customers the opportunity to compare industry prices. Now, with the emergence of fully automated and much cheaper services, the industry will have to get up to speed, or many traditional companies will disappear.

MANY INSURANCE AGENTS WILL BECOME DATA ANALYSTS

Instead of relying on professional experience, intuition, or past data, insurance companies will need more data analysts to get ahead of the facts and anticipate future trends. These analysts will mine data that people make public in their social networks or on their cell phone apps, and use that information to offer them tailor-made insurance policies. The industry's data analysts might, for instance, send an email to a potential client who uses the FitBit app to measure physical exercise, saying something like: "We've noticed that you spend an hour a day on the treadmill. We'd like to offer you a special rate normally available only to star athletes!"

An insurance company may want to offer clients a smartwatch or a free virtual assistant like Alexa in exchange for access to their information. The insurance company may then learn, for instance, that a particular client goes on a trip the third weekend of every month. Acting on that information, the company may offer a specialized insurance policy to cover every risk during the homeowner's absence. Why pay a full month's worth of insurance, if you really need coverage only for a week? Or if the insurance company's data miners learn that a client walks ten thousand steps a day or brushes his teeth three times a day, they will be able to offer reduced rates for health or dental coverage, thus winning over clients from competitors. Conversely, data analysts will be on the lookout for clients engaging in dangerous activities: if a client describes himself as a yoga instructor or church choir singer in his insurance application but posts pictures of himself on Facebook bungee jumping in Tanzania or paragliding off the top of a mountain in the Alps, the insurance company's data analysts will recommend increasing that person's premium once it comes up for renewal. Like bankers, many insurance agents will become explorers in the wild world of social media.

LAWYERS, ACCOUNTANTS, AND PSYCHOLOGISTS WILL BE WORKING TOGETHER

Judging by what I learned from interviewing innovation chiefs at law and accounting firms, I wouldn't be surprised if professional offices devoted exclusively to one specific line of work—such as providing legal or accounting services—will soon be extinct. Instead, we will have multidisciplinary practice offices, in which lawyers will work together under the same roof with bankers, accountants, insurers, doctors, psychologists, data analysts, public relations specialists, and perhaps even spiritual gurus. And they will jointly evaluate the best strategies for each client.

Does it make sense for divorce cases to be handled exclusively by attorneys, without the presence of a psychologist who can advise divorcing parents on how to do things in a way that will do the least harm to their children? Or does it make sense for lawyers to draw up a will without the help of an accountant who can help evaluate the document's tax ramifications? And when a law office represents a company in a lawsuit, wouldn't it be wise to involve a public relations expert in the whole process, so as to prepare for the media reaction? Soon enough, multidisciplinary practice offices will have all these professionals sitting at the same table. Gone are the days when people would say, "I need to check with my attorney" or "Let me talk to my accountant." Instead, we'll be saying, "I'm going to meet with my team of professional advisers."

In fact, this is already starting to take place, with multidisciplinary consulting firms like MSI Global Alliance, World Services Group (WSG), and the Geneva Group International (GGI), all of which are international alliances between law firms, accounting offices, financial advisers, lobbyists, and public relations agencies. GGI, for example, claims to consist of more than 538 independent professional law, consulting, and auditing firms in more than 120 countries across the globe, which collectively employ some 26,000 people.

These international alliances will soon be mirrored at the national and local level through the spread of multidisciplinary practices. For example, in 2010, Eversheds Sutherland, a multinational law firm with headquarters in London, opened a subsidiary called ES Consulting, which offers services in corporate strategies, technology, and human resources. And in 2015, the giant law firm DLA Piper announced the launch of a subsidiary called Noble Street, which focuses on financing, corporate, and mergers and acquisitions activities in the media, entertainment, technology, and sports industries. The consolidation of professional service firms has already begun.

MULTIDISCIPLINARY PRACTICES ARE THE FUTURE

Multidisciplinary practices, or MDPs, as they're known—joint operations between attorneys, accountants, and other related professionals—are expanding rapidly in the United Kingdom, Australia, and parts of Canada. Within the next decade, we are likely to see Ross and other robots like it handling the routine work that today is done by young professionals or paralegals, while the lawyers, accountants, and insurers will become members of multidisciplinary consulting teams that look to solve our problems in a comprehensive way. We might meet with our team of professional consultants once or twice a year for a routine checkup, even if we're not having any problems, the way many of us currently do with our doctors.

"The bottom line is, we can make certain predictions about what the future of the legal profession will be like," Mark Silow, chair of Fox Rothschild, told me, "but the one thing we can agree on is that it's going to be different, and the lawyers and law firm leaders that are simply saying that we have to keep doing whatever we're doing now will not succeed in the long run. Change is inevitable. You can't freeze time, and you have to be open to everything."

6

THEY'RE COMING FOR DOCTORS!

THE FUTURE OF HEALTH CARE

CAESAREA, ISRAEL

Moshe Shoham, the robotics lab director at the Israel Institute of Technology, better known as the Technion, is one of the people who are quietly reinventing modern medicine. I didn't even know he existed until someone told me about how he was developing a micro-robot the size of a grain of rice that will soon be able to clean human arteries the same way larger robots vacuum homes and swimming pools. When I heard about what he's doing, it sounded like something out of a sci-fi film. But after reading his bio, I realized he wasn't someone to be taken lightly: when I first met him in December 2016, Shoham had registered more than thirty international patents in robotic medicine and smart machines, and one of the companies he had cofounded, Mazor Robotics, was listed on the New York Stock Exchange with an estimated market value of $550 million.

Shoham agreed to meet with me at the Mazor Robotics headquarters in Caesarea, about an hour's drive north of Tel Aviv. The company was located in a nondescript industrial park along with pharmaceutical, engineering, and computer technology companies. Its offices were anything but flashy. On the contrary, they were located in an unembellished building that didn't even have a reception desk in the lobby. When I walked in the building's front door, the only other person there was a woman sweeping the floor, who led me to the elevators.

But the Mazor Robotics offices on the second floor were a hive buzzing with activity. While I waited for Shoham, I saw more than a dozen engineers and scientists—many of them in jeans or shorts and sandals—walking swiftly up and down the hallways. Most of them appeared to be in their thirties, and went in and out of cubicles where they seemed to be holding intense meetings. The cubicles' walls were covered with whiteboards filled with notes that, as they explained to me later, were due dates for pending assignments. Despite their casual attire, they seemed to be a fairly structured group.

The interview with Shoham didn't exactly get off to a great start. The scientist, in his midsixties, was a shy man who seemed somewhat uncomfortable talking with a journalist. He was dressed in a rather wrinkled white shirt and wore a knitted kippah on his head. His small office seemed the very definition of austerity: there was just one table surrounded by a number of plastic chairs, and posters of the human spine and limbs plastered across the walls. When I asked him about his personal life, he told me that he studied aeronautical and mechanical engineering at the Technion, and that he later founded a robotics laboratory at Columbia University in New York, where he had been a professor for a number of years before deciding to go back to Israel. He had returned because he wanted his children to grow up in his home country, he said. It was there that he cofounded Mazor Robotics, whose automated surgeon, known as Renaissance, had already performed more than 25,000 spinal surgeries in over 150 hospitals across the United States.

Unlike most businesspeople who brag about their products,

Shoham seemed to play down his accomplishments. When I asked him about his more than thirty international patents—which is more than what most of Israel's neighbors and many other countries have registered in recent years—he tried to change the conversation. After I insisted, he talked about his innovations as if they were collective projects in which he had played only a small role. When we finally got onto the topic I was there for—the micro-robot that could unclog human blood vessels, which he was developing along with another company called Microbot Medical—Shoham started reciting a long list of names of people who had worked with him on the project, and looked somewhat annoyed when he noticed I wasn't jotting down the names. I tried to explain that I wouldn't have enough space in this book to get into so much detail, but Shoham didn't accept that answer. He told me, in a polite yet firm tone, that he was morally obliged to give me all the names of his colleagues who had worked with him to develop this micro-robot. He then repeated their names and waited for me to write them down. And so I did, realizing that it would be the quickest way to move forward with the interview.

THE MICRO-ROBOT THAT CLEANS ARTERIES

Shoham explained that his Microbot Medical micro-robot would be among the first to be used to clean and drain the urethra and even vascular tubes in the brain without the need for invasive operations. It's essentially a titanium robot one millimeter in diameter and up to four millimeters long that is inserted into the body and operated externally by remote control. But in the very near future, he explained, it will also be used to remove plaque from coronary arteries, reducing the risk of heart attacks. Asked how long before it will be used on patients, Shoham replied that they were just then finishing up the animal testing phase and that the product could be available to the public as early as 2020 or 2021.

The micro-robot, known as ViRob, will do much more than cleaning. It will perform biopsies without the need for doctors to open up the body to take samples of potentially malignant tissue, he said. For instance, ViRob will travel—perhaps "swim" is a better word—through the body to reach the hidden cavities that are difficult for even the most skilled surgeons to reach, and perform the biopsy. And perhaps even more important, ViRob will also be used to detect and discharge localized treatments for diseases such as cancer. It will be able to release cancer-fighting medication directly into the tissue without the need for invasive treatments like chemotherapy, Shoham said.

Like many other inventions, the idea of a micro-robot to clean out the body's internal plumbing came to Shoham almost by chance. A few years after developing his robot-surgeon for spinal operations, Shoham and his team of Ph.D. students at the Technion had begun working on a robot to clean cities' sewage and water pipes and to fix leaks in their plumbing systems. Their original theory was that cities could save millions of dollars a year by using a robot that could clean up the filth that clogs pipes or locate leaks in the pipe system. But after Shoham made a speech about his new project at an interdisciplinary conference, he was approached by Menashe Zaaroor, a fellow professor of neurosurgery at the Technion and director of the department of neurosurgery at Rambam Medical Center in Haifa. Why not create a miniaturized version of that robot for medical uses? Zaaroor asked. If a robot can be used to clean up clogged city pipes, why not create one that does the same with the human body's plumbing system? Zaaroor had explained to Shoham that such a mini-robot could be extremely useful in cases of hydrocephalus, a condition in which there is an accumulation of cerebrospinal fluid in the brain. Until now, doctors had not been able to solve the problem of blocked drainage tubes in these cases. Patients had to undergo multiple operations to clear out these tubes. So, the neurosurgeon asked, why not use micro-robots to clean them instead? Soon enough, Shoham and Zaaroor founded Microbot Medical.

Shoham laughed when I asked him if his microbot would be replacing human surgeons in the near future. He said the first time he'd been asked that question was seventeen years earlier, at a robotics conference. Since then, journalists inevitably turned out articles about his research with provocative titles like "Robots to Replace Surgeons," he commented. Responding to my question, he said that "robots will not replace surgeons. What they will do is change the sort of work that surgeons do. Surgeons will have to program the robot, and they will need a lot of experience in programming and engineering." In other words, surgeons—at least for now, until artificial intelligence evolves further—will be directing the surgical robots.

Shoham showed me on his laptop an illustration of what a typical operation will look like in the future. It showed a patient laid out on a stretcher while a robot was arched over him performing the surgery, with the doctor directing—or rather, controlling—the procedure from an insulated room next door to protect him from radiation. Or in the case of microbots, the doctor in the adjacent room will be using a joystick to steer the micro-robot toward a tumor and will press a key to shoot the medicine directly into the malignant tissue. Like with other nano-robots that are being developed in other countries, the device will disintegrate and dissolve into the bloodstream once it has fulfilled its mission, leaving no need for it to be removed from the body. "Micro-robots have several advantages," Shoham explained. "They give the surgeon more accessibility, because they can reach nearly inaccessible parts of the body without the need for invasive surgery, and they also have much more precision, because a well-programmed robot makes fewer errors than humans," he said.

THE INVENTIONS THAT ARE CHANGING MODERN MEDICINE

Shoham's inventions are just a few of many examples of how medicine will be transformed thanks to robots, micro-robots, sensors inserted in watches or clothes, chips implanted under our skin, smartphones with self-diagnosis apps, telemedicine, preventive medicine, predictive data analysis, 3-D printers that will produce tailor-made organs, and virtual reality treatments.

The most elementary and revolutionary medical innovation is one that most of us are already using in everyday life: the Google search engine, and virtual assistants like Siri or Alexa. In coming years, we will see more specialized versions of these all-purpose assistants that will be able to answer any medical questions, much as if we were talking with our personal doctor. Plus, they will send us daily reminders about exercising and taking our medicine. Alexa can already give precise instructions on what to do if you have a heart attack or how to perform CPR on someone in an emergency. Increasingly, we will be doing our medical consultations with our virtual assistants, at home or wherever we are.

Medical virtual assistants, digital sensors, and many other similar innovations are already being used by millions of people, but in separate and disorganized ways. That will change, however. Just as smartphones existed for several years before the iPhone set the standard and became a global phenomenon, it's only a matter of time—perhaps even as you are reading these lines—until someone comes up with a device that integrates most existing apps for medical consultations, and that will allow us to diagnose and treat many of our illnesses.

Most gurus of medical technology say that it's time for medicine to stop being a practice or an art, and become more of a hard science. And for that to happen, human physicians will have to turn over much of their work to computers and robots, they say. Indeed, today's doctors are still using ancient tools, as if they had been frozen in time. Does it make sense for physicians to still use pretty much the same stethoscopes they have been using for a hundred years to listen to our heartbeats? Or to measure our blood pressure with a sleeve that is inflated with a rubber ball, much as they did a century ago? Today, digital sensors have made many of these devices look prehistoric, technologists say.

EVERY DOCTOR CAN BE UPDATED

The number of medical discoveries is growing so fast, with tens of thousands of new scientific studies being published every year around the world, that it makes no sense for doctors to continue working based on the knowledge they acquired in medical school many years ago, or on their own intuition. No human being is capable of either capturing or retaining the amount of new medical information that is coming to light every day. While in the past one of medicine's primary problems was the lack of information, today's problem is that there is too much information.

When it comes to diagnosing diseases, doctors just can't beat computers. A doctor can make a diagnosis based on his experience with the few thousand patients whom he has seen, but a computer can make its judgment based on data obtained from hundreds of millions of cases. And if Watson, the IBM computer that is already being used by a number of hospitals across the United States, determines that 300 million patients did better with one medication than with another, its diagnosis is much safer than one made by a human doctor, the medical futurists say.

According to IBM, Watson can digest information and

make recommendations by processing up to 60 million pages of text per second, including all the handwritten notes doctors might have added to medical records on file, academic articles in specialized publications, online figures from public health departments around the world, and other periodicals. And since Watson isn't just a computer but an artificially intelligent machine, not only does it instantly read all available information about a specific medical issue and make recommendations, but it can also follow a patient's treatment step by step and learn even more from that case's results. Watson is constantly acquiring and analyzing data, just as it did when it beat the world champions in chess and Go. And when it diagnoses a disease and recommends a treatment, it can offer a number of different possibilities and their projected success rates.

TECHNOLOGY WILL REPLACE 80 PERCENT OF WHAT DOCTORS DO

Vinod Khosla, the Silicon Valley medical technology tycoon and cofounder of Sun Microsystems, has predicted that technology will eventually replace 80 percent of what doctors currently do. But this doesn't mean that 80 percent of doctors will lose their jobs, he says. Rather, it means that many of the routine tasks they perform—such as checkups, tests, diagnoses, prescription of drugs, behavior modification programs, and data centralization—will be performed much more efficiently by intelligent machines.

"Most doctors couldn't possibly read and digest all of the latest 5,000 research articles on heart disease," Khosla argues. "And, most of the average doctor's medical knowledge is from when they were in medical school, while cognitive limitations prevent them from remembering the 10,000+ diseases humans can get."

To back up his argument, Khosla points out that more people die today due to errors by doctors and nurses than they do from many diseases. According to a study by Johns Hopkins, as many as 40,500 people in the United States die every year in an ICU due to misdiagnoses, rivaling the number of deaths from breast cancer. Medicine should therefore be less intuitive and more scientific, Khosla says. We should forget about the television series *House*—in which the main character was incredibly rude but had a remarkable ability to solve complex medical cases—and start to let computers handle most tasks that are currently performed by doctors.

PATIENTS CAN LIE TO THE DOCTOR, BUT NOT TO THE ROBOT

According to Khosla, besides making better decisions, computers and sensor equipment are much more accurate than doctors when it comes to collecting data on the medical history, the symptoms, and even the mood of patients. Today a doctor will ask us how we're feeling, and he or she will work with a pen or a tablet and write down whatever we say. But this is an archaic way of doing things, because a patient can easily forget hidden symptoms or even lie if, for example, he's ashamed to admit that he's not getting enough sleep because he's having an extramarital affair. But when patients are wearing a smartwatch with sensors that can track their vital signs all day and night, recording among other things how many hours they slept, this data can be transmitted directly to the doctor's office via the Internet. Those data will be much more accurate. Patients will always hold back from or even lie to their doctors, but that will be much harder to do when they have a robot connected to their wrist.

And even when patients don't lie, they often are not paying close enough attention to their own symptoms. "Today most heart disease is identified only after patients have heart attacks. But imagine having preventative cardiac care, enabled by machine-learning software that identifies abnormalities and *predicts* episodes," Khosla wrote back in 2012, before smartwatches with built-in sensors became popular. "We could discover most heart disease before a heart attack or stroke."

Finally, artificial intelligence is much more effective because it can consolidate a patient's entire medical history and solve one of modern medicine's primary problems: the fact that we go see different specialists, and none of them ever speak to one another. An average person over the age of seventy has at least seven different conditions, and usually goes to a specialist for each of them. As Khosla asks, wouldn't it be much more logical for a single AI computer to gather all that information and advise us whether the various treatments are compatible or may work against one another? Instead of skipping from one specialist to another, patients in the future will have just one doctor who will help them understand the computer's diagnosis and recommendation for treatment, he says.

But what sort of effect will all of this have on a doctor's work? According to Khosla, computers will free them up from routine checkup diagnostic tests and treatment plans, allowing them instead to focus much more on their role of supporting their patients psychologically and helping them interpret the computer's data. As Khosla puts it, instead of Dr. House, we'll have "Dr. Algorithm." "Eventually, we'll need fewer doctors," he says, "and every patient will receive the best care."

FROM INTERMITTENT AND REACTIVE MEDICINE TO CONSTANT AND PROACTIVE MEDICINE

When I interviewed Daniel Kraft, the futurist doctor and chair of Singularity University's Exponential Medicine program, he did the exact same thing he had done four years earlier when I visited him in Silicon Valley: he showed me all the smartwatches, rings, and clothes with embedded sensors he wears, and—like a magician—started taking out of a box the latest gadgets that he thinks will radically change modern medicine. He explained that these and other devices will allow each of us to make our own diagnoses in the comfort of our own homes without having to go to a doctor or to a hospital.

Kraft is an authority on the medicine of the future. He studied traditional medicine at Stanford before working in internal medicine and pediatrics at Harvard. But soon enough he launched a parallel career as an inventor of medical products, including a system for growing bone marrow in a faster way, and as a promoter of the latest advances in medical technology.

While he has long been donning the latest wearables, or external sensors, on the market, Kraft is doing something new these days: he is having all of them linked to his personal doctor's office at Stanford, where nurses can follow his vital signs twenty-four hours a day and can alert him in advance if they notice anything unusual. It won't be long before most of us will be wearing sensors that are permanently connected to our primary doctors, he says.

"We're moving from an intermittent and reactive medicine to a constant and proactive medicine," Kraft told me. He added that we already have in our smartphones most of the apps and sensors that are needed to monitor our bodies 24/7. Instead of getting a blood test done every six months or going to the doctor when we're already feeling sick, medicine will be focused on prevention and early detection of diseases through external sensors and cell phone apps that will be checking on us constantly, he said.

"The future of medicine will be much more about being preventative and proactive, using your genetic information and your behavioral information to help guide prevention," he said. "If you have a higher risk of getting a type of cancer or diabetes or Alzheimer's, then maybe with both exercise and diet, maybe drugs and other interventions, you can do things early to prevent those diseases from occurring. So instead of spending all our dollars on sick care, I think we're going to see more and more use of technologies that will be much more on the preventative side." Not only is this in the best interest of the patient, but it will also help society save money, he added. Countries are going to be emphasizing preventive medicine much more in the future because it's much cheaper than the current ways of fighting diseases, he explained.

GOING FROM SICK CARE TO HEALTH CARE

Kraft then showed me his Fitbit bracelet, which tracks his daily steps; his Apple watch, which measures his pulse; and a ring on his finger that he described as a "sleep lab" for monitoring his sleep at night. All these sensors represent what he calls the "Internet of the body."

"What, exactly, do you mean by that?" I asked.

"All these types of connected devices are interesting," he replied, "but we're starting to now connect the dots between them. With my physiological data, my medical record, my genomics . . . You know, when we talk about the Internet of health care, we're taking the information from many sources and using them to guide health and prevention, diagnosis and therapy." Just as the so-called Internet of Things connects multiple devices without the need for human beings, the Internet of the body allows for all of our medical data to be integrated and even condensed down into a single fundamental report.

But if these watches, sensors, and apps are so great, then why do doctors still listen to our hearts with a stethoscope and check our blood pressure with old cuffs and pumps? I asked. Is it possible that doctors don't trust these new sensors because they just aren't accurate enough?

"Well, health care is being practiced like it has been for hundreds of years," Kraft responded. "It's actually not always health care. It's more sick care. We have very intermittent data, an occasional blood pressure or blood sugar test or some other lab information. Then we're quite reactive. We wait for disease to happen, like a heart attack or a stroke or a cancer."

Today, for example, we go to the dermatologist to see if a spot we have on our skin might be a sign of cancer. But there's already a cell phone app that allows us to take a picture of the suspicious spot, and—thanks to artificial intelligence—we can find out immediately whether it's normal or malignant, Kraft explained. This is just a hint of what medicine in the future will be like, he added. It will be something that any of us can do at home every single day, instead of having to go to the doctor.

DOCTORS USED TO PRESCRIBE MEDICINE; NOW THEY'LL PRESCRIBE APPS

"Healthcare—or sick care, as we have it today—has long been practiced the same way: make a phone call, wait two weeks, see the doctor, go to the pharmacy, take a pill," Kraft explained. "We're now in an era where we can use a prescribed app to help someone prevent getting diabetes. If I'm going to prescribe you a new medicine, I can prescribe you an app that's going to help you manage taking that medicine, maybe manage your symptoms. Especially for complex diseases like multiple sclerosis or Parkinson's, where we can measure tremors or other behaviors that might be impacted by how much medicine you take."

Based on the data it gets from our body and according to our particular case, the application can tell us exactly how much of the medicine we should be taking, he explained. No two patients are the same, and not everyone reacts similarly to each treatment, so medicines themselves are going to be increasingly personalized. "I don't think we're going to be prescribing just drugs or devices, but a combination of these things, the combination that's going to help connect the dots in managing prevention, disease, and therapy," he added.

All the external sensors in our watches and clothing, and all the internal ones we'll be carrying in our bodies—whether it's hearing aids, smart contact lenses, embedded chips, or camera-equipped pills that will constantly transmit information—will make preventive medicine both easier and better than reactive medicine, Kraft told me. And this trend will continue to grow as more people come to realize that our behavior is more important than our genes. If we can eat better or be more active, for example, we'll have a much better chance of avoiding chronic diseases, he said.

Kraft gave me a number of examples of how smartwatches can change habits that are bad for our health. Sensors that are already on the market today can alert us when we're making bad decisions, like eating junk food, not being active enough, or smoking; when we're stressed or not sleeping enough; when we're dehydrated; when we've had too much to drink; even—if we want them to track this sort of thing—when we're biting our nails. All these devices, from smartphones to smartwatches to smart clothes to internal sensors, will let us know when we're doing something wrong. And the more we become accustomed to using them, the healthier we'll be, Kraft said.

There are even low-cost sensors available for tracking the quality of your breathing, and microphones attached to your clothes that can determine your mood based on the tone of your voice. Just as cars have red lights on the dashboard that turn on when the oil needs changing, our internal and external sensors will light up or send out some other signal when our body needs a checkup or maintenance, Kraft said. To put it another way, these sensors will become our own low-cost personal trainers available around the clock to keep us healthy and in shape.

SMART HEARING AIDS MONITORING HEALTH

Low-cost smart hearing aids are now on the market that can not only count our steps and track our heart rate, but—thanks to AI—can also answer just about any medical question we might have. Instead of saying, "Hey, Siri," into our cell phones, we can ask the hearing aid instead. But they're not just for people with hearing loss: they're for athletes in training and the general public in just about any circumstance, Kraft said.

There are also external sensors that can detect signs of disease: saliva readers that can pick up early warnings of diabetes or cancer, or Breathalyzers that can check for lung cancer. And that's not even counting the internal sensors, or "insideables," like new contact lens technologies that can measure blood glucose, chips under your skin, and exploratory pills that can give you all sorts of continuous medical data. All of these will not only greatly reduce the number of unnecessary trips to the doctor or hospital, Kraft says, but will also prevent many illnesses from occurring.

Kraft pulled another device out of his box and showed it to me. It's a new product for testing urinary problems at home. "If

I have pain when I urinate, I might use a diagnostic kit like this to test my urine and then use my smartphone to take a picture of the signal and use that to diagnose a urinary tract problem," he said. "All that without ever having to call the doctor."

MUCH OF OUR HEALTH CARE WILL TAKE PLACE AT HOME, NOT AT THE HOSPITAL

Pulling another gadget out of his box of surprises, Kraft told me it was a tricorder like the device Dr. McCoy used in the *Star Trek* TV series, a pocket-size device capable of measuring all vital signs and diagnosing many of the more common diseases. There are already a number of companies developing these mini home laboratories, and the X Prize Foundation has offered a $10 million award to whoever invents the best tricorder. It is expecting one of the participating teams to come up with a winning design sometime during the next five years.

Tricorders will "detect our temperature, our heart rate, our blood pressure, our oxygen saturation," Kraft said. "They'll talk to our smartphones and they'll give us an incredible amount of data that can help us diagnose a disease or manage a disease or triage it, and figure out whether we need to go to the doctor's office or the emergency room. . . . I think we're going to see more and more things that we can measure that used to require an entire laboratory. Now they can be done in our pocket."

Just about every medical futurist agrees with Kraft in that the spread of home diagnostic devices will decrease the number of visits to hospitals and waiting periods at doctors' offices. Much of the work of detecting and diagnosing diseases will be performed by patients in their own homes using tricorders or smartphones, which will become de facto portable health care centers.

DOCTORS WILL BE INTERPRETERS AND PERSONAL COUNSELORS

Skeptics argue that the new technologies for self-diagnosis won't be a panacea because patients will be flooded with information they simply cannot understand. Patients will be so confused that they'll need to see a doctor, the skeptics say. But, as was the case with computers and other technologies, new medical cell phone apps will be able to translate the complex medical jargon used by physicians into a much easier vocabulary that everyone can understand, and at the very least they'll be able to tell us whether a particular symptom we have is serious or not.

Vivek Wadhwa, a Silicon Valley futurologist with whom I consult frequently since first meeting him at Singularity University several years ago, believes that the doctors of the future will "serve as a filter, interpreting information and presenting it in a friendly and compassionate way." At first glance, this might seem like a less vital role than what doctors are performing now, but it's not: in the new reality—one in which we have at our disposal all the information from our sensors and tricorders, plus the data on our personal genetic code—we'll need the advice of doctors to put everything in context and avoid overreactions, Wadhwa says.

Soon enough, DNA tests to determine your chances of developing a certain illness will be as common as blood tests are today. Still, though, many people are worried. "When a genome test tells you that you are predisposed to a disease, you could take it very seriously and become demoralized, when in fact the factors that lead to disease are much more complex and often include aspects under our control," Wadhwa writes. "The readouts that consumer devices produce could lead people who don't have experience in medicine to make poor decisions." Doctors will continue to be important, especially when it comes to helping us understand the prognoses provided by all these new technological innovations, Wadhwa says.

ELECTROSHOCKS TO KEEP US FROM EATING MORE CHOCOLATE?

During my talk with Kraft, I told him that I'm somewhat skeptical about smartwatches that track our steps and measure our sleep. My wife has given me a few of these devices as birthday presents in recent years. Most often, I'll use them for a few days until I get bored with them, at which point they usually end up in a drawer. Many of us see them as a fad, as something fun, but when the novelty wears off, we decide not to keep using them. So what makes you think that they'll become an essential part of our lives? I asked Kraft.

"We know changing your behavior is hard," he said. "If you're my patient and I want you to lose weight, I can give you, in most cases, a little pamphlet and say, 'Oh, read this. Go to the gym. Eat better.' But we know behavioral change is hard. Now we can use connected tools on our wrists, sensors in our mattresses to track our sleep, apps that can track our diet, and use that to hopefully give us insights into our behaviors and answer questions like how many steps am I taking a day, how little sleep am I getting, and how much stress do I have in my life." The more we know about our life habits, the easier it will be to modify them through small, gradual changes, especially when all the data are collected together and not spread across a number of platforms, he explained.

Could you give me some concrete examples of that? I asked.

"When we get insights into our behaviors, we can use that to adjust them. So, small changes in behavior, like walking an extra five hundred feet a day, eating one less cookie . . . over months and years, that can dramatically impact our weight, impact our overall health," Kraft replied. "We're going to see interactive images in our bathroom mirror that might show us our health score for the morning, and help remind us to take our vitamins or go to the gym."

In addition to the wearables that measure our vital signs, Kraft also expects us to be using more shockables, or sensors that give us little electric shocks. Really? I asked, chuckling as I pictured people getting electroshocked every time they smoked a cigarette, ate a piece of candy, or drank one too many glasses of wine. Yes, he said, adding that we'll also be using trainables, showing me what looked like a strip of adhesive tape that's already on the market and which is designed to help you with your posture. "You put this on your back for an hour a day, and it buzzes and gives you feedback when your posture isn't good," he explained. "After about a week of wearing this, people's postures are dramatically improved. That's an example of a trainable, and we'll see other examples that might help you quit smoking, or give you feedback about your diet."

While Kraft was talking, the image that crossed my mind was that—with all these wearables, insideables, shockables, and trainables—we are going to become a society of wired individuals, like little Frankenstein monsters, who will experience little spasms every time we engage in some sort of inappropriate behavior. Science fiction? Probably most people won't be eager to strap on sensors that produce electric shocks, but I wouldn't be surprised if we end up wearing some benign version of these devices sooner or later. It could well be devices that produce a beep instead of an electric shock, or embedded chips that send some sort of silent—and mildly unpleasant—signals when we're doing something unhealthy. If millions of people nowadays are willing to undergo cosmetic procedures and painful operations such as gastric bypass surgeries to look better, why wouldn't they opt for a tiny invisible chip that would help them lose weight in a much less invasive way?

DERMATOLOGISTS AND RADIOLOGISTS WILL BE THE MOST AFFECTED

When I asked Kraft what kind of medical specialists will be most affected by the new technologies, he didn't have to think much: dermatologists and radiologists, he replied. Whenever we have a skin irritation, instead of scheduling an appointment with a dermatologist, we will use applications in our smartphones that can already do a quick scan and instantly tell us whether it's a melanoma or a harmless blemish, he explained. Asked whether dermatologists will lose their jobs, Kraft said no, but they will be doing a completely different job. Instead of seeing dozens of patients a day just to tell them whether they have a skin irritation that presents any danger, they will spend most of their time focusing on patients who really need medical care. Dermatologists will "spend more time on the therapy side, rather than looking at patients and going 'Normal, not normal, normal, not normal,'" he said.

The good thing about this is that many people with malignant skin lesions who wouldn't otherwise find out in time will now be able to do so. "By using some of these sorts of artificial intelligence dermatology apps, patients will catch more lesions early, and then press a button and make an appointment with a dermatologist to do the biopsy or the therapy," Kraft said.

And Kraft believes the same thing will happen with radiologists. "Today radiologists see thousands of images," he said. "They're almost overwhelmed with chest X-rays and MRIs and ultrasounds. We'll see more and more that machine learning and apps will read the basics and send the most concerning cases for a final reading by the radiologists, which could mean that we'll have fewer radiologists."

In time, even pathologists, who study patients' tissues and cells in search of cancer and other diseases, will let smart machines perform their more routine tasks. For years, Google has been working on its GoogleLeNet project—which was originally intended to interpret images for self-driving cars—to magnify, read, and recognize scans with better accuracy than pathologists with their microscopes can. According to some early studies, while an experienced pathologist is successful in diagnosing certain types of cancer in 73.2 percent of cases, GoogleLeNet has a 97 percent success rate. Google's intelligent machine still has too many false positives among its cancer diagnoses, but according to its creators, it's just a matter of time before it learns from its mistakes and eliminates them.

ROBOTIC SURGEONS WILL SOON BE AUTONOMOUS

Asked whether robotic surgeons and the microbots that will swim in our arteries and deliver medicines from inside our bodies will one day leave surgeons unemployed, Kraft told me that "we already are in the era of robotic surgery today." He explained that there are thousands of robots around the world performing all sorts of operations every single day, and with greater precision and in less invasive ways than human surgeons can do. Robots controlled remotely by human surgeons make much smaller incisions, avoid unnecessary blood loss, reach parts of the body that were otherwise difficult to get to, and leave much less significant scarring.

In most cases, the robot is perched above the patient in the operating room while the human surgeon is sequestered in a separate location directing the action through a computer, much like the image that Shoham showed me on his laptop in

Israel. But as the robotic surgeons hone their skills and develop their artificial intelligence, it will be less necessary to have a human doctor nearby to direct the robot's movements, Kraft said. "Today the surgeon is literally controlling every move of the robot. But I think that, in the next few years, we'll start to see parts of the surgery done autonomously," he said.

Surgical robots have been used since the 1980s. Their use expanded in the 1990s, when laparoscopies—in which small incisions allowed for cameras and surgical devices to be inserted into the body without the need to make major cuts—became more common. These operations were popular because they were less invasive and left less scarring, and patients were able to leave the hospital sooner. More recently, robotic surgeons became even more popular with the appearance of two creations by the U.S.-based Intuitive Surgical firm: da Vinci, which was first used to perform cardiovascular procedures and later also used for gynecological and urinary operations, and Renaissance, which performs spinal surgeries. According to a survey of American surgeons, operations performed by robots will increase from 15 percent today to 35 percent by 2021. The primary reason why there aren't more robotic surgeons today is the high cost of the robots—over $1.5 million each, the study says.

Critics argue that the growing use of robotic surgeons is mostly a marketing phenomenon. Many private hospitals in the United States are using robots as an advertising strategy to portray themselves as cutting-edge institutions in order to attract more patients, skeptics say. Many people naturally assume that robots are superior to human doctors, and are automatically attracted to hospitals claiming to use the latest medical technologies. When I asked Kraft about this, he acknowledged that there's a grain of truth to it, but added that the growing use of robotic surgeons is a gradual, unstoppable trend. "We're still many years away from fully autonomous robotic surgeons," he said. In the meantime, there will be a "partnership" between human and robot surgeons. "It's not a surgeon being replaced by a robot, but being helped and augmented, so the surgeon can do less invasive, safer, and smarter surgeries," he explained.

CARDIOLOGISTS WILL BE USING A LOT MORE TECHNOLOGY

What about cardiologists? Besides becoming more preventive, cardiology will be much less intuitive and much more technical. "The number one killer in most of the Western world is heart disease," Kraft told me. "Most folks learn that they have heart disease only after they have a heart attack or a stroke. In the future, a cardiologist will be able to use new tools like cloud-based computing to do a CT scan of the heart and send that data to the cloud and compute how narrow the blood vessels might be without being invasive like with the angiogram, where you insert a needle into the groin and run it all the way up to the heart." Other tools cardiologists will increasingly use are stents and other devices that can be custom fit to an individual patient with the use of a 3-D printer, instead of having them mass produced as they are today.

And patients will have new tools as well to monitor their own heart. The simplest of these will be virtual assistants on our phones, like Siri, or in the form of boxes, tubes, or more humanoid robots like Alexa. But there are other devices available to patients that are much more sophisticated. "You can go on Amazon and buy a little sensor you can put on your phone to look at your EKG," Kraft says. "Patients can use this to screen themselves to see if they have a heart condition, or a doctor can use it to keep better track of a problem remotely."

Pulling another gadget from his box, Kraft went on: "For example, this little patch: it's like a Band-Aid that I can wear under my shirt, and it tracks my EKG 24/7 as well as my posture, my respiration rate, my temperature, and it sends all that information to a physician. Now, it's true that most cardiologists won't want to look at that data 24/7. We're going to need to use smart software to look at those signals and alert the doctor and the patient only when something seems wrong," he explained.

MICROBOTS WILL BE WIDELY USED WITHIN THE NEXT TEN YEARS

Kraft believes that microbots and nanobots like the one Shoham is developing in Israel to clean the plaque from inside the blood vessels will become widely used within the next ten years. "The trend for many technologies is to get exponentially smaller, smarter, and less expensive," Kraft said. "We already have some robots the size of a pill that you can swallow and that will go down to your stomach and take pictures, replacing the need for an endoscopy. At MIT, we've seen similar little robots that can crawl through your GI tract and possibly help remove foreign objects or do a better job of diagnosis and treatment. We've also seen some work at Stanford, where they're making little microbots that are small enough to go through blood vessels."

Isn't it overly optimistic to think that we'll be using these microbots in less than a decade? I asked. Kraft shrugged. "Well, think of what's happened in just the last ten years," he replied. "Ten years ago, we didn't have smartphones, we didn't have Twitter, we barely had the early versions of Facebook. Those are just some of the things that have happened in just the past decade. A lot more will happen in the next ten years as technology accelerates with Moore's law and computing becomes cheaper. You know, we now have 4G smartphones. In a few years we'll have 5G smartphones, which will be able to transmit a hundred times more data in terms of speed and power. . . . In ten years, we may have things that would look as magical as some of the technologies we have today would have looked ten years ago."

INTERNISTS HAVE A BRIGHT FUTURE

Much to my surprise, Kraft said, "I think the future of the general practitioner, the internist, is actually quite bright. We still need that quarterback primary care doctor who is going to be using some of these technologies and tools to be able to do their job." But he also expects the role of the primary care doctor to change: instead of sitting in an office with a line of patients waiting to see him, he'll do most of his work over the phone or through Skype sessions. "I think many appointments in the future will be done through our computers, through our laptops, through chat bots like Siri," both in big cities and in rural areas, he explained.

"You might be a physician in rural Brazil, in the Amazon, or a nurse in a rural village in Argentina or Chile, where it might be a hundred miles to the closest city," Kraft said. "Using some of these tools and technologies you can fit in your pocket will allow you to do a much better job of taking care of patients, in terms of both diagnostics and therapy. I think the general practitioner will be able to use these new tools, whether it's digital electronic detection devices or mobile devices that can be used to perform an ultrasound anywhere. They might even be using drones to deliver drugs and devices to remote locations. I don't think the role of the primary care doctor is going away, but their ability to use technology and to use it to communicate with their patients will change."

Indeed, in 2018, my insurance company sent me a promotional printed brochure offering me—without being asked—a telemedicine service. For what it said would be a much lower cost than a trip to the doctor's office, Aetna offered virtual medical consultations "24/7 by web, phone, or mobile app." The service, called Teladoc, allows you to "talk to a U.S.-licensed doctor by video or by phone for diagnosis and treatment plan. If medically necessary, a prescription will be sent to the pharmacy of your choice," it said. What Kraft had predicted as a trend of the future was already spreading far and wide just months after I had interviewed him.

PSYCHIATRISTS AND PSYCHOLOGISTS HAVE NOTHING TO FEAR

Virtually all studies on the future of jobs agree that psychiatrists, psychologists, and other mental health professionals are among the least likely to be replaced by robots. According to the Oxford University study by Carl Benedikt Frey and Michael Osborne, mental health professionals will have less than a 1 percent chance of being replaced by intelligent machines. Out of the 702 jobs that were included in their index, psychiatrists and psychologists ranked among the 5 safest from technological disruption.

Kraft agreed with that forecast, but added that intelligent machines will help psychiatrists and psychologists do a much better job. "We know that mental health is very important to our overall health, and we also know that folks with mental disorders or psychiatric disorders have a hard time accessing a good psychiatrist or psychologist. But now we're seeing new tools, like your wearables on your clothes or on your wrist, or your smartphone, that can tell a lot about your mental state," Kraft explained. These tools will gauge the tone of your voice and read your text messages and social media postings, and will alert the doctor—or the patient's mother—if there are any signs of danger. "All these tools can, I think, be very helpful. I believe in digital psychiatry," he said.

WE CAN ALREADY HAVE A 24/7 CONNECTION WITH OUR DOCTOR

Toward the end of our interview, I asked Kraft whether he himself has all his wearables and shockables directly connected with his doctor's office. "That's right," he answered. Until recently, he used a health app on his phone that let him monitor all his vitals and that was also connected to his bathroom scale at home so he could see how much his weight varied over time, he told me. The app also tracked how many steps he walked, how many sets of stairs he climbed, and how many hours of sleep he got per day. But now all that information goes to his doctor as well, he added.

"About a year ago I was the only person who could look at that data, but now I can hit a button on my smartphone and connect that data with my medical records at my doctor's office at Stanford," he said. "So now data from my watch, from my bathroom scale, from my blood pressure cuff, from my glucose monitor (if I had one) can all flow to my doctor's office. He can see that information, and if he needed to, he could use it to help guide therapy or help me manage my medications or other issues. All of this is just now starting to happen."

Of course, doctors and nurses aren't going to be glued to their screens tracking stats from each and every one of their patients, Kraft said. "But they're going to use software like AI machine learning to understand what's relevant to each particular patient." And as is the case in hospitals, doctors will get an alarm if there's any imminent danger to a patient, or perhaps even a series of alarms, depending on the urgency of each particular case.

ADVICE FOR THOSE WHO WANT TO STUDY MEDICINE

Finally, I asked Kraft about what advice he might have for young people wanting to study medicine, considering the current technological threats to the profession. He responded that medical students will have to study much more than medicine, because medicine will become a much more interdisciplinary profession. Students will have to learn to work with scientists, data analysts, engineers, and other professionals who until recently had no place in a doctor's office.

"I think it's a really exciting time in medicine," he said, "particularly for young folks who come from many different fields, and who will play a role in reshaping health care as we know it." Even medical students who don't simultaneously study other disciplines will have to be well versed in computer programming, data analysis, and genetics in order to work in the hospitals of the future. Others might want to study engineering so they can specialize in robotic surgeries, or so they can design, manufacture, and perfect devices that help elderly people get around better, or help those suffering from paralysis, as Hugh Herr of MIT has been doing. In other words, "it's going to take people young and old from many different fields coming together," Kraft concluded.

In the end, thanks to preventive care, data analysis, personalized home diagnoses, increased connectivity with our doctors, and virtual medical consultations, we will have to make fewer trips to the hospital or doctors' offices in the future. To use a car-racing metaphor, hospitals will become like pit stops where drivers can pull in to have a wheel changed before getting back on the racetrack. Instead of going to the hospital for an emergency, we'll periodically pop in for a quick tune-up and then get back out on the road of life.

DEEPAK CHOPRA: PHYSICIANS WILL HAVE TO EVOLVE INTO NEW PROFESSIONS

While writing this book, I also interviewed Dr. Deepak Chopra, the alternative medicine guru who is a staunch critic of traditional doctors' habit to prescribe pills for almost everything. Considering his deep skepticism of traditional medicine and his penchant for ancient meditation and Ayurvedic practices, I expected Chopra to have a very negative view of the medical technologies supported by Kraft and other futurists. I had interviewed Chopra several times before, and he had always assured me that he didn't take any sort of medication besides herbs and other natural products. He has always been very mistrustful of the pharmaceutical industry, so I was quite curious to hear what he would have to say about automated surgeons, microbots, and artificial intelligence to track and maintain our health.

Much to my surprise, Chopra didn't lash out against the technological innovations that are revolutionizing modern medicine. "Technology is the next phase of human evolution, and it can't be stopped," he told me. "So if you resist the emergence or evolution of technology, you will become irrelevant." Physicians will have to work with things such as vibrational therapies, ultrasonics, augmented reality, virtual reality, and artificial intelligence, "or they will be condemned to irrelevance. That's the number one principle," he said.

"Principle number two is that technology is neutral," Chopra continued. We can use it to destroy the world or to improve it. "I see a world five years down the road where, instead of prescribing you a drug, a doctor will put you through a thirty-minute virtual reality or augmented reality session, after which you'll feel better." Or there could be brain wave technology and sleep training, and nanobots running through your blood vessels and cleaning out the plaque or suppressing genes that cause disease. "All of these things will be computerized and all regulating themselves," he said.

So what will doctors do? I asked. "Just like everyone else, doctors will either adapt or become extinct," Chopra replied. "I believe that the role of physicians, and health caretakers in general, will be more collective. Medical treatment will not be a one-to-one relationship anymore. It's not going to be me consulting a doctor maybe once or twice a year . . . I will feed my information, and algorithms will come in and give me the best and latest treatments available. And then I can engage in a personal relationship with a caretaker, just to feel good." Instead of a doctor-patient relationship, we'll consult with groups of experts in all areas of health and wellness. We'll have a lot of them, and they'll all interact through technology to improve our health, help us sleep better, manage stress, or encourage exercise, he added.

"There will be a role for someone to hold your hand, and to be there in a very compassionate way, that we have lost already, to guide you through the process. But physicians as we see them today will become a lost species," he concluded.

Chopra—who is prone to grandiose statements—is probably exaggerating a bit, but the fact is that medicine will quickly become a much more precise, personalized, participatory, preventive, and predictable profession. Certain specialists will be replaced by intelligent machines, and others will be working side by side with data analysts, geneticists, and robotic engineers. Doctors will continue to exist, but their primary mission will be to constantly monitor the information they receive from our sensors, interpret the data sent by our smartphone apps and home medical labs, help us select the best diets, medicines, and treatments recommended by intelligent machines, and give us practical advice and encouragement throughout the whole process. To put it in another way, doctors will cease to be repairmen for our diseased organs and instead become counselors on how to improve our health. Whatever you think of Chopra's critical views of traditional medicine, he is absolutely right about one thing: doctors who don't adapt to the new technologies will soon become irrelevant.

7

THEY'RE COMING FOR TEACHERS!

THE FUTURE OF EDUCATION

MIAMI

In a televised interview with Professor Einstein—the small humanoid robot with white hair, a thick walrus mustache, and the other unmistakable features of the Nobel Prize–winning physicist—it couldn't have gone worse. Hanson Robotics, the company that created the robot, had just launched the promotional campaign for its new educational robot after having been granted a five-year license by the Hebrew University of Jerusalem to use the name of the famous physicist. According to the company, Professor Einstein would be the first of many robots that would revolutionize education by teaching students in a more fun, interactive, and effective way than human teachers do.

When I saw Professor Einstein on the screen—I was in a Miami TV studio, and he was in a New York studio—the just-over-one-foot-tall robot looked very funny. In addition to having an Einstein-like air of absent-minded professor or crazy genius, he could laugh, move his eyes in all directions, and even stick out his tongue. He walked and could make more than fifty facial expressions. The little robot was standing on a desk at the set in front of Andy Rifkin, the chief technology officer at Hanson Robotics. Before the start of the show, we had agreed that I would ask questions directly to Rifkin, who would relay them to Professor Einstein, because the robot was operating on a voice recognition program, and we didn't want to run the risk of the robot's not understanding me. According to Rifkin, Professor Einstein could recognize only familiar voices like his.

Rifkin began by explaining the advantages of his robot. Professor Einstein could describe the theory of relativity in a number of different ways depending on the strengths and weaknesses of each student, he told me. "All individuals are unique: some of us learn visually and others perceptively, so we're constantly modifying the way we present a topic based on your personal way of learning. If Professor Einstein can't get you to understand what he's explaining, he'll change the way in which he's explaining it and keep trying until you understand," Rifkin said.

But the interview quickly went downhill. No sooner had Rifkin begun to discuss the advantages of Professor Einstein than the robot started swinging his head from side to side instead of looking directly at the camera. Visibly anxious, Rifkin started typing on his laptop in an attempt to return the robot to his original position. But the robot was still staring off to one side, as if he wasn't interested in being interviewed at all. Noticing that something was going wrong on the other side, I stretched out my next question for as long as I could, trying to give Rifkin more time to straighten out his robot. Finally, I asked Rifkin to ask Professor Einstein what kinds of things he was able to do. Rifkin relayed the question, and the robot, still looking off to one side, responded in a rather robotic accent: "I can walk, talk, teach games, forecast weather, and answer all kinds of questions about science." He finished up with a joke that fell a bit flat, since he still wasn't looking into the camera: "In short, I'm your personal genius, or at least that's what it says on the box."

When I asked a follow-up question through Rifkin, the robot remained speechless. Several seconds passed, and Professor Einstein still didn't react. Rifkin—visibly nervous—asked him the question again, but now the professor was silent and expressionless, as if absorbed in his own thoughts. After a number of failed attempts to interact, Rifkin explained on the air that the robot had probably been muted because the Wi-Fi connection had gone down. With the cameras still rolling, I jokingly suggested that Professor Einstein probably had a case of stage fright because this was his first live television interview, and we cut to a commercial break. After several more attempts, we were finally able to resuscitate the robot, and it told us a little bit more about the things it was able to do.

TEACHERS WILL NO LONGER BE THE ONLY PURVEYORS OF KNOWLEDGE

Although Professor Einstein's television debut left much to be desired, I came out of the interview convinced that educational robots and other intelligent machines will quickly find their way into classrooms and homes. While they won't replace most teachers, they will take over a number of their current tasks. After all, robots have virtually all the qualities of an ideal teacher: they have unlimited patience, never get tired of their students' questions, are able to explain their lessons in multiple ways depending on each student's preferred way of learning, and are available twenty-four hours a day, anytime and anywhere. Plus, robots are able to monitor their students' progress using sensors that detect their levels of comprehension based on the tone of their voice and dilation in their pupils, thus eliminating the need for regular testing. They can make learning seem more like a game and less like torture. All this will force teachers and professors to reinvent themselves and their profession.

Until now teachers "taught" their students. That is, they passed on their knowledge. But now, with Google's and YouTube's search engines, as well as Siri and other virtual assistants who are able to answer any and all questions, the teacher's role as a transmitter of knowledge has been completely taken over. Any Internet search engine has immensely more information than a human teacher, can deliver it more quickly, and can explain it in many more different ways. And robots don't get impatient when a student goes off on a tangent with a string of questions that veer off the issue being discussed.

"When children find something interesting, teachers often don't have enough time to fully explain it," Rifkin told me. "But Professor Einstein does. We can ask him as many questions as we want the deeper we get into a topic. We can ask him, 'What's a dumpling?' and Professor Einstein will say that 'it's a kind of food made with dough, water, vegetables, and meat.' Then we can ask him, 'What's dough?' He will tell us that it's a food made from flour and water. Then the kid might ask, 'Where does flour come from?' and so on."

But since any virtual assistant can easily handle a string of questions, Professor Einstein's biggest advantage is that he can help students solve problems from many different angles. If we don't understand the way he's explaining a particular topic, the robot will try another and another until we get it. He can see us and listen to what we're saying. He can tell from our tone of voice if we're not truly grasping a particular concept, and he'll try to find a better way to convey it, whether it's visual or auditory, through humor or with games. If a student learns better visually, for example, Professor Einstein will use his hand

and point to a computer screen showing an illustrated explanation of the lesson. If we learn better by listening, he will tell us a story.

TEACHERS WILL BECOME MOTIVATORS, COUNSELORS, AND PERSONAL THERAPISTS

As their traditional role as conveyors of knowledge gradually fades away and is replaced by robots and virtual reality, teachers will have to reinvent themselves, becoming motivators, academic counselors, spiritual guides, and personal therapists. They will still teach certain things, but they will be "soft skills" like intellectual curiosity, personal initiative, mental flexibility, teamwork, and ethical behavior. At least for the foreseeable future, robots won't be able to match human educators when it comes to instilling people with moral principles, a sense of purpose, and a desire to change the world for the better.

In this sense, the growing use of robots and virtual reality to impart knowledge could be good news for teachers: it will free up time they ordinarily spend preparing their classes, which they can then use to focus on the ethical aspects of education. They will also be able to devote more time to work on the strengths and weaknesses of their students, and encourage them to be more creative and enterprising. A robot like Professor Einstein won't be able to teach these skills as well as a human, at least for now.

"It's great to have a tutor who never gets tired of your questions, who has infinite time, and cares only about your needs," says Randall Bass, the executive director of the Center for New Designs in Learning and Scholarship at Georgetown University. "There is tremendous potential, especially for people who don't have access to good education. But there are those of us who think education isn't just about technical knowledge: we have to be thinking also about the moral aspect, helping the students be good people, to work for positive change, and be able to make complex moral and ethical decisions. I don't think Professor Einstein can do that very well, at least not yet."

WITHIN THE NEXT FIVE YEARS, THERE WILL BE A ROBOT IN EVERY HOME

I asked Rifkin how long it might be before his creation or other robots like it will work their way into our homes. "Within the next three, four, or five years," he said. How could he be so sure? Because it's already happening, he said. "Look at the case of Roomba: it's a robotic vacuum cleaner, and just look at how many people are using it all across the world. So when it comes to a personal robot like Professor Einstein, I think within the next three to five years people will have them for all sorts of reasons, from medicine to day care, classroom supervision, help with homework, and many others."

Part of this inventor's enthusiasm is that the prices for these humanoid robots are already within the budgets of many consumers. Professor Einstein was released in early 2017 and retailed for $300 through an offer on the crowdfunding site Kickstarter .com. Its creators had set a goal of raising $750,000, and within just a few weeks they had raised more than $850,000. Whether it was out of curiosity or necessity, people wanted to buy this robot.

Skeptics will argue that just a few years ago, the "One Laptop per Child" program was supposed to revolutionize education and replace teachers with computers. That, of course, didn't pan out. But even if Professor Einstein doesn't end up being a hit, some other robot, tablet, or virtual reality headset equipped with artificial intelligence most likely will be. The

X Prize Foundation in Silicon Valley—the same organization that is offering a prize for whoever can invent the best *Star Trek*–style tricorder—announced a $15 million competition to develop a robot or other electronic device that can teach Tanzanian children how to read and write in eighteen months without the aid of any human teachers. Under the rules of the competition, whoever wins the prize will be obligated to publish online for free how the device works. It is likely that shortly thereafter, there will be tens of millions of new robotic educators out there teaching kids across the world in a much more effective way.

WILL ROBOTS IN OUR HOMES SPY ON US?

I asked Rifkin whether these educational robots, with their eyes and ears, won't invade our privacy. How do we know that they won't be filming and recording us all day long, and perhaps sell information about us to governments or companies hungry for data about us? Just a few weeks before our interview, news had broken that during the course of a criminal investigation, police in Arkansas had seized an Amazon virtual assistant from a private home.

The police had charged James Bates with murdering a friend who had attended a party at his house and whose body was found in a hot tub in the backyard the next morning. Investigators confiscated the Amazon Echo as evidence and demanded the manufacturer, Amazon, turn over everything the device recorded. The prosecutors argued that, since the virtual assistant was sitting right there in the living room, it had likely heard—and possibly recorded—everything that happened the night of the murder. The case made headlines across the country when Amazon refused to turn over any data, and many defenders of the right to privacy began to wonder whether home robots could be used—or worse, were already being used—to spy on their owners.

Rifkin assured me that, at least when it comes to Professor Einstein, there's nothing to fear. Any filming and recording done by the robot is contained within the robot itself. "We don't retain any information. When the camera records you, it's just to recognize your face. We don't upload photos, we don't store images, we don't transfer anything. Anything the camera sees stays in the robot locally, and again, it's just for facial recognition purposes. The microphones don't transmit any audio, either. They only transmit voice patterns, not your voice itself. Absolutely nothing is stored in the cloud. Everything in the device is encrypted: it's as secure as your credit card," he claimed. But the big question will be whether robot manufacturers will be able to resist the temptation of selling the information they will be collecting from inside our own homes. For many companies, that could be a much bigger business than the robots themselves.

VIRTUAL REALITY WILL REVOLUTIONIZE TEACHING

When I visited Google's headquarters in Mountain View, they made me a presentation that absolutely convinced me that virtual reality will be as effective as, if not more effective than, educational robots. Basically, augmented reality and virtual reality can do something neither a human nor a robotic teacher can: transport us through space and time. It allows us to place ourselves into a geographic or historical reality—whether it's the Egyptian pyramids or a Roman market in the second century B.C.—just as if we were in a movie.

Benjamin Schrom, a project manager at Google Expeditions, the company's virtual reality educational division, showed me the Google cardboard viewfinder sitting on the table in the conference room where we were meeting, and invited me to look through it. Instantly I found myself in the middle of a jungle. As I turned around in a 360-degree circle, I saw mountains, waterfalls, and rivers. And these were real images: the same things I would have seen if I were actually standing in that actual location in the real world. "This tool turns teachers into superheroes. They can take their students on field trips to places they would otherwise never be able to visit, and without even having to leave the classroom," Schrom told me as I looked, mesmerized, at the landscape around me.

Google put these VR cardboards on the market alongside a virtual class on jungles and has been going full speed ahead to develop other virtual courses. There are already more than five hundred apps that let students use these devices among other things to virtually swim with sharks, travel through space, or stroll through a museum, and there are soon to be thousands more. As more students buy it, more developers will be creating apps, Schrom explained. The young executive, a man in his thirties who, like most of his colleagues at Google, wore jeans and a T-shirt—in fact, I didn't see a single tie at any Silicon Valley tech company—told me he had been a teacher before entering the world of technology and had experienced firsthand the limited access to materials that educators have.

"Imagine you want to dissect a frog in biology class," Schrom offered by way of example. "It can be complicated to do that in real life, so many schools just use a blackboard or photographs. But with virtual reality, it's a lot easier: each of the students can dissect their own virtual frog, remove the heart and other organs, all of that. It's a visual and very personal experience, not a symbolic and abstract one."

WILL CHILDREN CONFUSE VIRTUAL REALITY WITH REAL LIFE?

Despite all its advantages, virtual reality has its problems, such as the danger that children might confuse it with real life. A study by Bank of America and Merrill Lynch indicates that virtual reality will lead to a new global technological revolution not unlike the massive boom in smartphone use during the first decade of the current millennium, but it comes with a warning: "We also identify longer-term risks around the psychological and neurological impacts, social isolation, hindered vision, privacy and cybersecurity."

According to another study, by Stanford University, a group of children who had participated in a VR experience of playing with whales couldn't distinguish between reality and false memories a week after the experiment. So what would happen if—just as today's young people are able to find pornography on the Internet—children start accessing virtual reality sites of, for instance, radical or racist groups? Will we end up with legions of young racists or fanatics? If a white supremacist group or hackers from Russia or North Korea want to destabilize Western democracies by posting fake virtual reality videos of young people being attacked for no reason by a group of African Americans, what can we do to prevent young people from developing racial prejudices? The social consequences of not being able to differentiate between fantasy and reality can be quite serious.

Another risk is that virtual reality could produce even more social isolation than laptops or smartphones. As the aforementioned study points out, "role-play VR games can exacerbate social isolation. There are rising numbers of teens and young adults who stay at home and display depressive and obsessive-compulsive tendencies." In Japan, one of the countries where video games are most popular, it is estimated that there are between 700,000 and 1.5 million *hikikomori,* or people who refuse to leave their homes, and their average age is thirty-one, the same study says. In 2018, the UK government created a minister for loneliness to deal with the growing number of people who live in virtual isolation. Prime Minister Theresa May said that "loneliness is the sad reality of modern life" and added that it is causing an increasing number of health problems. In our push to improve education, will we end up creating a society of antisocial young adults addicted to their virtual reality goggles?

THE TREND OF THE FUTURE WILL BE "FLIPPED CLASSROOMS"

Virtual reality and robot teachers are likely to speed up a new trend known as "flipped classrooms" in schools that are turning the traditional model of education on its head. In this education system, children study at home and do their homework in school. Increasingly, with tablets, educational robots, and virtual reality, instead of studying at school like most of us did, young people will be studying at home in the mornings, and then go to school in the afternoon or evening to do their homework with the help of their teachers and in collaboration with their classmates. By some measures, this system has proven to be much more effective and socially fair than the traditional one.

The traditional system of going to school during the day and doing homework in the afternoon or evening is a recipe for social inequality: only middle-class and rich kids whose parents were fortunate enough to finish high school or get a college degree can help their children do their homework or get private lessons from a tutor. That gives them a head start over children from lower-income homes; such children often don't have parents who can help them with their homework or who can afford a tutor. So the traditional model leaves children in underprivileged homes at a huge disadvantage. Over time, they fall further and further behind their better-off classmates, and many end up dropping out of school altogether.

Also, several studies have shown that, with the advent of interactive games, many students learn better by interacting with their electronic devices than they do by sitting in a classroom listening to a teacher. As we noted earlier, each student has his or her own pace and needs: some concentrate well in the morning, while others function better in the evenings. So why not let young people study on their own time, at their own tempo, and with whatever method they prefer, and do their homework at school with the help of their teachers?

Our traditional school system comes from the Prussian system of education that originated in the eighteenth century. The king of Prussia had established free elementary education, which was both collective and compulsory. The king's idea was to produce a working class of obedient subjects who learned from a young age to go to work at the same time every day and to respect authority. By replacing individualized education—the apprenticeship model—with a collective one, the king of Prussia tried both to create a large group of disciplined workers and to shape the minds of the citizens by having them study from the same books, developed by the government. As part of this educational system, students had to sit in rows, stop whatever they were doing when the teacher entered the room, and listen silently to their educators as they gave their lessons. It was a model designed to churn out disciplined laborers ready for the factories during the Industrial Revolution, but that is becoming rapidly outdated in the innovation economy of the twenty-first century. Today, robots and algorithms are handling growing numbers of routine tasks that workers used to perform at factories, and nations need increasingly more creative people with critical minds, who can invent new products or processes.

According to Salman Khan—the great Silicon Valley educational innovator whose Khan Academy (www.khanacademy.org) offers free educational videos that have already been seen over a billion times—today's world needs a working class of creative and curious people who can come up with new ideas and implement them. That's the exact sort of student that the Prussian model was designed to discourage. The flipped classroom, he says, allows students to develop critical thinking to the best of their abilities and assures that nobody is left behind. Thanks to educational videos, virtual reality, robots, and other technologies, "what was once done in the classroom can now be seen by the children on their own time and at their own pace. Students can rewind videos, ask the robot teacher to explain something again, or rewatch something on their virtual reality headsets that they didn't quite understand the first time. And the teacher can figure out the level each student is at and help them solve problems," Khan told me.

THE FOCUS WILL BE ON LEARNING, NOT ON TEACHING

A similar concept to that of the flipped schools, one that also emphasizes learning over teaching, is the "democratic education" model. It has existed for centuries but was developed more recently by Yaacov Hecht in a number of schools in Israel. There, it's the children who decide what they want to study and how their development should be handled. In these schools, a child's vote is equal to that of an adult, and they can use a majority vote to decide—within certain parameters, of course—school policies like how long recess should last or which disciplinary measures should be taken.

The guiding principle of democratic education is that children learn much more when, instead of receiving lessons with materials dictated from above, they are asked every six months about what they want to be when they grow up. If the child says, "An architect," the "moderator"—formerly known as the teacher—centers his or her math classes on examples from the field of architecture. At the end of the year, students will have developed the same skill sets and acquired the same knowledge as those at traditional schools, but they will also have learned leadership and teamwork, and honed their democratic instincts.

None of this is anything new. As far back as the seventeenth century, John Locke had written in *Some Thoughts Concerning Education* that children shouldn't be taught anything that seemed tedious. In his book *Émile,* Jean-Jacques Rousseau described an imaginary student who only learned things that seemed useful to him. Later thinkers like John Dewey and Margaret Mead, among others, developed similar concepts. And more recently, Hecht created the Institute for Democratic Education in Tel Aviv, which ran a number of schools under that particular model. In 2010, with Hecht's support, the Institute for Democratic Education in America—or IDEA—was founded. It now supervises some forty educational institutions across the United States. According to the institute's directors, the centuries-old theory that children learn more when they participate in the development of their lessons is being tested and proven.

A TEACHER'S PRIMARY MISSION: HELPING CHILDREN FIND THEIR PASSION

At a Singularity University conference in Silicon Valley that I attended in 2017, a person in the audience asked Peter Diamandis—founder of the X Prize Foundation and coauthor of *Abundance*—to name the most important soft skills that educators should be teaching in schools. I liked the one Diamandis picked as the most important one.

Diamandis, fifty-five, started his answer by saying that he had two young children who were about to enter kindergarten, and that after some careful research, he and his wife decided to choose a school based on three priorities. The first one, he said, was that it had to help children "find their passion." Whatever that may be, it's important for schools to help children be excited and enthusiastic about something, he added. Diamandis said his own devotion to space exploration and the search for habitable worlds in space was driven by his childhood passion. He also offered up the example of a friend of his, the billionaire Richard Garriott, whose father was an astronaut and who had grown up in a neighborhood filled with other astronauts and NASA astrophysicists. All his friends wanted to grow up to become astronauts like their parents, but Richard was passionate about video games. That was his calling. He told his parents that video games were what he wanted to do as a grown-up. So in high school, he started programming video games, which eventually made him hundreds of millions of dollars. So much money, in fact, that he was able to book a sightseeing trip to the Soyuz space station, thus becoming the first second-generation astronaut.

"A lot of times in my life, I've done things to make my parents happy or to make my teachers happy, or because someone else was doing it and I felt that I had to do it too," Diamandis said, getting back to his own situation. "But at the end of the day, doing anything big and bold in the world is hard. And if you don't love it, then you'll give up before you get there. So for me, for my children, the number one thing is passion. Can you help them find their passion? Whether it's comics, Barbie dolls, whatever it may be. Find out what it is, and then drive them to learn."

Passion awakens interest and intellectual curiosity. It's one of the best gifts that life can give you. "You'd be amazed at how many people don't have a mission in life," Diamandis has written. "A calling . . . something to jolt them out of bed every morning. The most valuable resource for humanity is the persistent and passionate human mind, so creating a future of passionate kids is essential."

Today's schools should help children explore their passions, and the best way to do that is by exposing them to new and different things. "The key to finding passion is exposure," Diamandis says. "Allowing kids to experience as many adventures, careers, and passionate adults as possible. Historically, this was limited by the reality of geography and cost, and implemented by having local moms and dads go to school and talk about their careers. They'll say, 'Hi, I'm Alan, Billy's dad, and I'm an accountant. Accountants are people who . . .' But in a world of YouTube and virtual reality, the ability for our children to explore 500 different possible careers or passions during their K–6 education becomes not only possible but compelling." For example, schools should ask students to share their current passions with the class once a month, using videos or virtual reality devices, and explain why they like the topic they chose, he said.

A TEACHER'S SECOND MISSION: PROMOTING CURIOSITY

The second important soft skill that Diamandis said schools should be teaching is curiosity. As parents, we must "create a culture of questioning," because that's what leads to experimentation and discovery, he said. Considering that we all have access to Google's search engine, it's increasingly important to make sure our children don't become lazy or uninterested. "In a world of Google, robots, and AI, raising a kid that is constantly asking questions and running what-if experiments can be extremely valuable," he said. "It will be the quality of your questions that will be most important." The futurist went on to say that he lives just a few blocks from his children's kindergarten, and when he walks them to school, he asks them, "What questions do you have for me today?" And when he drops them off, he adds, "Make sure you ask good questions today."

"Coupled with curiosity is the process of experimentation and discovery," he said. "The process of asking questions, creating and testing a hypothesis, and repeated experimentation until the truth is found. As I've studied the most successful entrepreneurs and entrepreneurial companies, from Google and Amazon to Uber, their success is significantly due to their relentless use of experimentation to define their products and services. Curiosity is innate in children, and many times lost later in life. Arguably, it can be said that curiosity is responsible for all major scientific and technological advances—the desire of an individual to know the truth." It's no coincidence, then, that Albert Einstein—not the robot, but the real one—reportedly famously said that "I have no special talent. I am only passionately curious."

A TEACHER'S THIRD MISSION: TEACHING PERSISTENCE AND GRIT

According to Diamandis, the third priority for schools should be teaching persistence and a tolerance for failure. In a world where technology is expanding exponentially, it's increasingly important to have long-term goals and to never give up on them, he said. What I found most interesting about what he said on this topic was that it's much more important to be an expert in a problem than to be an expert in a solution.

"Now, if I said to you, 'Become an expert in quantum physics or in gene editing,' that's what it is like today," he explained. "I don't think it's about becoming an expert in any one thing, because that one thing is going to change massively at a rate of increasing exponential change. It's actually better to become an expert in a problem. Like, for example, if you are the expert in why housing is a problem around the world, and you understand every culture around the world and what the issues are in housing or food or energy as new technologies come online, you're in a beautiful place to say, 'Take this or that technology and plug it into the problem.'"

SUCCESS IS OFTEN THE FINAL LINK IN A CHAIN OF FAILURES

During that conference at Singularity University, Diamandis didn't spend much time talking about the need to teach children to deal with failure—maybe because we were in Silicon Valley, where the vast majority of entrepreneurs are already fully aware of the fact that success is usually the final link in a long chain of failures. But in much of the rest of the world, especially in Asia and Latin America, it's very important to develop a culture of social tolerance for individual failure. As I wrote in my book *Innovate or Die!,* one of the things that impressed me most in my first few trips to Silicon Valley was the number of young people who casually mentioned to me—without my having brought it up in the first place—that they had failed in a number of start-ups. In other parts of the world—and even in other parts of America, as Donald Trump exemplifies—the last thing a businessperson would do is admit a failure, and the fear of failure is one of the biggest obstacles to innovation.

Nearly all the great innovators in human history failed many times before making their signature discoveries. Thomas Edison, who patented nearly 2,000 other inventions, including the gramophone and the camera, went through many thousands of failed attempts with lightbulb filaments before finally succeeding with the one that worked. According to his biographers, Edison said, "I have not failed 10,000 times—I've successfully found 10,000 ways that will not work."

Another story that's taught at many graduate schools of business administration—though not as much in elementary schools, as it should be—is that of Alexander Graham Bell, inventor of the telephone. According to some of his biographers, Bell offered to sell the patent to his invention for $100,000, but an executive at the Telegraph Company, a predecessor of today's Western Union, rejected it for allegedly being "hardly more than a toy." Another version of the same story says that a member of the Telegraph Company committee that rejected the proposal wondered, "Why would any person want to use this ungainly and impractical device when he can send a messenger to the telegraph office and have a clear written message sent to any large city in the United States?"

In much the same way, aviation pioneers Orville and Wilbur Wright made 163 failed attempts before completing their first successful powered flight. And according to an unconfirmed yet famous story, Henry Ford, who created the world's first successful mass-produced car, called it the Model T because he had started with a Model A and had to reinvent it nineteen times before he came up with his final product.

Shouldn't schools be teaching children at a young age stories like these about the importance of not being intimidated by failure? As I've been told by some of the world's leading innovators whom I have interviewed, these stories aren't exceptions, they are the rule. Persistence in the face of failure is the key to most successful innovations. The stories of Edison, Bell, the Wright brothers, and Henry Ford before they became rich and famous should be taught in every classroom. And doing so is something that teachers can do much better than tablets, robots, or virtual reality.

ETHICS AND EMPATHY CAN BE TAUGHT

As we said at the beginning of this chapter, technology will be replacing or assisting teachers in "hard" subjects such as math, history, or geography, but it can't easily make up for them when it comes to teaching students about ethical values. Flesh-and-blood educators will continue to be important for years to come as moral guides for our children. But can ethics be taught in schools in a way that's not a series of boring lectures that put students to sleep? The answer is yes, it can.

At Ad Astra, the school founded by Elon Musk, creator of Tesla cars and the SpaceX exploration corporation, teaching ethics is a top priority. At this ultra-exclusive school, which has only about thirty students, Diamandis says he once sat in on a class in which the teacher presented the students with the following question: "Imagine a small town on a lake, in which the majority of the town is employed by a single factory. But that factory has been polluting the lake and killing all the life. What do you do? Shutting down the factory would mean that everyone loses their jobs. On the other hand, keeping the factory open means the lake is destroyed and the lake dies." According to Diamandis, these sorts of moral dilemmas should be constantly presented to children in all schools, not only to teach them about real dangers such as environmental pollution, but also to get them used to facing moral dilemmas starting at a young age. Teachers can bring up these sorts of situations, ask children to make decisions, and then change the variables, helping students to adapt to all sorts of situations, he said.

Empathy, like ethics, can also be taught. In Denmark, public schools offer classes in empathy to students between the ages of six and sixteen, and the results have been excellent. Danish children must spend one hour of class time a week discussing something that affects them—whether it's a problem between two students or a current global issue—and finding a solution. At the end of each of these sessions, everyone shares a cake that students take turns bringing to class. Several studies show that these empathy classes have helped among other things to reduce bullying. For all sorts of classes like these, the teachers—or rather, the moderators—will continue being much more effective than robots for many years to come.

HIGH SCHOOLS MUST TEACH TEAMWORK

Argentina's Instituto Nacional de Educación Tecnológica (National Institute of Technological Education), or INET, surveyed 876 private companies in 2016 to learn what skills they wanted from incoming high school graduates. The response was almost unanimous: they wanted young people with soft skills like teamwork, a willingness to learn new things, the flexibility to adapt to changes, and a strong work ethic. What was also nearly unanimous was the fact that nearly every company that participated in the study said that it was very difficult to find high school graduates with these sorts of skills.

According to Gabriel Sánchez Zinny, at the time head of INET, which oversees some 4,500 technological institutes throughout the country, the survey showed that 92 percent of the companies said they wanted high school graduates who were good team workers, followed closely by those who had other skills such as a strong work ethic and flexibility. "The employers told us, 'We're not interested in hearing from young candidates who can only show degrees in mechatronics or agrotechnics, because their outdated school programs often teach things that were true twenty-five years ago but were never updated.' So instead they want people with soft skill sets that the companies can later update and upgrade."

So I asked Sánchez Zinny what high schools should do to

catch up with the times and help reduce youth unemployment. Like so many other experts in the field, he told me that schools should be teaching skills like teamwork, and that countries should be promoting vocational programs the way Germany, Australia, and South Korea do. In several of these countries, the government either gives tax breaks to companies or pays them directly in exchange for internships for high school students who want on-the-job training in fields where there is a shortage of workers. That, he said, was the path forward.

THE RETURN OF VOCATIONAL SCHOOLS

In America, there is a growing movement to restore vocational and technical schooling. These high school and private-sector mentorship programs were created on a large scale after World War II, during the boom in the automotive and airplane industries when large companies needed growing numbers of mechanics and electricians. But these schools and mentorship programs started losing popularity with the expansion of white-collar jobs in the 1960s, when young people started preferring working in offices to working in factories. In 1963, Congress moved to approve the Vocational Education Act to subsidize vocational schools, but even that was in vain: vocational schools had gained a reputation as institutions of last resort for students with bad grades who couldn't get into college. As a result, it was hard for these vocational schools to attract top-notch candidates.

But all that could soon be changing, because America will need growing numbers of technicians to repair and maintain the robots that will replace many workers in manufacturing plants. In 2017, President Trump signed an executive order to "expand apprenticeships and vocational training to help all Americans find a rewarding career, earn a great living, and support themselves and their families and love going to work in the morning."

One of the examples cited by the U.S. government is that of Germany, where vocational schools have always been on the front lines of education. To this day, 55 percent of German students choose to attend vocational schools where they can take academic courses while at the same time participating in paid internships with various companies. When they graduate, students take an exam for one of the 350 available occupations, from electricians to nurses, and if they pass, they're often hired by the same company for which they interned. That helps Germany maintain very low levels of youth unemployment—just 6.9 percent—and one of the most skilled labor forces in the world. South Korea, which also has a large number of vocational schools, is a similar case.

SOUTH KOREA'S ROBOTICS SCHOOL

One of the most interesting things I saw during a recent visit to South Korea was the Seoul Robotics High School, a public vocational school where students specialize in manufacturing and maintaining robots. The school has 455 students—95 percent of them male, 5 percent female—and is one of seventy-nine vocational schools in the nation's capital that produce skilled technicians through courses proposed by some of the nation's largest companies. When young South Koreans are ready for high school, they can choose between public schools with a more academic orientation, or public schools with a more vocational focus. About 35 percent opt for the latter, South Korean officials told me.

According to Shin Sang-yeol, the school's principal, these programs are funded by the government to help solve the country's labor shortages. In South Korea, he explained, "our population is getting older, and we're having fewer children, so the government needs to invest in vocational schools to meet the demand from companies for qualified workers." It's the same problem many other nations have: a shortage of technical personnel for manufacturing industries and an overproduction of college graduates who can't get a job because they don't have technical skills. So the government is subsidizing vocational schools and giving tax breaks to companies to offer internships to their students in order to turn out more and more technicians, he said.

Seoul Robotics High School is the crown jewel among South Korean vocational schools. It has seventy teachers and thirty teaching assistants, which amounts to roughly one educator for every five students. During my tour of the school, I saw groups of young students in their blue uniforms working in labs with computers and robots of all shapes and sizes. The principal proudly told me that 93 percent of seniors have a job lined up on the day they graduate, which is a much higher percentage than traditional high schools. Parents send their children to the robotics school because they know they'll have internships and a much better chance of landing a good job, he said. And for the 7 percent of students who aren't offered a job by the companies for which they interned, the school has a career services department to help them. That department, he told me, was the most important in the school.

I STUDY AN AVERAGE OF SIXTEEN HOURS A DAY

In one of the classrooms, I asked Surim Kim, a seventeen-year-old senior who was close to graduation, what an average day in her life looked like. The young lady, sitting in front of a computer in her blue uniform, told me that she lives on campus because her family is a long way away in the countryside. The school has dorm facilities for students like her, and both lodging and meals are covered by the state. "I get up at six-thirty in the morning for breakfast, and class begins at eight," she told me. "I'm in class until four in the afternoon, and after that, from Monday through Thursday, I go to a private institute to get my national certificate of competence in math." I followed up by asking her if she needed that certificate to graduate. "No," she replied, "but it will be a lot easier to get a job with it."

So when do you do your homework? I asked. "At night," she replied. "Usually after dinner, usually until eleven at night, but sometimes I'm up till one in the morning." Seeing the look of astonishment on my face, she shrugged and said, "That's pretty normal here. We all study like that. I average about sixteen hours a day." And when do you go home to visit your parents? I asked, still somewhat perplexed. "One weekend a month," she replied, "and for summer vacation."

While I have heard stories like this many times from students in China, Japan, Singapore, and several other Asian nations, they never cease to amaze me. Not only do these young people study many more hours per day than Americans, Europeans, or Latin Americans, but they're also in class many more days a year. In most parts of the United States and Latin America, the school year lasts 180 days; in South Korea, it's 220 days. It should come as no surprise, then, that students in Shanghai, China, Singapore, and other Asian countries are among the top scorers on standardized tests like the PISA exam of fifteen-year-olds around the world. These Asian countries have a family culture of education—and often a national obsession with it—that simply doesn't exist in many Western nations.

THE UNIVERSITY CRISIS

It's no secret that universities—and the traditional careers they teach—are at risk of becoming irrelevant in a world where technology is advancing so rapidly that much of the "hard" knowledge students learn is instantly worthless the minute they graduate. But Salim Ismail, the former head of Brickhouse, Yahoo's internal incubator, and founding executive director of Singularity University, surprised me with a prediction that when I first heard it seemed rather extreme: "Universities are going to implode," he told me over dinner in Miami one night in 2017. Ismail was devoting a good part of his time to a number of educational projects, and from what I could see in his face, he was not kidding.

Seeing my skeptical reaction to what I thought was an exaggerated statement, Ismail pointed to the example of what's happening in Silicon Valley with college graduates who have majored in computer science. "The value of a college degree has fallen to zero, because start-ups are much more interested in a 100 rating on GitHub than a programming degree from even one of the most prestigious universities in the world," he said.

"GitHub?" I asked, admitting that I'd never heard of it. Ismail explained that it's an Internet platform that programmers use for posting their projects to the cloud and getting feedback from their peers. It has more than 12 million registered users, who evaluate one another, and many of the top-scoring programmers—those most admired by their peers—never graduated from college. "Today, your rating on GitHub is worth much more than a college degree," he told me.

So how do you picture higher education in coming years? I asked. Ismail said that the future of education will be "project-based" learning. There will be a practical training system in which students will be asked to take mini-courses, and over the course of four years, they'll complete a specific project that has real-world application, he said. And this system may or may not be run by a school, he added. It's quite likely that we'll be seeing new institutions popping up in the margins of traditional universities: institutions like Singularity University or the TED conferences, which serve as tutors in this new learning environment. He claims that conventional universities have become so stagnant and reluctant to change that there's no way they can keep up with the latest technological advances. "Currently, if you want to be an expert in blockchain, you don't go to a university, you go to the best guy you can find who's an expert in blockchain," he said. "We're going to see more and more of that: institutes that provide apprenticeship-style tutoring and mentoring."

THE MYTH OF THE SUCCESSFUL COLLEGE DROPOUT

Ismail may well be right when he says that many universities run the risk of becoming irrelevant because of their failure to update their courses and keep up with technological changes. But while it may be true that start-ups in Silicon Valley often prefer to hire a computer expert with a 100-point GitHub rating rather than a Harvard graduate, the same does not happen in the labor market as a whole. On the contrary, I believe that a college or master's degree will become an increasingly more important requirement for getting a good job, especially for those looking for their first jobs in well-paying occupations.

The much-publicized cases of Bill Gates and Mark Zuckerberg—both of whom dropped out of Harvard and never graduated—are the exceptions to the rule, rather than examples to be followed. A study of 11,745 professional success stories in the United States, conducted by Jonathan Wai of Duke University in North Carolina and Heiner Rindermann of the Chemnitz University of Technology in Germany, looked into the educational backgrounds of leaders in several fields—from CEOs and entrepreneurs to federal judges, politicians, multimillionaires, and billionaires—and found that the vast majority of them have college degrees, if not master's degrees. There are many more success stories like those of Amazon founder Jeff Bezos, who graduated from Princeton, and Facebook COO Sheryl Sandberg, who graduated from Harvard, than cases of successful dropouts like Gates and Zuckerberg, the researchers found.

"While it's true there are successful college dropouts, statistically speaking, they are not the norm. As researchers in education and talent, we found that the vast majority of the country's success stories are college graduates," the authors wrote. "If you're a student thinking about not going to college or considering dropping out, remember that even Gates and Zuckerberg got into college. Even if you're not aiming for mega success, doing the work to get into and graduate from college today may open important doors."

And that is likely to continue being the case in the future, according to a 2018 study by the Organisation for Economic Co-operation and Development (OECD), an economic research group for most of the world's thirty-five richest countries. The higher academic degrees people have, the lower their chances of being displaced by automation will be, the study says. "The occupations with the highest estimated automatability typically only require basic to low level education," it says, citing the case of manufacturing and agricultural jobs, as well as some service jobs such as postal workers or food attendants. "At the other end of the spectrum, the least automatable occupations almost all require professional training and or tertiary education," it adds. And that will continue to be the trend, because people with college or graduate degrees tend to get more on the job training or engage in lifelong learning programs, which allows them to constantly ride the waves of new technologies, it adds.

THE RISE OF ONLINE EDUCATION

But that doesn't mean that traditional universities won't have to change, and do so rapidly. The growing popularity of online courses is a clear indication that traditional universities—with brick-and-mortar campuses and students sitting at classrooms—are in crisis. The number of massive open online courses, better known as MOOCs, has skyrocketed in recent years, and colleges are increasingly offering not only individual classes online but also majors and master's courses with certificates and diplomas. And while the early meteoric rise of online students has stabilized recently, there are around 78 million people taking online courses at more than 800 universities worldwide.

Coursera, the largest MOOC provider, offers classes by professors from several U.S. universities that are attended—virtually, of course—by 30 million students. Its top rival, edX, has 14 million registered users, while China's XuetangX has over 9 million. These independent university platforms are now in direct competition with traditional universities. Coursera, which has already begun offering a master's of business administration degree online, planned to start up to twenty new degrees by 2019. Will brick-and-mortar universities be able to compete with independent online education platforms, which have infinitely fewer expenses and can thus offer lower fees to their students? Probably not, unless they diversify and offer increasingly more of their courses online. They will have to offer a combination of virtual and physical programs.

THE FUTURE OF UNIVERSITIES: 50 PERCENT FACE-TO-FACE, 50 PERCENT ONLINE

When I interviewed Rafael Reif, president of MIT, which according to some rankings is the world's best university, he did not dispute the assertion that traditional universities are at risk of becoming irrelevant. Reif told me that brick-and-mortar higher education institutions will have to ride the wave and offer a roughly equal number of face-to-face and online classes.

"In some fields, the ratio could be 70 percent in the classroom and 30 percent online, and in others it could be vice versa," Reif told me. "But overall, I think it's going to be a fifty-fifty mix."

Not to be outdone by Coursera and other MOOCs, MIT had just started a pilot program for an Internet-based MicroMasters degree, Reif told me. After completing the online courses and passing a final exam, the school gives graduates an academic certificate. And if students want to complete a full-fledged master's degree, they can attend physical classes for the second part of the program and obtain their master's degree. But the biggest novelty of this MicroMasters program is that students don't need a college diploma to be able to enroll in it. In other words, major universities are already adapting to the trend popularized by the MOOCs of allowing virtually anybody to enroll in graduate courses. It was either that or facing a gradual death.

In addition to the rise of blended education—partly online, partly physical—universities will have to rethink their four-year college programs and make them more flexible, Reif told me. "Traditional college programs will come to an end," he said, adding that the technical knowledge that is currently passed on to students in college will end up being outdated by the time they graduate. In the future, universities will become a permanent source of education. "Instead of paying tuition for four or five years and getting a degree, you will pay to be constantly connected to your university so that you can continue learning throughout your entire life," Reif told me. "Starting college will eventually be like subscribing to a magazine: you will take courses, and then you will have access to courses to keep you up-to-date for the rest of your life."

WE WILL BE LIFELONG STUDENTS

Julio Frenk, president of the University of Miami and former dean of the Harvard School of Public Health, agrees that universities will have to become higher education centers for people of all ages. "There's an educational revolution going on, created in part by the change in the nature of the labor market, which is forcing us to get out of this notion that higher education is something that happens to people during a specific time in their lives, a time when they go into a tunnel and come out with a diploma," Frenk told me.

"Now, we're going to have a more open structure, where people can go in and come out all the time, at every stage of life," he said. "Not only for personal enrichment but also because of the demands of a changing job market. So we'll have to develop the students' analytical skills, which will give them the flexibility to adapt to a changing job market throughout their lives." When I asked him if he agrees with MIT's Reif that the future of higher education will involve a fifty-fifty mix of face-to-face and online learning, he said yes. "The best models are the hybrid ones," he added.

According to Frenk, when it comes to higher education, there are three levels of learning: informational, formative, and transformative. "They are very different," he told me. "Informational learning, which is the transmission of information and concrete skills, is the one most suited to online education. But education must also be formative, since we must develop critical thinking and create ethical frameworks, because we want people like doctors and lawyers to abide by ethical standards. And finally, education must also be transformative: it has to be able to turn people into agents of change. It has to develop leadership skills and the capacity to understand the world and transform it." Formative and transformative learning are more difficult to teach online, and work best in face-to-face classes, he said.

"THERE WILL BE FIVE TYPES OF COLLEGE PROFESSORS"

Randy Bass, the Georgetown professor who is somewhat skeptical about teaching robots like Professor Einstein, told me that there will be five types of college professors in the future. First, there will be teachers like the ones we currently have: we can call them expert performers, or people who use their oratory skills to teach their classes in front of students. Then, there will be personal mentors or motivators, who will be in charge of helping students find their passions and develop them. Other teachers will be academic advisers, others will be evaluators, and the last group will be that of personalized class designers.

"Historically, all five of those roles have been included in what we have called a professor," Bass said. "In the future, there will be an unbundling, a split in these functions. Some professors will be just one of these things, or some combination of them. It's inevitable." When I asked him whether that will translate into a larger or smaller number of professors, he said that "it might lead to fewer professors who perform all five roles, but there may still be just as many people doing that work. They might not all be what we call professors today.

They may not all need to be Ph.D.s, but could be psychologists or people with master's degrees."

Most likely, we will see an increase in the number of professors—all types of them—over the next few decades. That's among other things because of the world's population growth and the fact that more people will be studying on and off for their entire lives; it's also because the jobs of the future will increasingly require college and graduate degrees. Not surprisingly, the 2018 OECD study on the impact of automation on jobs placed teaching professionals, alongside business managers and health workers, among the least likely to lose their jobs because of automation. But the role of professors will change, as there will be less of a need to simply impart knowledge and a greater demand for psychologists, mentors, and motivators for students, and engineers to prime and oil the robots.

Intelligent machines will play a big role in the new educational universe. Thanks to their infinite patience, unlimited time, and ability to tailor their answers to the personalized needs of each student, robotic teaching assistants will be unmatched in their ability to pass along information. But it will still take human teachers to guide, motivate, and develop their students' ethical standards. And as time goes by and more robots take over routine jobs in factories, restaurants, and hotels, there will be an increasing demand for more highly skilled workers with university-level educations. In the future, if people don't want to work for robots, they'll need to learn how to manage them.

8

THEY'RE COMING FOR FACTORY WORKERS!

THE FUTURE OF TRANSPORTATION AND MANUFACTURING

MOUNTAIN VIEW, TOKYO, SEOUL

Elon Musk, the founder of the Tesla motor company and one of the world's most innovative billionaires, wasn't kidding around when he said that in less than twenty years, driving a car will be as old-fashioned as riding a horse. "Any cars that are being made that don't have full autonomy will have negative value. It will be like owning a horse. You will only be owning it for sentimental reasons," he said. Musk has earned an international reputation for making bold predictions and investing hundreds of millions of dollars of his money in daring projects. In 2002, he founded the Space Exploration Technologies Corporation, better known as SpaceX, to produce reusable spacecraft, which he says—seriously—that he wants to use to establish a colony of 80,000 people on Mars. Since then, SpaceX, with roughly 6,000 full-time employees, has become a leading force in the aerospace industry and one of NASA's primary partners in space research.

And while it remains to be seen whether Musk will achieve his goal of establishing a human settlement on Mars, he's already well on his way to making Tesla one of the automotive industry leaders in self-driving cars. Unlike General Motors, Ford, and other automakers, Tesla has started from day one to produce electric cars and to experiment with self-driving technology. In 2016, the company was already selling electric cars with automatic driving, braking, and parking. For legal reasons, a person had to be behind the wheel, but instead of driving the car, the driver could be resting or checking emails. And while a fatal 2016 accident in Florida involving a Tesla S made headlines around the world, the company rebounded from that public relations fiasco when an investigation later revealed that the car had warned the driver several times to take over manual control, and the driver had failed to do so.

Experts have long concluded—and investors seem to agree with them—that self-driving cars will be much safer than human-driven ones. According to Google, whose subsidiary, Waymo, has been producing sensors for automated cars for years now, autopilot technology will reduce the number of deaths from car accidents by more than 90 percent. The reason is that the vast majority of today's accidents are caused by human error, whether it's drunk driving, texting, or falling asleep at the wheel. As Brad Templeton, a member of the Google team working on self-driving cars, once told me, "Since robots generally don't drink or fall asleep at the wheel, self-driving cars are much safer than the ones we're using today." Indeed, according to the World Health Organization, every year more than 1.2 million people around the world die in car accidents. If Google's estimate is correct, cars driven by robots could save over a million human lives a year.

And many investors have bet that Musk will be a major player in the self-driven car industry. So many that in 2017, Tesla exceeded the market value of General Motors, even though Tesla produced just 76,000 cars per year compared to GM's 10 million vehicles. Obviously, investors and their financial advisers were taking Musk seriously when he said that driving a car would soon be a thing of the past, just like riding a horse.

IN CALIFORNIA, SEMIAUTONOMOUS CARS ARE ALREADY ON THE ROAD

It didn't take much investigating to conclude that self-driving cars will be hitting the streets very soon. I have already seen many of them wandering along the roads of Mountain View, California, and Miami, Florida, as part of test runs by Waymo—Alphabet's self-driving car subsidiary—as well as Uber, GM, Ford, Volvo, Audi, and several other car and tech firms. Semi-automated Teslas were everywhere in 2018, and several other companies are planning to produce fully automated cars commercially by 2020, if not sooner.

Driving along Route 101 from San Francisco to Mountain View for several interviews at Google and other companies working on self-driving cars, I was struck by how many semi-automatic Teslas were on the road. I could spot them easily: the ones ahead of me kept their course with almost absolute precision, without drifting an inch to either side. Obviously, they were on autopilot. Their human drivers were behind the wheel, but they were reading or texting on their cell phones, quite confident in their vehicles' automatic brakes.

When I visited my friend Vivek Wadhwa, the Mountain View–based professor at Carnegie Mellon and Harvard and author of several books on technological innovations, he told me that driverless cars are already a reality in Silicon Valley. He said he had bought a Tesla the previous year, and that for all practical purposes, it was already a self-driving vehicle. "I'm behind the wheel because legally I have to do that," he said, "but the car drives itself just about all the time."

Wadhwa, who had just published a book titled *The Driver in the Driverless Car,* told me that one of the main reasons autopilot technology is progressing so rapidly is that all autonomous vehicles on the road are constantly learning from one another. Collectively, they have already traveled millions of miles, and they share the information they pick up on the road each and every day.

SELF-DRIVING CARS WILL BE MUCH CHEAPER

"Few people seem to fully grasp the profound improvements in our lives that driverless cars will bring," Wadhwa wrote in his book. "Their adoption will slash accident and fatality rates, saving millions of lives. As well, it will remove one-third to one-half of all vehicles from city streets." Fully automated cars in New York, San Francisco, or other big cities will no longer have to be on the streets at the same time looking for a parking place, because they won't need to park. They will be able to continuously circulate, picking up and dropping passengers, or parking themselves outside the cities, he said.

In addition, growing numbers of people will stop buying cars. Instead, they will use Uber, Lyft, and other car-sharing services that offer cheaper and more efficient transportation in cities. And these companies' services will become increasingly cheaper. Today, about 60 percent of what you pay when you take a ride with Uber, Lyft, or another private taxi company goes to pay for driver-related costs. Once Uber, Lyft, and other ride-sharing companies start using robotic cars without human drivers, their prices will plummet, and even more people will use them.

According to a UBS study, the number of private car owners will drop by 70 percent by the year 2050. Plus, private taxi companies will be able to reduce costs even more because self-driving cars will cost much less to produce than traditional cars: they don't require steering wheels or brake or gas pedals, nor many of their other current features. As accidents are gradually reduced to near zero, autonomous cars may not need steel-reinforced doors and fenders, airbags, or even seat belts. And since almost all self-driving cars will be electric, the savings in terms of gas will be tremendous.

Why own a private car if it spends 95 percent of its time parked in your driveway or garage? Growing numbers of people will conclude that it makes more sense for them to use automated taxis. Robotaxis will be responsible for a quarter of the total number of miles driven on U.S. roads by as early as 2030 and will reduce the number of cars in cities by a whopping 60 percent by then, according to BCG consulting firm projections.

"My grandchildren will ask me to tell them what it was like to drive a car in an old city. I'll tell them it was scary, dangerous, and wasteful, and that they are lucky to have a better way of living," Wadhwa wrote. He added that he will tell his grandchildren that the few accidents that did happen during the transition from human-driven to self-driven cars "were because of the pesky, ill-mannered, and dangerous humans that they had to share the road with."

MY EXPERIENCE WITH A SELF-DRIVING CAR: BORING!

Lauren Barriere, a spokeswoman for Waymo, had arranged for me to take a ride in one of its autonomous vehicles during my visit to Google's headquarters in Mountain View. As we had agreed several weeks before, a Google engineer came to pick us up in one of the company's driverless cars. It was a white Lexus sedan equipped with a radar dish on the roof and small cameras with sensors poking out from all sides.

After the standard introductions and presentations, the engineer sat at the wheel, just as he would in any conventional vehicle. He was required to do so by law, he explained, even if he didn't so much as turn on the radio. And we had to wear our seat belts just as we would in any other car. Inside, there was nothing special, save for a laptop connected to the dashboard that was positioned next to the engineer and which he would use to drive—or rather, control the car's movements. When all of us were strapped in, the engineer hit a key on the laptop, and the car started to move.

What followed was the most boring ride of my life. The Lexus left the Waymo offices at a snail's pace. At first I assumed it was just a precaution to avoid any accidents there in the parking lot. But when we got out onto the road, the car was still crawling along at less than twenty miles per hour, despite the fact that the streets were almost empty. Barriere and the engineer explained that their self-driving cars are programmed to never exceed the speed limit on any street. And in that part of the city, the speed limit was twenty miles per hour.

Soon enough, the ride went from boring to excruciating. Not only were we moving at an annoyingly slow pace, but the driverless car wouldn't pass any other vehicle. Even when the car in front of us was going much slower than we were, ours hung back obediently, waiting patiently for it to get out of the way or for everyone to turn onto a wider road where it could change lanes. And to make matters worse, every time we came to a stop sign, the car came to a complete halt—as is the law—before waiting three never-ending seconds before moving forward. It was a special precaution to avoid any potential accidents caused by a careless human driver who might be coming in from one side or another, the engineer explained.

About fifteen minutes into our ride, I looked pleadingly at Barriere, hoping that she could put an end to this torture. Ever the PR manager, she explained that a self-driving car's primary objective was precisely that: to avoid accidents. "The biggest compliment you can give to our engineers is that the trip was boring," she said, obviously repeating a line she had delivered to other guests before. I nodded as politely as I could. But at the same time, I was thinking to myself that transitioning from traditional cars to self-driving models won't be all that simple. People stuck behind an autonomous car moving at a snail's pace on an empty road will get impatient, honk, and look for any opportunity to pass it. It won't be easy to get used to it!

AUTONOMOUS CARS ARE ALMOST READY TO GO

Although the autonomous car revolution probably won't shake up the world economy until the early or mid-2020s, these cars have been built and tested for decades. The reason that they are attracting so much attention now is because they have become much more reliable in recent years thanks to new sensor technology that allows them to react most of the time to unforeseen situations, like a dog running across the street on a foggy night. With a few exceptions, like the 2018 accident in which an Uber driverless car killed a woman who was crossing the street outside the designated path during the night in Tempe, Arizona, these problems have been overcome. At the time of this writing, technicians are working feverishly to get automated cars to detect increasingly complex signals, like the hand signs of a police officer directing traffic around an accident and other nonverbal communications, such as a cyclist trying to make eye contact with a driver in order to get permission to pass.

Just about every major car maker or tech company experimenting with robotic cars is on the verge of removing the last few obstacles remaining in the path of the fully autonomous car. These companies have hundreds of these cars on the streets in several cities, with engineers behind the wheel ready to take control if some unforeseen problem arises, but such cases are becoming less and less frequent. In fact, as Waymo's Barriere told me, the number of emergency cases where engineers had to step in and drive fell from 0.5 percent per 1,600 kilometers driven in 2015 to 0.2 percent in 2016. And everything indicates they will be hitting the final goal of 0 percent in the very near future. "The car is now ready to drive," she said, "and very soon you'll be seeing them on the road in places where it's relatively easy to drive, like where there's no snow. Bit by bit, they'll be operating in more complicated conditions."

THE DRIVERLESS CAR ACCIDENT THAT KILLED A PEDESTRIAN

The 2018 accident involving an Uber driverless car that killed a woman in Tempe, Arizona, drew worldwide attention because it was believed to be the first pedestrian death caused by an autonomous vehicle. Shortly after the crash, Uber announced it was temporarily suspending its experimental program in Arizona, fueling speculation in the media that it could be a serious setback for all autonomous car companies. But shortly after the accident, Tempe police chief Sylvia Moir told *The Arizona Republic* that the initial police investigation and review of the car's video had revealed that the accident was most likely "unavoidable." In other words, it would have been difficult for a human driver to see a woman crossing that street on a dark night at ten P.M. outside any crosswalk.

Months later, I had a chance to interview Uber CEO Dara Khosrowshahi, the forty-eight-year-old Iranian American tech executive who had previously been CEO of Expedia, and was a member of the board of directors of Hotels.com and *The New*

York Times. He is a media-shy tech executive—his press handlers insisted that we didn't take video of the interview, because they said he was not yet feeling comfortable with doing TV interviews—who had taken over Uber in 2017 after a tumultuous year that had led to the resignation of the company's founder, Travis Kalanick.

I asked Dara—as he is referred to by virtually everybody—to what extent the Tempe crash would delay or halt the development of autonomous cars. Dara said the crash was "a tragedy" and "a step back for our company," but added that "ultimately self-driving will improve safety across the board." He told me that "these machines will get better and better on an infinite basis. A self-driving robot learns how to drive, and then keeps getting optimized. The equipment and the sensor packages are going to continue to improve. So, at maturity, I can confidently say that this accident would not have happened in a mature self-driving environment."

He added that "this mature driving ecosystem will take a lot of work, but I'm 100 percent confident that at the end it's going to be much safer than where we are now." When I asked him when he expects that to happen, he responded, "In the next eighteen to twenty-four months, in 2019 or 2020." In other words, the fatal accident in Tempe, Arizona, was not likely to stop the development of autonomous cars, much like the early fatalities in the first flights didn't stop the development of commercial aviation.

TRUCKERS WILL BE AMONG THE FIRST TO FEEL THE IMPACT

One of the first places where we will see commercial driverless vehicles will be the highways. An increasing number of fully automated big-rig trucks like the ones produced by Otto, a company founded by former Google engineers and recently acquired by Uber for $700 million, are already being used on an experimental basis in California. According to Matthias Kässer, a transportation industry analyst at McKinsey, more than a third of the trucks on American highways will be fully autonomous by 2025.

That will affect the jobs of large numbers of truckers. While most of us who live in big cities don't see them very often, there are tens of millions of truck drivers in the world. The American Trucking Association estimates that there are 3.5 million professional truck drivers in the United States, not including several million more who do related jobs—from maintaining engines to handling paperwork—and are not sitting directly behind the steering wheel. It's a fairly well-paying job in most countries, especially for those who are both truck owners and drivers. But what will happen to them when their vehicles become fully automated? In the short term, human drivers will still be needed to get their trucks in and out of congested cities, but it won't be long before the autopilots can handle even those tricky stretches.

Lior Ron, one of the cofounders of Otto, is convinced that the new technology will make life a lot easier for truckers, especially those who own their vehicles. He reasons that a new tractor-trailer costs between $160,000 and $200,000, and can be driven by a human for only nine hours at a stretch. But with self-driving technology, the driver can take as many naps as he wants while the truck drives itself. That doubles or triples the driver's performance. "The truck is always productive," Ron said. "They're making more money, because they can use it more. They're seeing their families more often, because they can finish their long-haul routes faster. And most important, they're safer."

"IT WOULD MAKE THE JOB NOT WORTH DOING"

But what Ron didn't say was that many truckers who don't own their own vehicle may lose their jobs. Wade Dowden, a thirty-two-year-old truck driver, told *The New York Times* that he doesn't see much of a future in his line of work in the age of autonomous vehicles, because the pay will get progressively worse. The idea that automated trucks will drive themselves while human drivers sleep won't work for most truckers, he said. "It would make the job not worth doing. Once you're only paying a guy to drive the final miles into a city, we're certainly not going to get a raise for that," Dowden said.

In many countries, truckers' unions will be able to hold off layoffs of salaried drivers for some time. And in some of them, governments—facing the threat of truckers' strikes—may ban the use of autonomous trucks altogether. But how long will they be able to do that? If a country tries to outlaw autonomous trucks, how will it compete with other countries whose exports will become increasingly competitive thanks to lower transportation costs? And conversely, how will domestic industries in countries that prohibit autonomous trucks compete with cheaper imports from countries where transportation costs are much lower? Sooner or later, it will be all but impossible to keep this technology from taking over the trucking industry, let alone the streets.

THE SELF-DRIVING PIZZA DELIVERY CARS

In 2017, Domino's Pizza began using experimental self-driving cars to deliver pizzas in Ann Arbor, Michigan. And in 2018, I saw these same cars on the streets of Miami. Through an arrangement with Ford, Domino's began using several dozen self-driven Fusion sedans to gauge the public's reaction to automated pizza deliveries, in hopes of starting that service commercially in 2021. The cars—with big signs that read "Experiment" and "Self-Driving Delivery Vehicle"—carried the pizzas in the back seat.

It worked like this: You ordered your pizza through a cell phone app, received a code via text message, and when the delivery arrived, you punched the code into a tablet attached next to the car's rear window. Then a speaker on the roof of the car confirmed your order, the back window rolled down, and the pizza was there—hot and ready—sitting in a box waiting for you to grab it. Why would people want their pizzas to be delivered that way? Among other things, because they won't need to leave a tip, saving at least 10 percent of their order's price.

"It's going to be a real learning experience," Dennis Maloney, Domino's chief digital officer, said. "No one really knows what's going to happen when customers walk out to the car. They're faced with a car. There's no human interaction. What happens if they approach the car from the wrong direction? Will people mind coming out of their house? We want to understand all that."

In the beginning, all of Domino's self-driving delivery cars had an engineer on board to keep an eye on everything, but the idea is that soon these cars will be on their own, a Ford spokesman told me. The experiment could pave the way for a possible new niche for big car companies such as Ford or GM, which could help them offset their expected losses once autonomous taxis become the norm and fewer people buy their own cars. Interestingly enough, the title of the *New York Times* article on the new trend in pizza delivery wasn't focused so much on the future of Domino's, but on the future of Ford. It read, "There's a Pizza Delivery in Ford's Future, by Driverless Car."

WHAT DOES THE FUTURE HOLD FOR CABDRIVERS?

Up to this point, most headlines about self-driving cars have not focused on their potential for distributing packages or delivering food, but on their likely use as taxis. What will happen to cabdrivers once Uber, Lyft, and other ride-sharing services start using driverless cars? The taxi industry is one of the most labor intensive in big cities across the globe. There are no fewer than 38,400 registered cabs in Buenos Aires, 35,000 in Tokyo, 24,000 in Mexico City, 23,000 in Seoul, 15,000 in Paris, 13,400 in New York, and 7,300 in Washington, D.C. And that doesn't include Uber and Lyft's privately owned taxis.

Already, even before the commercial introduction of driverless taxis, traditional cabdrivers have protested—sometimes violently—against human-driven Uber and Lyft cars. In some places, like Buenos Aires, traditional taxi drivers have managed to stave off the legal use of Uber for several years. But that's an exception to the norm. In most large cities, the protests failed to stop the wave of private taxis. Sooner or later, market forces prevail over government regulations, and growing numbers of people will choose to moonlight as private cabdrivers to bring in some extra income.

Traditional taxi drivers may be a species on the verge of extinction. "Uber and Lyft Have Devastated L.A.'s Taxi Industry, City Records Show," read a 2016 headline in the *Los Angeles Times.* Since the appearance of Uber and Lyft three years earlier, the number of traditional taxi rides had plummeted by nearly 30 percent, the article said. In San Francisco, that drop was an even steeper 66 percent. In many states, traditional taxi drivers—who have to pay as much as $600,000 for a medallion—can't compete with these new private taxi startups that don't need to pay these fees and thus can offer much cheaper rides. The impact of ride-sharing platforms on the taxi industry has been "brutal," the story said.

THE FUTURE OF UBER AND LYFT LIES IN SELF-DRIVING TAXIS

Some studies are less ominous for traditional taxi drivers. Carl Benedikt Frey—the Oxford economist who coauthored the 2013 study predicting that 47 percent of jobs would disappear over the next two decades—raised eyebrows in 2017 with a new study arguing that Uber's impact on the transportation industry hadn't been as significant as previously thought. The study examined rides by traditional taxi drivers in several U.S. cities between 2009 and 2015, and concluded that Uber's net impact on wages was not dramatic: it caused a 10 percent reduction in traditional taxi drivers' income and a 10 percent increase in Uber drivers' income. As for actual jobs, the study found that Uber's arrival hadn't significantly reduced the number of traditional taxi drivers.

But the study was retrospective and conducted during the early years of Uber and other ride-sharing services. In addition, it didn't take into consideration the fact that Uber and Lyft are focusing on the development of self-driving cars, with which they may soon replace many—if not all—of their human-driven taxis. When I asked Uber CEO Dara Khosrowshahi what will become of his company's drivers once autonomous taxis start hitting the streets, he told me, "I don't believe that 100 percent of our demand is going to be able to be served by robots. There are always going to be exception cases, where people will want people to drive them." And considering that Uber plans to grow exponentially as more people stop buying cars and use private taxis—the company currently accounts for 0.5 percent of all miles driven in the United States and projects its share to grow to 30 percent—the pie will grow for both automated and human-driven taxis, he said. In the end, the boom in ride-sharing services could even have "a net labor positive" impact, he added.

But the fact is that Uber and Lyft are betting much of their future on self-driven cars, and that human drivers will most likely be—to use Dara's word—"exception cases." In 2014, Uber cofounder Travis Kalanick traveled to Pittsburgh and, in one fell swoop, hired almost all members of the robotics team at Carnegie Mellon University, one of the most advanced in the world. Overnight, Kalanick snatched about fifty Carnegie Mellon engineers. And in 2016, Uber announced with great fanfare its first fleet of experimental, self-driving taxis in Pittsburgh. At the same time, Lyft sold a chunk of its shares to General Motors in exchange for a $500 million investment to develop autonomous taxis. Most likely, human-driven taxis will begin to disappear in the early 2020s.

THE FLYING TAXIS OF DUBAI

In addition to Google, Apple, General Motors, BMW, Ford, Mercedes-Benz, Uber, Lyft, and several other companies that are developing self-driving vehicles, the Chinese corporation Ehang is already producing autonomous flying taxis. In 2017, Dubai bought several of these drones, which are powered by eight propeller engines and can carry a 220-pound person with a small suitcase, and began using them experimentally on predetermined routes.

"This isn't just a test," Rohan Roberts, director of the Dubai Science Festival and host of the 2017 Global Innovation Summit, told me in an interview. "It's a real service, one we'll be putting into operation soon. People are going to be taking rides in flying cabs, and what's even more amazing is that these electric drones will be able to carry a person as far as thirty miles at a top speed of nearly one hundred miles per hour."

But have these drones been thoroughly tested? I asked him, wondering to myself whether I would want to take a ride in an autonomous flying taxi. Roberts responded that Dubai had already tested these drones in more than a hundred flights with real passengers, without any problems. One of the main reasons why the flying taxis will be safe is that they will leave no room for human error, he said. "It's a completely autonomous vehicle: the passenger sits inside the vehicle and has no control over it. The drones will be monitored remotely from a central command station, and at the first signs of any trouble, they are programmed to land immediately," he explained.

What if the passenger is drunk or falls asleep? I asked. "Again, the passenger won't have any control whatsoever over the drone," Roberts said. Asked about the possibility that parts of the drones will break loose and fall, hitting pedestrians on the streets, he replied, "Well, there really aren't many parts that can just fall off. These vehicles fly at an altitude of a little under a thousand feet, and of course, as with any new technology, there are certain risks, so the important thing is to keep the drones well maintained. But the same could be said about airplanes: thousands of them are flying across the skies at any given time, and you could certainly make the argument that a piece of metal could fall from the sky. But they don't, because they have good maintenance and are serviced frequently. The same goes for the drones."

When I asked him if flying taxis wouldn't create havoc over city skies, Roberts told me that "at the moment, they are only going to be used for certain, predetermined routes, so they won't be flying all over the city. We are starting on a small scale, and later will expand these routes to make the drones available to a larger number of passengers. As with any large city, Dubai has occasional traffic jams. That could make for an interesting experiment: to see how flying drones could help solve some of our traffic problems."

DRONES WILL DELIVER PACKAGES TO YOUR FRONT DOOR

For several years now, Amazon, FedEx, UPS, and DHL, which account for a significant amount of the world's package transportation business, have been developing drones able to deliver products to your front door. The skies above our cities most likely won't become a whirlwind of unmanned flying vehicles carrying packages in all directions. Rather, shipping companies will use self-driving trucks with drones mounted on their roofs, from which the drones will take off to deliver packages to addresses far away from their standard driving routes.

In fact, UPS estimates that if the use of drones could cut just one mile per driver per day, the company and its fleet of 66,000 trucks would save around $50 million a year. FedEx, on the other hand, has said that using autonomous trucks will be much easier than using drones, in part because automated trucks won't have to comply with regulations that prohibit air traffic over densely populated areas. Either way, drones delivering packages will become increasingly common across the world. Walmart, America's largest retailer, announced it will begin challenging Amazon in delivering packages with drones. But it won't be using trucks. Instead, it will use blimps.

In its patent application for blimp-style floating warehouses that would also serve as drone launching platforms, presented in 2017, Walmart said these airships would fly at heights between 500 and 1,000 feet, and their movements would be determined by which areas have the greatest demand for deliveries. "Movable warehouses are a really nice idea," says Brandon Fletcher, an analyst at Sanford C. Bernstein, "because any flexible part of a logistics system allows it to be more efficient when demand varies widely. The e-commerce world suffers from highly variable demand, and more creative solutions are needed."

ROBOTS ARE TAKING OVER FACTORIES

After several decades of failed forecasts that robots would soon be everywhere, these predictions are finally beginning to materialize. According to the International Federation of Robotics, annual sales of industrial robots tripled from 81,000 units in 2003 to 245,000 units in 2015. And annual industrial robot sales will triple again in the near future, reaching some 900,000 units by 2025, according to the tech consulting firm ABI Research.

Why such a sudden explosion in industrial robots? It is mainly because robots are getting increasingly cheaper and smarter, and because the population in industrialized countries such as Japan and Germany is aging rapidly, which is driving up the demand for robots to replace their shrinking labor forces. Also, the steep increase in wages in China is forcing companies there to buy robots in order to remain competitive. In part because of its economic success in recent decades, China is no longer a cheap labor country, and Chinese businesses are now buying huge numbers of industrial robots to replace workers they cannot afford.

Back in 2011, Terry Gou, founder of Foxconn, the company that produces iPhones and many other electronic products in China, announced that he would be buying a million robots over the next three years to supplement the million people he had working in his factories. Not only were Chinese workers too expensive, they also brought with them too many problems, he said. Gou was quoted by the Chinese news agency Xinhua as saying that "as human beings are also animals, to manage one million animals gives me a headache."

In Japan, industrial robot manufacturers are thriving. When I visited the Japan Robot Association, I was told that more than 70 percent of the robots produced in Japan are for export and that China is their number one client. Hiroshi Fujiwara, executive director of the association, told me that while China had 189,000 robots in operation in 2014, the association was projecting the number for 2019 to reach 726,000.

It is believed that the word *robot* was first used by the Czech writer Karel Čapek in a 1920s play set in a factory where an android did the work of two humans at a much lower cost. Čapek initially called his work machine a *labori,* the Latin word for labor, but later changed it to *robot,* very similar to the word *robota,* which means work in several Slavic languages. In Čapek's play, titled *Rossum's Universal Robots,* one of the characters says, "Robots are not people. Mechanically they are more perfect than we are, they have an enormously developed intelligence, but they have no soul." Čapek's play ends—let us hope mistakenly—with the destruction of the world at the hands of the robots when the intelligent machines discover love.

Today, in part because of skyrocketing robot purchases in Asia, robot prices are plummeting. According to a Bain & Company consulting firm study, while in 2010 the payback period in China for replacing workers was about 5.3 years, by 2016 it had fallen to 1.5 years. Industrial robots are also becoming increasingly efficient thanks to technological advances like sensors that let them "see" better and perform the more meticulous tasks that they weren't able to do before. And many multinationals, encouraged by the declining costs of industrial robots, are moving their manufacturing plants from China to their home countries or to places closer to their markets, to reduce transportation costs and delivery time. Chinese companies and those in other major manufacturing nations don't have many options: they either robotize their factories to remain competitive or go out of business.

IN SOME FACTORIES, THERE ARE 20 WORKERS TO 400 ROBOTS

It's no coincidence that South Korea, Japan, Germany, and the United States are the countries with the largest numbers of industrial robots per capita in the world. According to the International Federation of Robotics (IFR), in 2015, South Korea had an average of 531 robots per 10,000 manufacturing workers in all industries, followed by Singapore with 398, Japan with 305, Germany with 301, the United States with 176, Spain with 150, France with 127, Slovenia with 110, the Czech Republic with 93, China with 49, Mexico with 33, Argentina with 16, and Brazil with 11.

However, in certain specific fields, like the automotive industry, the percentage of robots is much higher. The IFR estimates the overall density of industrial robots in Japan's automotive industry at 1,276 robots for every 10,000 workers. But according to what a couple of executives at Yaskawa—one of the world's largest manufacturers of industrial robots—told me in an interview in Tokyo, there are some car plants in Japan that have only 20 human workers and 400 robots. "Right now, robots in car factories mainly perform welding and painting tasks," Kei Shimizu, one of the sales managers at the Yaskawa robotics facility, told me. "Human workers are totally separate from the robots for safety reasons, and are mostly involved in engine and cable assembly, which robots aren't so good at. But that's changing very quickly. We figure that at least part of the work being done by people will be automated within the next five years."

Shimizu also told me that over the next decade or so, the biggest expansion of the use of robots will take place in the food industry. In factories, supermarkets, and restaurants, "the cost of labor is still low, but sooner or later we'll reach a point where robots will be even cheaper," he said. "In Japan, for example, we have an old tradition of having lunch with the food inside a wooden container known as a bento box. Today that box is filled by human workers, because for now the robots don't quite have the dexterity of human fingers. But that's changing fast. It won't be long before robots take over the job of filling the bento boxes with food."

THE FUTURE OF ROBOTS IS NOW

I doubt Shimizu was exaggerating, because robots are already everywhere in Japanese factories. A few years ago, in what you might call an exercise in science fiction, McKinsey & Company painted a picture of the factories of the future:

> Imagine you are a manager in a manufacturing plant in 2035. At your plant, injuries are virtually unheard-of. In fact, there are few people on the floor: a small group of highly skilled specialists oversee thousands of robots, interacting naturally with the robot workforce to produce goods with unprecedented speed and precision, 24 hours a day, 365 days a year. When a new product or design improvement is introduced, factory workers train robots to follow new routines, using simple touch-screen interfaces, demonstration, and even verbal commands. Most of your day is spent optimizing processes and flows and even assisting with product designs based on what you see on the factory floor and the data that your robots generate.

McKinsey did make one mistake, though: this scenario will not take place in 2035. It's already a reality in many factories in Japan, and across the globe.

THE JAPANESE GOVERNMENT IS SUBSIDIZING ROBOTS

The labor shortage in Japan due to low birth rates is so pressing—the country's workforce will drop from 76 million people to 70 million by 2025—that the government is giving subsidies to companies so they can buy robots. Under a $1 billion public-private sector plan launched by Prime Minister Shinzo Abe, designed to turn Japan into a robotic superpower, Japan pays large corporations up to 50 percent of the cost of each robot they buy. In the case of smaller businesses, the subsidy is as high as 69 percent.

"For example, if a small bakery doesn't have the manpower to mix flour and water, and can't afford to pay someone to do that work, the government covers up to 69 percent of the cost of a robot," Atsushi Yasuda, director of the robotic policy office at the Ministry of Economy, Trade, and Industry (METI), told me in an interview in his office. "We've already delivered robots to bakeries for mixing their dough and shaping their bread."

Some industries, such as health care facilities or homes for senior citizens, are getting higher-than-average government subsidies to buy robots. The government considers that because of the country's rapidly aging population, that's an area that needs urgent help. There are already 67,824 Japanese citizens who are a hundred years of age or older, according to official statistics. And that figure is growing every year. Faced with this problem, the government is subsidizing more than five thousand nursing homes so they can buy robots to monitor the elderly, transport them from place to place, and even keep them company.

According to Takeshi Kobayashi, an official at the Japanese Ministry of Health, there are more than 5.3 million senior citizens in the country who require constant medical attention, and by 2020 there will be a shortage of 250,000 nurses and nursing assistants to take care of them. "We need robots to assist our elderly people," he told me. "It's a very hard job, and many nurses can't be carrying patients around all day because they simply don't have the strength to do so. These robots won't replace the nursing staff, but they'll help the sick and elderly get from place to place, which is a great help."

Prime Minister Abe's plan to turn Japan into a robotic superpower called for quadrupling the country's robot production by the 2020 Tokyo Olympics, so among other things there should be plenty of multilingual robots—like Nao, the one I met at the entrance to the Bank of Tokyo-Mitsubishi branch in the airport—ready to serve tourists in museums and restaurants. Abe also aims to stage a Robot Olympics that will coincide with the Summer Games, whose motto will be "Robots for Happiness." According to Japanese officials, the idea is to share the nation's optimistic view of robots and help make it the largest exporter of robots in the world.

THE ROBOTIC PET TO KEEP THE ELDERLY COMPANY

In Tokyo, I visited the Silver Wing nursing home, one of the most robotized homes for the elderly in the nation's capital. Its building is several decades old and crumbling a bit in places, but it has a wide variety of robots to care for the elderly. When I entered the building, I was asked to remove my shoes in favor of a pair of paper slippers, and wait in a small conference room. A few minutes later I was greeted by Kimiya Ishikawa, the home's director, along with several of his colleagues, who gave me a tour of the place.

In one of the first rooms we visited, a woman in her eighties was sitting on her couch watching the television with her eyes fixed on the screen while her hands were caressing something that looked like a pet. But it wasn't a real animal: rather, it was a hairy little robot that looked like a pet. The small, furry, blue-colored robot looked like a mix between a dog and a seal. Its name was Paro, I was told. When the elderly woman ran her fingers through Paro's thick fur, the robotic animal looked up and wagged its tail the way a real dog would. Ishikawa told me that Paro was dearly loved by everyone at the nursing home. Many even kissed him goodnight and let him sleep in their beds, he added. I found that a bit hard to believe, but I took him at his word, and we continued on with the tour.

Next they showed me a room containing several robotic chairs that looked like first-class airline seats that turn into beds. Once these chairs were in a horizontal position and set up against the side of a bed, an elderly person who wasn't very mobile could still move back and forth from seat to bed without any help. In another room, I saw a "robotic suit" that nurses use to help move the patients around. It was something of a metallic belt with extensions covering the legs that were activated when the nurse began to walk.

In another room I saw Pepper, the humanoid robot I had seen before at the entrance to the Hamazushi restaurant and at the men's clothing store at Tokyo's Akihabara station. There in the nursing home, Pepper played the role of aerobics instructor. The robot was standing in front of a group of residents. When he raised one arm, the class of elderly men and women followed suit. When he turned his body to one side, the humans did as well. When he sang, everybody chimed in. Pepper led these classes several times a day at regularly scheduled times.

When we finished our tour of the nursing home and were

heading back to the conference room to get my coat, I saw something that made me a bit sad. There, sitting in the same position on the same couch, was the same elderly woman I had seen at the start of my tour more than an hour earlier. She was still staring at the television with a lost look in her eyes, caressing her robotic pet. The image was a perfect symbol of the loneliness in which many people spend the last years of their lives in modern societies. I didn't say a word, but the directors of the nursing home must have known what I was thinking because they immediately came out in Paro's defense. "Pet therapy is really important: when a person who was at home or in a hospital arrives at a nursing home, they usually feel very lonely and anxious. And for those people suffering from dementia and call for a nurse every five minutes, this robot can help calm them down," one of the administrators told me.

CHINA WILL MAKE ROBOTS "UNTIL THERE'S NO MORE PEOPLE IN FACTORIES"

Much like Japan, China launched a ten-year plan in 2015 called Made in China 2025, aimed at creating what President Xi Jinping called a "robotic revolution." The goal is to automate Chinese factories, increase their productivity, and thus counter the negative impact of manufacturing plants fleeing the country because of its growing labor costs. The International Federation of Robotics says China is increasing its purchases of industrial robots by 20 percent a year, buying up more units than the twenty-eight nations that make up the European Union combined. According to the federation, by the 2020s, China will be the largest buyer of robots on earth, followed by South Korea, Japan, and the United States.

"China is by far the biggest robot market in the world

regarding annual sales and regarding the operational stock," federation president Joe Gemma says. The federation anticipates that China's demand for robots won't be limited to automotive companies, but will extend to electronics and several other industries. "We will make robots until there's no more people in factories," Max Chu, general manager of E-Deodar, a robotics start-up, told Bloomberg News only half-jokingly.

THE UNMANNED FACTORY IN DONGGUAN CITY

Recently, official Chinese newspapers proudly announced—in an apparent effort to prove that the Made in China 2025 plan is working—the emergence of the nation's first "unmanned factories." The Changying Precision Technology Company, a cell phone manufacturing plant located in the manufacturing city of Dongguan, had laid off 590 of its 650 workers and replaced them with robots, the state-run *People's Daily* newspaper reported. And beyond that, the company plans to let the rest of its human workers go in the very near future, the firm announced with a seeming sense of pride. Luo Weiqiang, the company's general manager, boasted that the sixty human workers remaining at the factory would be reduced to twenty going forward.

According to the *People's Daily,* the factory, located in Guangdong Province, represents "a vision of future manufacturing" in which all the manual work of production and shipping will be handled by computer-controlled robots and self-driving trucks. Changying Precision Technology replaced the laid-off workers with sixty robotic arms on ten production lines that cut and polish the cell phone pieces twenty-four hours a day, 365 days a year, increasing productivity by 250 percent, the paper reported.

The robots make "far more and better products than well-trained workers and experts," the report added. The mere fact that they can work day and night is the equivalent of an entire third shift's worth of work at no cost to the company. Monthly production capacity increased from 8,000 units per person to 21,000 with the robots. And contrary to what some might think, using robots didn't reduce the quality of the product. In fact, since robots took over the factory floor, the rate of defective pieces fell from 25 percent to less than 5 percent, the report said.

"This company is only a microcosm of Dongguan, one of the manufacturing hubs in China," the article said, adding that the city was planning somewhere between 1,000 and 1,500 "robot replace human" programs within the next year. "With the implementation of Made in China 2025 strategy, a growing number of 'unmanned workshops or factories' will come out," the *People's Daily* concluded.

In addition to the exodus of foreign companies due to rising labor costs, the Chinese government is facing a problem previously seen only in industrialized nations: few young people want to work in factory jobs. Plus, China is anticipating a dramatic technological change that will affect all major manufacturing countries: 3-D printers. Nations that until recently imported a large part of their clothes, electronics, and other products from China will now be producing them at home using new technologies like 3-D printers. Today, a manufacturing plant in China churns out hundreds of thousands of identical shirts, which it exports all over the world. But as people are increasingly looking to design their own styles and create their clothing with a 3-D printer at home or at a nearby store, there will be less of a demand for mass-produced shirts imported from China or anywhere else.

FROM MASS PRODUCTION TO INDIVIDUALIZED PRODUCTION

As I pointed out in my book *Innovate or Die!,* 3-D printers will revolutionize the manufacturing industry, even if the excitement around them has somewhat diminished since their first commercial prototypes made a big splash a few years ago. Just as a traditional photocopier can reproduce a piece of paper, 3-D printers can do the same for just about anything, from a button to a shoe to a house. In much the same way as the steam engine led the way for the Industrial Revolution in the early nineteenth century, and personal computers changed the world in the late twentieth century, 3-D printers may eventually change the way goods are produced. It won't be long before we move from mass production to individualized production.

For example, 3-D printers will one day allow each of us to produce our own customized shirts. We will select a design on our computer screens, add or remove any details we want—whether it's blue stripes, white polka dots, or whatever it may be—and print them out in the comfort of our own homes. And if our personal 3-D printer doesn't have the right fabric or material we want, we will send it off to a nearby 3-D printing store. As we go forward, it's the designs that will be exported, not the clothes themselves.

The 3-D printer was invented in 1986 by Chuck Hull, an introverted engineer whom I interviewed a few years ago, and they began gaining popularity in the early 2000s when NASA started using them to produce replacement parts for damaged equipment during space missions. Soon, 3-D printers were being used by the aerospace industry for the same purpose, to repair planes without having to send them back to the hangar. The shipping industry followed suit and included 3-D printers in the engine rooms of ships so they wouldn't have to waste time stranded in ports waiting for spare parts. These printers also became increasingly popular in the medical field, where they are used to generate teeth, bones, and even ears that are perfectly tailored to each and every patient. After that, the personalized 3-D printer emerged, allowing people to replace a lost knob from their stovetop or create a new home-made object. But that was just the beginning of something much, much greater.

ADIDAS IS ALREADY TURNING OUT 3-D PRINTED SHOES

The sporting-goods giant Adidas has already announced the start of new automated mass-production plants in Germany and the United States that will use 3-D printers to turn out one million pairs of sneakers previously made in China and other Asian nations. Thanks to 3-D printing in factories close to its customers, Adidas will be able to bring products to the market much more quickly, and will always be up-to-date with the latest fashion trends, a company spokesman said. In many cases, the process of bringing a new shoe model to the market took—from the moment it was designed until delivery—between twelve and eighteen months, he added. Now, the time span will be much shorter.

"This is a milestone not only for us as a company but also for the industry," said Gerd Manz, Adidas's head of technology innovation, in announcing a new model of 3-D printed shoes known as the Futurecraft 4D. "We've cracked some of the boundaries." Manz was referring to the fact that thanks to industrial 3-D printers, the production time of a shoe sole has been reduced from 1.5 hours to around 20 minutes. Nike has also recently announced that it has started using these printers, and is producing soles ten times faster than when it was using traditional injection molding.

And the major sports equipment companies are already offering their online customers the opportunity to choose their own colors, designs, soles, and shapes for their shoes, based on their personal tastes, weight, shape of the foot, and the specific sport for which they'll be using them. "What you can do is introduce more types of products without a cost penalty," says Terry Wohlers, head of Wohlers Associates, a U.S. consulting firm specializing in 3-D printing. "With this technology, you can produce one or a few [pairs of shoes] inexpensively."

A GADGET INVENTED BY THE MEDIA?

Despite all the publicity surrounding 3-D printers, some are skeptical that they will ever result in a new Industrial Revolution. Terry Gou, the founder of Foxconn who said that human workers give him headaches, astonished the world again a few years later when he said that 3-D printers are a "gimmick" whose importance has been exaggerated by the media. According to the *South China Morning Post,* Gou even joked that he was so confident in his belief that if he turned out to be wrong, he would legally change his last name and write it backward: Uog. If he intends to keep his promise, it seems likely that sooner or later Gou will have to rename himself, because everything indicates that 3-D printers—while they may be advancing more slowly than some anticipated—will eventually prevail.

As we've seen with self-driving cars, there is almost always a certain amount of lag time between an invention and its massive commercial use, and 3-D printers are no exception. Aviation pioneers Orville and Wilbur Wright made their first flight in 1903, but it was another eleven years before the world witnessed the first commercial flight, and the age of commercial aviation didn't fully begin until 1926 when federal regulations for pilots became mandatory. Similarly, automobiles didn't hit the market until long after they were invented. German engineers Nikolaus Otto, Gottlieb Daimler, and Wilhelm Maybach patented the four-cylinder engine in 1870, but mass-produced cars didn't arrive until almost three decades later, when Henry Ford launched his Model T in 1913. Something similar is most likely happening now with 3-D printers.

THE RISE OF THE "TECHNICIANS"

Until recently, workers in manufacturing companies were divided between those performing white-collar jobs in offices and those who had blue-collar jobs on factory floors. While the former were often university graduates or had some other sort of higher education, the latter performed routine mechanical tasks that didn't require a college education, and sometimes not even a high school diploma. But this division of labor is changing very rapidly with the emergence of a new group whom we might call the technicians.

"Today, a third group has emerged in the contemporary manufacturing environment, and is poised to eclipse at least one of the two traditional groups in importance," says a study by the consulting firm Manpower. It notes that "often called technicians or 'techs,' it is the job of this category of workers to program, operate, troubleshoot, and maintain the increasing number of computer- and network-driven manufacturing devices in the contemporary factory." These technicians are people who require more training than traditional workers because they are in charge of operating the robots, 3-D printers, and computer networks that are doing an increasing amount of work in modern factories, the study adds.

Todd Teske, president of the engine manufacturer Briggs & Stratton, explains that "now we have lots of robots—as many in a single manufacturing cell as we once had in the whole factory. The skill levels required to work in our plants have gone up substantially. We need people who can program the robots and CNC machining centers, operate them, and fix them." He points out the fact that despite the increasing demand for labor, companies are finding it difficult to hire technicians because "there is a stigma against going to a tech school vs. getting a four-year college degree. We have misdirected our youth. High schools have become prep schools for college, and not industry. People don't seem to know that there are good jobs available that pay good wages off technical degrees and certificate programs."

FACTORY WORK DESERVES MORE RESPECT

How can we solve this problem? In the United States, as we saw in the chapter on education, the government is already trying to copy the German system of training and vocational schools, and other countries are creating tech-based high schools like the Seoul Robotics High School in South Korea. But there won't be any great leaps forward in vocational and technical schools until young people see technicians as role models, or at least as people whose jobs are not boring. The study Manpower conducted suggests that it might take a TV series glorifying their work, like what *CSI: Crime Scene Investigation* did for forensic investigators. That show sparked a huge increase in enrollment at schools that offer degrees in forensic science, and these investigators do a job that's not nearly as glamorous as a manufacturing technician in real life.

"Perhaps the ideal situation would be to develop a glamorous fictional movie about tech careers and show it to middle schoolers. Whatever the specific method used to overcome these cultural barriers, it is important to recognize that they exist. We will not see North American students flocking to these important tech jobs—and getting the preparation they need to perform them successfully—without dealing with current stereotypes about manufacturing and jobs in it," the study concludes.

IT WILL BE HARDER TO TELL BOSSES FROM WORKERS

The factory workers of the future will be doing the kind of work that won't require getting their hands dirty. Factories will be needing designers and mechanics specializing in virtual reality so that engineers are able to check products and train workers remotely. In the not-so-distant future, engineers at a factory in China or Mexico will be able to work together to solve a technical problem by handling the same object through their virtual reality headsets, saving companies a lot of time and money in travel expenses. Expert technicians will be needed to install and maintain the VR equipment so that this new mode of long-distance work can take place.

There will be a need for technicians to program and repair robots, and specialists in 3-D printers to maintain these machines, and know which materials they should use and how. One of the great upcoming revolutions in engineering will be the creation of multimaterials—combinations of different materials—that 3-D printers will be using to create all sorts of new objects. There will also be self-repairing materials, which will patch themselves up if they're damaged, like the metallic armor and flesh in Arnold Schwarzenegger's *Terminator* films, which can melt down and build themselves back up after taking a direct hit from a shotgun.

With the expanding Internet of Things, which allows

machines to communicate with one another online, there will be a growing demand for programmers and experts in sensor technology, who will be needed to monitor the interactions between various machines. Factories will increasingly have their machines connected and communicating with one another through sensors and Internet messages, which will allow them to let others know when to start or finish a production cycle. But the machines will need human specialists who know how to monitor the sensors, repair them when they break down, and make sure that everything is coordinated to perfection.

That's why as manufacturing plants become increasingly automated, they will need qualified technicians who are much more highly trained than the workers of the past. It will be harder to tell the bosses from the workers, since most will be doing similar jobs overseeing the machines. Everyone will be side by side, monitoring the rows of robots and 3-D printers, solving problems and thinking up new products or more efficient production processes. The humans who will be working on the factory floors, coexisting with the robots, will not be there to do manual work, but to do mental work.

9

THEY'RE COMING FOR ENTERTAINERS!

THE FUTURE OF THE ACTING, MUSIC, SPORTS, AND LEISURE INDUSTRIES

NEW YORK

Until recently, having a child actor, musician, athlete, or tour guide wasn't much of a cause for celebration for parents who had followed more traditional career paths. The most desirable occupations were lawyers, doctors, and business executives, just as they had been for centuries. But all this could be changing soon. With so much work being automated, people will find themselves with more and more free time, and they'll need growing numbers of actors, musicians, writers, visual artists, and tour guides to entertain them. And while there is an oversupply of labor in parts of the entertainment industry, creative endeavors may well be entering a golden age.

In most countries, the number of hours in the workweek has been falling for centuries. In ancient times, there was only one day of rest per week—Shabbat for the Jews, Friday for the Muslims, and Sunday for the Christians. Peasants worked from sunrise to sunset, roughly eighty hours a week. But as we transitioned from agricultural societies to industrial ones, and most recently to service-oriented ones, working hours have fallen by nearly 50 percent in the industrialized world. In 1870, the average workweek in the United States, Germany, and Sweden was nearly 70 hours per week. By 2015, it had dropped to 38.6 hours per week in the United States and 35 hours in Germany and Sweden. There is a clear world trend toward shorter workweeks.

THE CREATIVE INDUSTRIES ARE GROWING AT A DIZZYING RATE

Creative or cultural industries—including film, television, visual arts, music, and literature—already employ 29.5 million people worldwide, according to a study by the consulting firm EY. That figure is higher than the number of people working in the automotive industry in the United States, Europe, and Japan combined. Activities that were previously considered mere sources of entertainment or spiritual growth are now being seen as engines of economic growth. Bilbao, in Spain's Basque country, became a center for world tourism when the Guggenheim Museum opened a branch there, reviving the city's economy. Something similar happened with the Cannes Film Festival, the Art Basel fair in Miami, the Guadalajara International Book Fair, the Hollywood film industry, and hundreds of other cultural ventures that gave a big boost to local economies. According to Irina Bokova, the former director-general of UNESCO, "the cultural and creative industries are major drivers of the economies of developed as well as developing countries. Indeed, they are among the most rapidly growing sectors worldwide. It influences income generation, job creation and export earnings. It can forge a better future for many countries around the globe."

THE FILM AND TV INDUSTRIES WILL ALSO LOSE JOBS TO AUTOMATION

Of course, the boom in the movie and television industries will not prevent some of its workers from losing their jobs to automation. The huge crowds of extras who worked on the great Hollywood blockbusters of the past have largely been replaced by computer-generated images. For several years now, film studios have been using computer effects to create stadiums filled with virtual crowds or massive armies with tens of thousands of virtual soldiers. The 1982 film *Gandhi* used 300,000 human beings in its scenes of the Indian independence hero's funeral. But today a similar scene could be done digitally with a few dozen extras whose images are duplicated and differentiated with computer programming. And technology is ready to go a step further: replacing the movie stars themselves with digital facsimiles and doing so without viewers even realizing that what they're seeing isn't an actor but a virtual image of one.

The best-known example of this is the case of Paul Walker, star of *The Fast and the Furious* series of films, who continued to act after his death—metaphorically speaking, of course—thanks to the digitization of his face.* Walker died in a car accident while filming the seventh installment of *The Fast and the Furious.* After a time of mourning and some legal consultations, the producers finished the project using a digital replica of Walker. What's most amazing about this is that most people—if they hadn't read about the case—didn't even notice. Walker's virtual stand-in performance raised a question that

* There are previous cases of actors whose images were used to create computer-generated scenes after their deaths, like Brandon Lee in the final minutes of *The Crow.* But Walker's case is considered a milestone because it was the most technically complex at the time.

remains a hot topic of conversation in Hollywood to this day: Will flesh-and-blood actors eventually be replaced by digital ones? It's no trivial matter: big studios could be eager to use computer-generated images of dead movie stars because virtual actors would be much cheaper, and significantly easier to work with, than many Hollywood celebrities.

PAUL WALKER AND THE CASE OF DIGITIZED ACTORS

Walker died on November 30, 2013, in the Porsche Carrera GT sports car driven by a friend who crashed it into a utility pole. The accident occurred at 3:30 P.M. in Santa Clara, California, when the two were returning from a charity event. The police found no traces of alcohol or drugs at the scene, but investigators determined that the car was traveling at more than 100 miles an hour on a road with a 45-mile-an-hour speed limit.

At the time of Walker's death, Universal Studios had already invested a significant part of the film's $190 million budget. Facing the possibility of adding a massive economic loss to the tragic loss of Walker's life, Universal decided to finish the movie with digitized images of the late actor. Similar visual effects had been used for years to Photoshop the faces of Hollywood stars over those of their stunt doubles in high-risk action sequences, but most of those had been fleeting scenes shot from a distance. In this case, Universal set out to finish the film with a computerized version of Walker and hired the New Zealand visual effects studio Weta Digital to digitize his face. Walker's two brothers were also brought in to film physical movements similar to those of the late actor. At least 350 additional scenes were filmed with Walker's simulated voice and image.

According to *Variety* magazine, the producers could have digitally put Walker's face on another actor's body, but they didn't do so because many moviegoers had learned of the actor's death and might have noticed the trick. Using digital imagery, the filmmakers achieved an amazing virtual performance in which movements, gestures, and even the small marks on the late actor's face seemed real. Joe Letteri, one of Weta Digital's visual effects managers, told *Variety* that the technology for producing virtual actors had advanced so quickly that the prospect of replacing Walker would have been impossible five years earlier. "It was barely possible last year when we did it," Letteri said. The film premiered in 2015, and became one of the biggest box-office hits of all time, grossing $1.5 billion that year.

PRINCESS LEIA OF STAR WARS ALSO PERFORMED AFTER HER DEATH

The 2016 movie *Rogue One: A Star Wars Story* had used digital doubles to film scenes of late actor Peter Cushing, who had played the role of Grand Moff Tarkin in the first *Star Wars* trilogy, and also of late actress Carrie Fisher, who had played the role of Princess Leia in the original movie. The plot of *Rogue One: A Star Wars Story* recounted a story that preceded the original 1977 *Star Wars* movie, and producers faced the problem that the two actors had since died. Technology took care of the problem. Welcome to the world of virtual actors.

The only reason why the virtual performances in *Furious 7* and *Rogue One: A Star Wars Story* didn't result in an actors' strike or major protests in Hollywood was that they coincided with a boom in the movie and TV industries. The success of Netflix, Amazon, HBO, and other new companies producing shows like *Game of Thrones* had created thousands of new jobs in the film business. However, virtual doubles will most likely be an increasingly common phenomenon in Hollywood movies, and that could make movie stars lose some jobs. Thanks to new computing programs such as Light Stage, film studios are already digitizing the faces of Angelina Jolie, Tom Cruise, and Brad Pitt, enabling them to act well beyond their deaths.

Light Stage photographs every millimeter of a movie star's face. It does so from various angles, using about twenty high-definition cameras while the actor makes fifty-odd facial expressions, such as smiling, crying, or showing concern. Then the Light Stage program reconstructs those faces in 3-D and uses that as the model for digitally inserting the actor into a movie. It's possible that by the time this book hits the shelves, there will be movies that will have been shot entirely with virtual actors. The big studios may prefer to buy the digital use rights to Hollywood stars instead of having them perform in person. And the actors in turn may want to grant studios the rights to their images in order to guarantee an income for their children and grandchildren for many years to come.

Skeptics argue that digital re-creations of late actors and actresses won't become the norm because audiences would eventually get bored. After all, Hollywood feeds on big headlines focusing on the sexual adventures and political passions of its stars, and dead actors don't generate juicy news stories. But few industry insiders doubt that film studios will be using this resource to at the very least resolve scheduling conflicts. Many performers concurrently work in more than one movie at a time or have other commitments that overlap with their film contracts. So movie stars may record only close-up scenes, leaving the rest of their performances to be handled by virtual doubles. Although, in the future, the new technologies will make it hard to prevent digital pirates from making their own films with images of their favorite stars or—perhaps even worse—political figures. How will we know if they're real or fictitious?

EVERY ACTOR YOU SEE JUMPING BETWEEN BUILDINGS IS DIGITAL

Carlos Arguello, a Hollywood visual effects director who worked on the *Fast and Furious* series, and who was nominated for an Oscar for his work on *The Chronicles of Narnia: The Lion, the Witch, and the Wardrobe,* told me in an interview that Hollywood studios started using increasingly more computer-generated imagery (CGI) since scoring big hits in the early 1990s with *Terminator 2: Judgment Day* and *Jurassic Park.* CGI has replaced what was formerly known as special effects. In the past, if moviemakers wanted to simulate a castle, they filmed a model of a castle and would later enlarge it on the screen to make it look real. Or if they wanted to film an action hero jumping from one building to another, they would use a stuntman suspended from ropes that viewers would not see on the screen. But now these effects are done much faster and cheaper on a computer, he explained.

"At first movies had maybe thirty or forty special effects. That quickly grew to fifteen hundred or two thousand, to the point where a ninety-minute movie today has a special effect about every three seconds," Arguello told me. "Now, every time you see a hero running and jumping off a building, like in *Captain America,* it's all being done on a computer." And this has turned visual effects into a huge industry in itself. Up until the early 1990s, Hollywood studios produced their own special effects, but today they most often subcontract to companies in Britain, Canada, and New Zealand, among others.

"When we did *The Chronicles of Narnia* back in 2005, we started by making visual effects for the same scene in different places," Arguello said. "We did the castle in Guatemala with Industrial Light & Magic (ILM), the eagle was done in San Francisco with Lucasfilm, and the lion was done in Los Angeles by a company called Rhythm & Hues. We merged all of that together later, to put the castle, the eagle, and the lion together in one shot."

He added, "The visual effects industry has really been globalized. Now there's a company that is known to make the best castles, another company that is known to do the best birds, another company that does the best dragons, and then everything is put together." And the CGI companies that are in the highest demand are those that can create digital crowds, like armies or stadiums filled with spectators, he added.

FROM 300,000 EXTRAS TO A FEW DOZEN

Before large crowds could be simulated digitally, Hollywood studios had to spend fortunes to hire huge numbers of extras and pay them daily stipends, as well as providing costumes, transportation, and food for them. The 1956 film *The Ten Commandments,* which told the story of the Jewish people's exodus from Egypt, used 14,000 extras and 15,000 animals, including goats, cows, and camels. *Ben Hur,* in 1959, used 15,000 extras. And as was mentioned earlier, *Gandhi* employed a grand total of 300,000 extras. For the funeral scene, the studio hired some 100,000 extras, but another 200,000 onlookers showed up at the scene and were filmed as part of the crowd.

A great technological leap took place in 2001 with the launch of the *Lord of the Rings* trilogy. Director Peter Jackson used a computer program from New Zealand called Massive that utilized artificial intelligence to create battle scenes involving thousands of digital warriors. And from that point on, all you needed to film a war was a few actors or extras who could be digitally multiplied and turned into huge armies.

With 2004's *Troy,* Warner Brothers wanted to re-create one of the greatest battles of all time. To do so, the studio created its own digital simulation with an artificial intelligence program nicknamed Emily, for M.L.E., or Motion Library Editor. Instead of hiring hundreds of thousands of extras, a mere ten programmers were used to create the digital battles. According to a description of the production, the process began with three weeks of motion capturing of about ninety different movements that were carried out by the actors. These movements were then stored in a database of around 1,000 clips, which were then mixed together to create 100,000 different combinations. At first, *Troy*'s producers had planned on digital war scenes pitting 50,000 Greeks against 25,000 Trojans. But thanks to Emily, they were able to add as many soldiers as they wanted and ended up with some shots featuring as many as 150,000 soldiers.

Since the filming of *Troy,* even fewer actors or extras are needed to shoot action sequences that are later turned into massive virtual armies. "With twenty or thirty actors, you can build an entire army of thousands of people, complete with spears and horses. Just about everything can be done on a computer," Arguello told me. "You film a scene with a couple of soldiers that have some good interaction between them, and then you multiply it by five hundred. The software can change each of the soldiers' outfits. It can make each of the fighters wear a different leather skirt or armor, and put a sword or a spear or a club in their hands."

RICHARD GERE: TODAY'S MOVIES ARE SHOT IN THREE WEEKS

One of the things that caught my attention when I interviewed actor Richard Gere was his assertion that today's movies are shot in half the time they once were. During the interview, shortly after he had presented his film *Norman* at the Miami

Film Festival in 2017, Gere told me that "before, we used to make films like *Norman* with budgets that let us film for forty-five or fifty days. But now we can do that in twenty to twenty-five days," with smaller budgets.

Shooting times have been cut mainly thanks to computer technology. Where you once had to build multiple sets in different locations, which required moving large numbers of people from one place to another and setting up new lighting and shooting equipment, technological advances such as virtual scenes and digital crowds are allowing producers to save time and money. And while all that is cutting the working time of actors and crew members, it is also allowing for many more low-cost independent films to be made, Gere told me. "I'm much more optimistic" than those who are predicting a future of growing unemployment for actors, he said. Thanks to lower production costs, "there are a huge number of independent productions being made every year," he added.

Stuart Dryburgh, an Academy Award–nominated cinematographer and director of photography known for his work on *The Great Wall, Emperor,* and several other Hollywood films, gave me a few more examples to further explain how moviemaking is becoming increasingly efficient. In the past, in order to film a car speeding down an empty highway from a helicopter, you had to start shooting at dawn so there wouldn't be any other cars on the road. And if a car showed up, you had to wait for it to pass and shoot the whole scene over. "Now we just remove the other cars in postproduction," he explained. In much the same way, it used to take cinematographers hours, if not days, to prepare a set so that the lighting and overall environment were perfect. "Now we know that we can simply take out everything we don't want," Dryburgh said. "We can change a cloudy sky to a blue one and vice versa."

MORE FILMS AND TV SERIES ARE BEING PRODUCED THAN EVER

The good news for actors, directors, visual effects artists, screenwriters, and everyone else working in the film industry is that the number of visual content companies has skyrocketed. Since 2013, when Netflix began streaming shows like *House of Cards* online—allowing viewers to binge-watch several episodes of a series in a single viewing, instead of having to wait a week for the next one—many tech companies have jumped into the moviemaking business. Where Hollywood and television studios once essentially had a monopoly on content production, they now have to compete with producers like Netflix and Amazon.

After the success of *House of Cards,* Netflix spent $6 billion on the production of TV series in 2017 and announced that it would spend $8 billion in 2018. Amazon invested $4.5 billion in visual content in 2017. Both Google and Apple launched their own film divisions to produce original content, and Facebook and Twitter were said to be considering following suit. All this has led to unprecedented investments in movie making, and all indications are that this trend will continue.

"It's only a matter of time—perhaps a couple of years—before movies will be streamed on social-media sites," writes Nick Bilton in *Vanity Fair.* "For Facebook, it's the natural evolution. The company, which has a staggering 1.8 billion monthly active users, literally a quarter of the planet, is eventually going to run out of new people it can add to the service. Perhaps the best way to continue to entice Wall Street investors to buoy the stock—Facebook is currently the world's seventh-largest company by market valuation—will be to keep eyeballs glued to the platform for longer periods of time. What better way to do that than a two-hour film?"

Which is probably why Facebook bought the Oculus virtual reality viewer company for $2 billion in 2014. With virtual reality headsets, Facebook users can digitally share a movie from the comfort of their homes, regardless of where they are in the world. And Facebook will be able to inject ads into the movies, which will allow the company to offer free visual content. When Bilton asked a Facebook executive why that hasn't happened yet, his response was, "Eventually it will."

According to industry data, the number of movies that people watched in American theaters—not counting those that are shown only at film festivals—increased from 478 films in 2000 to 736 in 2016. And while the number of theatergoers isn't growing, there are increasingly more pay-per-view online platforms where people are watching movies. According to the Motion Picture Association of America (MPAA), there are currently 480 legal websites such as Netflix, iTunes, and Google Play, where people can watch movies and TV shows for a small fee.

The booming movie production business is providing jobs for 2 million people in the United States, 4.1 million in China, and 1.8 million in India, according to MPAA figures.* Writers, too, are benefiting from the proliferation of movie and TV series platforms, to the point where many novelists who once dreamed of winning a literary prize are now focusing their efforts on writing screenplays for Netflix and Amazon. "The number of online platforms for legally viewing movies and TV shows continues to grow steadily, making more creative content from all over the world available to more audiences than

* The MPAA data account for all occupations connected to the film industry, including indirect jobs. According to more specific data from the U.S. Department of Labor, there were 250,000 people working specifically on movies and videos in 2016, up from 146,000 in 2009.

ever before," says Julia Jenks, vice president for global research for the MPAA.

WELCOME TO THE "VISUALIZATION INDUSTRY"

The future expansion of work opportunities for filmmakers, visual effects artists, and actors will come not only from TV series and independent films but also from a growing visualization industry. For instance, with the advent of virtual reality devices, there will be a need for more immersive video games, which will allow us not only to watch movies, but to enter them and become their stars. As in the science fiction novel *Ready Player One*—which Steven Spielberg adapted into a film in which the leading character participates in the virtual search of an Easter Egg for a multimillion-dollar prize in 2044—we will move from being passive viewers to active participants while sitting in our own homes wearing virtual reality headsets.

Beyond movies and TV, virtual reality will lead to a new visual content industry for schools, doctors' offices, and businesses of all kinds. As mentioned earlier in this book, restaurants will be producing their own videos to tell their story and feature their dishes, while supermarkets and department stores will be generating their own visual content in much the same way as they do on their websites today.

Growing numbers of medical students will be using virtual reality to digitally dissect corpses, instead of using real bodies. Schoolchildren who want to learn about the pyramids in Egypt will be able to tour them virtually and even "touch" artifacts as they explore them. All companies in every industry will have to be constantly updating their visual presentations, and to do that, they will need creative directors, videographers, writers, and actors. Even business cards may soon be replaced by electronic presentation videos, which people will send by cell phone and will tell others who we are, what we do, and what our life story is. We may even need multiple video presentation cards, depending on whether we want to use them for work or social occasions. In many cases, they could become major productions that will need to be renewed constantly, thus generating more work for content and visual artists. "There's an explosion of possibilities in what used to be called the film industry. Movies will be just one part of it, because we will be seeing a phenomenal growth in the visualization industry," Arguello told me.

THE FALL—AND RISE—OF THE MUSIC INDUSTRY

The music industry—which had reached record worldwide sales of nearly $24 billion in the 1990s—took a nosedive after the 1999 creation of Napster, which allowed people to listen to music online for free. It was a brutal crash that led many to predict that the industry was mortally wounded. But music sales began to recover in 2015 thanks to the fact that a relatively small but growing number of people started paying to listen to their favorite artists on legal platforms like Pandora, Spotify, iTunes, Amazon Music, and Google Play.

After fifteen years of declining sales, music industry revenues grew by 3.2 percent to $15 billion in 2015, by another 5.9 percent in 2016, and by an additional 8.1 percent in 2017, according to the International Federation of the Phonographic Industry (IFPI). While still below their all-time record, the new figures were a sign of hope that the industry could recover and that streaming—which had nearly killed the industry—could actually become its savior. According to a study by the investment bank Goldman Sachs, the music industry is "on the cusp of a new era of growth." It added, "The growth of streaming will help music revenues almost double by 2030."

One of the most hopeful signs for professional musicians is that young people in China—the world's biggest consumers of pirated music—are starting to pay for the songs they listen to. Revenues of legal music-streaming companies in China increased fivefold between 2012 and 2017 despite the fact that the vast majority of Chinese music fans continue to get their songs from illegal websites. According to *The Economist,* only 20 million Chinese online music listeners use legitimate sites, out of a total of 600 million listeners in the country. But the number of legal users is increasing rapidly, thanks in part to the fact that smartphones are making it much easier to download apps that allow you to listen to music legally through a monthly subscription. And that trend is growing worldwide.

IS SPOTIFY KILLING THE MUSIC INDUSTRY OR SAVING IT?

In the short term, however, this isn't of much help to professional musicians, who went from selling ten-dollar records just a few years ago to earning less than a penny for every song that someone listens to on a legal platform today. In 2017, a song had to be downloaded more than 700,000 times on Spotify—a free platform financed with advertising—in order for the artist to earn one hundred dollars.

Spotify does provide another pay-based service that offers musicians a better deal, where fans pay a monthly fee in exchange for access with no ads and better selections. But it will take many years for artists to live off the royalties from the streaming of their songs the way they used to live off their record sales. For now artists will have to see Spotify, Pandora, and other legal online music services as a means of promoting their music without expecting much in the way of compensation, at least not directly.

THE SAVING GRACE FOR MUSICIANS: LIVE SHOWS

As John Hartmann, the former manager of bands like Peter, Paul, and Mary and the Eagles, predicted some years ago, live concerts will be—and already are—the main source of income for musicians. Actual records, on the other hand, have basically become business cards for professional musicians. According to the concert trade publication *Pollstar,* live concert revenues in the United States have risen from $1.7 billion in 2000 to $7.3 billion in 2016, and are expected to continue growing at a rapid pace for the foreseeable future.

And while artists are always complaining about how little they get from streaming platforms like Spotify and Pandora, they are starting to see huge indirect benefits from them, says Cherie Hu, a music industry analyst with *Billboard* and *Forbes* magazines. In an interview, Hu told me that "artists aren't limited by geography anymore. Thanks to streaming services, young people in China are downloading 'Despacito' by Puerto Rican artist Luis Fonsi, and South Korean pop music is becoming famous in the United States. Music has become more democratized than ever before, and it's giving artists more opportunities to thrive and shine."

Plus, she told me, "streaming has given artists much more actionable data on who's listening to their music, which they can use to program their tours." Indeed, several streaming platforms now offer personalized dashboards to artists so they can know how many times their songs are being heard, and where around the world, as well as which are their most popular hits.

In the past, bands had to plan their tours randomly. They went to some part of their country—or some part of the world—and hoped for the best. Sometimes, after spending a lot of time and money, they ended up playing to an empty room. But today, with the ability to analyze their geographic data on streaming platforms, these bands can know in advance where they will have a sold-out show and where they won't. There's no better example of this phenomenon than the huge success K-pop—or South Korean pop rock music—is enjoying in Chile.

HOW A SOUTH KOREAN BAND ROCKED CHILE

Much to the surprise of many, the K-pop band Bangtan Sonyeondan—also known as BTS or the Bangtan Boys—was a huge success in Chile in 2017 despite the fact that its music had never been played by Chilean commercial radio stations and that most of the traditional media in that South American country didn't even know of its existence. The seven-member band, which was very famous in South Korea, went to the Chilean capital of Santiago to put on a concert and sold out the Movistar Arena for two nights in a row. According to *The New York Times,* the event promoters hadn't even bothered to advertise it.

The 12,500 seats for the first show sold out in just two hours. Thousands of teenagers had camped outside the stadium for days in advance, waiting to buy tickets priced between $38 and $212. Faced with such demand, promoters quickly set up a second show for the following night. More than $2 million in tickets were sold, plus whatever was brought in from sales of promotional T-shirts and other paraphernalia. Fans flocked to several parks across the Chilean capital to practice the band's dance moves.

How did this happen? It turns out that *Wings,* the BTS album that had topped the charts in South Korea the previous year, had become a global hit thanks to streaming services and social networks. Thousands of Chilean teenagers had become K-pop fans, and BTS lyrics that touched on teenagers' internal conflicts and sense of pessimism had resonated without

Chile's traditional media even realizing it. And thanks to the audience-tracking data and location maps offered by streaming platforms, BTS's managers learned that—no matter how strange it seemed—they had a huge fan base in Chile. So they planned a concert there. "We cross-checked with social-media-channel statistics to confirm the level of loyalty and fan base in the country," said Yandi Park, a concert business manager for Big Hit. "We did expect to have good ticket sales because the promoters were also confident but did not anticipate the sellout in minutes."

"THE NUMBER OF MUSICIANS WILL INCREASE SIGNIFICANTLY"

The growing globalization and democratization of music will make cases such as the surprise success in Chile of South Korea's BTS increasingly common, and live performances—whether they take place in stadiums, concert halls, or bars—will become much more frequent. When I asked Hu, the music industry columnist for *Billboard* and *Forbes,* whether people will not stay home and watch a show on a virtual reality device rather than go to a live concert, she told me she doesn't see that happening. "I don't think there's anything like being at a concert, being surrounded by a crowd of people, sharing the excitement of seeing an artist," she said. "Virtual reality just isn't the same."

In this new musical universe, big labels that once dominated the industry will lose some of their influence, and independent musicians will have more resources to make money and get their names out there. Indie artists can already fund their records with donations through Kickstarter.com, PledgeMusic.com, Indiegogo.com, or other similar sites where creative people can raise money for their projects. Thanks to social media, musicians can also make themselves known across the globe without the help of a record company to promote them. And thanks to the algorithms used by the streaming channels, they can pick up new followers in several new ways.

For instance, when we click on a music video on YouTube, we get a list of other artists with similar styles popping out on the right-hand side of the screen. This allows us to find artists we didn't know about before and greatly expands the range of music that's available to us. All of it works to the benefit of the musicians, helping them reach even broader audiences.

"The number of musicians will increase significantly," Gabriel Abaroa, Jr., president and CEO of the Latin Recording Academy, told me in an interview. When I asked him if it wouldn't be just the big-name performers who will be making money giving live concerts, Abaroa replied that more music is being made now than ever, and that will benefit all artists. "When I was young, how many of my friends dreamed of going on a reality show and singing? Not many. I would have made fun of them, and people would have labeled them as losers. But today everyone wants to perform, everyone wants to go to a karaoke bar and sing. You get on a plane and half the people around you are listening to music. You go to a restaurant and there's music playing. You go to your office and it's not uncommon to see the receptionist listing to music at her desk. Music is everywhere," he told me.

INDEPENDENT MUSICIANS MUST BE SMALL-BUSINESS ENTREPRENEURS

In the new music economy, more musicians will have to serve as their own managers, promoters, public relations agents, social media administrators, event organizers, distribution managers, and accountants. There will always be superstars who will have their own support teams, but most musicians will have to achieve success on their own, says Don Gorder, chair and founder of the Music Business/Management Department of the Berklee College of Music.

"The good news is that technology is making that possible," Gorder says. "Successful do-it-yourselfers will continue to leverage the latest social media platforms and analytic tools to connect with their fans and fund their projects, partner with product and service companies for branding and advertising campaigns, license their music for film, television, games, ads, etc., leverage relationships with electronic media as part of their marketing strategy, and book and promote their tours and concerts—all with an ultimate goal of getting their music to the ears of the curators of the outlets for consumption," he adds. To put it succinctly, the vast majority of musicians will have to become small-business entrepreneurs.

Independent artists/entrepreneurs will also have to learn to use technology to monitor and collect royalties without the need of a record company, promoter, or manager. "Independent artists and songwriters will continue to become more and more conscious of how to leverage their intellectual property into alternate revenue streams," says Tony van Veen, president of AVL Digital Group. "In addition to the companies that already exist, you will see many new businesses offering affordable services to DIY artists to capture performance royalties, Internet royalties, mechanical royalties, YouTube royalties, sync licensing for film, TV, games, and commercials. Each of these incremental revenue streams may be small, but in the aggregate they will become a needle-moving part of the artist's revenue mix."

Music marketing will also be increasingly automated and will often start with the consumers themselves, said Ira S. Kalb, professor of marketing at the Marshall School of Business at the University of Southern California. "People will have bots (or avatars) that are digital representations of them," he added. "These bot agents will know their music preferences and travel around the Internet buying songs, concert tickets, and related merchandise for their human bosses. It might even get to the point where musicians and record companies will have bots that market their services directly to customer bots," he predicts. In other words, algorithms for both consumers and artists will be able to communicate with one another, and they will give each of us the music they think we want.

ATHLETES, LIKE MUSICIANS, WILL BE MORE INDEPENDENT

Just as growing numbers of musicians are operating independently of the big record labels, athletes will also become increasingly independent from teams and television networks. In many cases, they will become small-business entrepreneurs themselves. A study titled "The Future of Sports" by Delaware North, a company that operates in the sporting and entertainment industries, predicts that Google, Facebook, and other social networks will increasingly invest in the sports industry, buying the rights to broadcast events and showing them on YouTube or other websites. Audiences for sporting events will be migrating from TV and radio to streaming, the same way they did with music and television miniseries. This will allow athletes to earn more from their speeches, endorsements, and merchandising outside the sports tournaments in which they participate. At the same time, growing numbers of individual athletes and entire teams will be creating their own mass media.

"Major networks become increasingly boxed out as leagues, franchises, players, and even fans themselves become popular content providers. Following the lead of Manchester United, sports franchises become their own media outlets, creating their own broadcast, radio, and online channels. Athletes increasingly step up to form their own media outlets. . . . Why would an athlete reveal news in an interview, when they can break news on their own media property?" the Delaware North study says.

The practice of having coaches give a press conference after a game could soon be a thing of the past and replaced by players' statements given through their own media outlets or through shared media with other colleagues. *The Players' Tribune,* which was created in 2014 by former baseball star Derek Jeter and which received $40 million in investment during a second round of fund-raising in 2017, has become many athletes' favorite site, and several of its columnists feel it's the best place for publicizing personal news or expressing opinions without having to deal with intermediaries who might inject their own comments into the conversation. According to its website, *The Players' Tribune* defines itself as "a new media company that provides athletes with a platform to connect directly with their fans, in their own words."

WILL CRISTIANO RONALDO AND LIONEL MESSI HAVE THEIR OWN NETWORKS?

When soccer star Cristiano Ronaldo announced to the world in late 2017 the name of the daughter he was expecting with his partner, Georgina Rodriguez, he didn't do it in an interview with a journalist. Instead, he posted a live video on his Instagram account, revealing that his daughter would be named Alana Martina and that he had picked her first name and his girlfriend chose the second. After making the announcement, and visibly moved, Ronaldo took several questions from the Instagram audience. That's just an example of how sports stars are—sometimes without even realizing it—creating their own media.

Basketball champ Kobe Bryant had already done something similar in 2015 when he announced his retirement. He didn't do it in a TV interview or through a press release, but in a letter to *The Players' Tribune,* thereby skipping the traditional news media. Another NBA star, Kevin Durant, did the same when he announced that he had accepted an offer to play for the Golden State Warriors. Since it began, nearly five hundred athletes from twenty-four different sports have written articles or recorded videos for *The Players' Tribune.* And just as athletes want to reach their fans without intermediaries, many fans also prefer to hear directly from their favorite players. As Jasneel Chaddha, a sports analyst for the *Huffington Post,* pointed out, "The authenticity of this 'direct touch' allows fans to get closer to the people they follow religiously and perhaps even idolize."

The success of *The Players' Tribune* has led several sports stars to set up their own media outlets. The NBA's LeBron James created the website Uninterrupted, where athletes can post their own videos and talk about whatever they want. Former tennis champ Andre Agassi and his investors launched Unscriptd, which—as the spelling of its name suggests—has a more rebellious air to it, and which allows for more daring content. How long will it take before every star is using his or her own social network as the one exclusive channel for his or her own statements? Most of them already have more followers than any traditional media outlet.

Soccer stars Ronaldo, Lionel Messi, and Neymar have respectively more than 122 million, 89 million, and 60 million Facebook followers, to whom they can promote their own brands for free. Why should they continue giving exclusive interviews to traditional media that profit from them? It's entirely likely that many sports journalists currently working for newspapers or TV networks will become content providers for the media outlets of famous players in all sports.

LIVE SPORTING EVENTS WILL CONTINUE TO GROW

Live streaming will make sporting events more accessible, and 3-D screens and virtual reality headsets will allow us to experience them more closely. Thanks to virtual reality, we'll be able to change the way we see a soccer match from the perspective of the referee to that of a striker or defender. Still, though, the number of fans who attend live events at stadiums is likely to continue to grow. "The world of video and connectivity is not threatening the stadium experience," says Chris White, former vice president of Cisco Sports and Entertainment Solutions Group. "Look at the way that jumbo screens have been embraced outside of venues—think Wimbledon or the World Cup. We are still human beings and we still yearn for human interaction. There is nothing more uplifting than being in a positive crowd environment with a bunch of people having fun roaring for a team."

Industry analysts are already forecasting arenas that seat 250,000 people and are integrated into city centers. Thanks to new construction materials and the use of carbon fiber modules, these stadiums will be multiuse facilities. And with self-driving cars able to take people to the event and then park themselves outside the downtown areas, stadiums will take up less space and be located in much more central locations. Increasingly, they will become giant social gathering places. At TD Garden, home to the NHL's Boston Bruins, an app is already available to LinkedIn members that lets them know which of their professional contacts happen to be at the arena. "The entire sporting complex—not just the seats at the game—will become an attraction," the study predicts. "Many more fans will come into the complex, and while not everyone has a seat, all will have a front-row experience."

SPORTS BARS WITH 360-DEGREE SCREENS ON THE WALLS

Meanwhile, there will be venues outside sports stadiums where people will use new technologies to watch games. They will be futuristic versions of today's sports bars and will pioneer many new technologies, such as the 360-degree TV screen. According to the Delaware North study, history shows that some of the biggest innovations in the entertainment world—such as cinema, video games, IMAX, and 3-D—were not launched at people's homes or in stadiums, but at other public places. That trend may continue, it suggests.

The sports bars of the future—which the study calls the "third venue" after the stadium and the home—will be a popular option not only because people will have more time to watch sports events but also because the prices of tickets to the games will continue rising. Going to a live sports event may be beyond the reach of much of the population. A bar with a 360-degree TV screen will be a great substitute for those who want a more exciting experience than watching a game on their laptop or on a virtual reality device in the privacy of their home. And these sports bars of the future may become family attractions, much in the way that Las Vegas hotels transformed themselves from adult entertainment places into family vacation destinations.

FANS WON'T JUST BE SPECTATORS ANYMORE

The explosion of social media is turning fans, who were once merely spectators at sporting events, into active participants in the decisions made by their favorite teams. Whether it's signing players or creating salary cap space, there are more and more cases in which the fans are changing the minds of once all-powerful team owners and managers. Fans sent a powerful message to the owners of Italy's Lazio soccer team when after sharing their frustration on social media, they boycotted a match against Atalanta following Lazio president Claudio Lotito's decision to sell Brazilian player Anderson Hernanes. Lazio was able to sell only about 2,000 tickets at the 82,000-seat stadium for the match. Since then, soccer club owners in Italy have become more conscious about the growing power of their fan base.

"The emerging generation of fans—armed with powerful media devices and always-on connectivity, and social media platforms with massive reach—have started to take control of the conversation, effectively becoming a major media entity in their own right," the Delaware North study finds. "Teams, leagues, and sponsors who fail to respond to activist fan movements risk major damage to ticket sales and brand equity." And in the coming years, fans may have an even greater influence on club decisions, since algorithms will be able to predict fan reactions and club authorities take such forecasts very seriously, the study predicts.

THERE WILL BE A NEW MARKET FOR EMERGING SPORTS

In addition to the new venues and technologies to watch sports events, the scope of professional sports will be greatly expanded. Until now the global sports industry was limited to a relatively small number of sports. People paid to watch American football, baseball, basketball, hockey, soccer, cricket, tennis, or golf. But all that is changing rapidly with the arrival of emerging sports such as various forms of skating, extreme sports like triathlons, parachuting, and bungee jumping, and the so-called e-sports, or video game competitions.

Many emerging sports that were already gaining an audience thanks to cable television, like surfing and skateboarding, will be further enhanced by the broadcasting of new competitions on YouTube and other Internet platforms. Dozens of new sports will emerge over the next two decades, including several that will use exoskeletons, prosthetics, and rocket packs, the Delaware North study says. Professional football or basketball games, which draw the biggest TV audiences, will now have to compete with online tournaments in which we and our friends will be the stars of the show, competing with others in walking, running, or biking contests.

Thanks to sports-oriented social media platforms such as Strava.com, anyone who engages in outdoor activities can already link his smartphone to the Internet and compare his results with those of other people of a similar age and physical condition anywhere in the world. If amateur joggers or cyclists, for instance, go to a track in their hometown, they can compare their times with the times of others who have used the same track in the past. These platforms are becoming giant databases that allow us to be part of all sorts of competitions, making them more participatory and attractive for many people. If the Internet is already letting us know who is the fastest cyclist on our favorite local route, how long will it be before corporations start sponsoring the top performers, drawing more viewers into our microcircuit competition? As sportswear companies increasingly focus their advertising on their most likely customers—instead of anonymous masses watching football games on TV—they will start to mine the data collected by these websites to target, for instance, weekend bikers. After that, how long will it take for companies to start sponsoring your top neighborhood cyclist? In fact, it's already happening, and it will become increasingly common.

THE RISE OF EXTREME SPORTS

Skateboarding, surfing, and ice and rock climbing will debut as new official sports at the 2020 Tokyo Olympics. The British Parachute Association reported that the number of jumps in the United Kingdom rose from 39,000 in 2006 to nearly 60,000 in 2016, and the British Mountaineering Council reported that its membership has grown from 25,000 in 2000 to roughly 55,000 today. And BASE jumping—parachuting or wingsuit flying from cliffs or mountains—is gaining in popularity as well, despite several deaths that made international headlines in recent years.

Sponsors are starting to flock to extreme sports. In 2016, Red Bull, the energy drink company, partnered with the sports camera company GoPro to jointly produce and promote some of these sports events. Now mountaineers, wingsuit fliers, and fans of any extreme sport can upload point-of-view footage of themselves to the Internet platforms of GoPro Channel and Red Bull TV. As Red Bull founder and CEO Dietrich Mateschitz said, the partnership between his company and GoPro "will expand not only our collective international reach but also our ability to fascinate people."

THE E-SPORTS PHENOMENON

Digital gaming competitions, also known as e-sports, which were previously confined to the bedrooms of teenagers, are now starting to fill stadiums. Tickets to the 2015 Dota 2 international gaming tournament, which was held in the 17,000-seat KeyArena in Seattle, sold out in just twenty-four minutes, and prize money totaled more than $18 million. According to a report by *The Seattle Times,* the competition—which was broadcast on ESPN—was watched by over twenty million fans. A year earlier, the League of Legends 4 video game championship, held in South Korea, filled the 40,000-seat Seoul World Cup Stadium. Video game players are becoming world-famous stars, though many of us wouldn't recognize their names. As advertisers discover and begin sponsoring them, these stars will find themselves on the same stage as professional football, baseball, or basketball stars.

Many young people across the globe have grown up idolizing e-sports champions like Lee "Faker" Sang-Hyeok from South Korea or Enrique "xPeke" Cedeño Martínez of Spain, and millions of other kids are now following the next generation of video game stars. For many youths, "the biggest sports upset story in recent memory is not Leicester City FC taking the Premier League title—it's CDEC Gaming taking $2.8 million at the International 2015 Dota 2 Championship," the Delaware North study says. It's no coincidence that Amazon spent $970 million to buy Twitch, the online channel that broadcasts video game competitions. James McQuivey, author of the book *Digital Disruption,* writes that "it's no longer just wanting to see how someone defeated the boss on Level 5. It's having that social experience and the comradeship of fellow gamers."

GYMS WILL BECOME COLLECTIVE EXERCISE CENTERS

The gyms of the future won't be places where people go to exercise individually. Instead of being filled with people training on their own, watching TV while they jog on a treadmill, gyms will become places where we'll be doing team exercises or even competing with one another. Forty-two percent of the U.S. health club market's facilities have already been modified to attract people who practice group exercises like yoga, Pilates, jiujitsu, dance, Zumba, indoor climbing, and CrossFit.

Gyms specializing in particular group activities such as CrossFit and yoga have been growing at a rate of 450 percent a year since 2010. The number of activity-specific health clubs could soon surpass that of traditional multipurpose gyms, industry analysts say. Yoga classes—including the sale of clothing, mats, and other products and supplies—are generating $27 billion in annual sales just in the United States.

And with new technology like smartwatches that monitor our movements, group classes and competitive exercises at gyms will become increasingly popular. "Alt-athletes have little interest in sitting in the stands and rooting for a traditional professional sports team. They don't want to watch—they want to play," the study, "The Future of Sports," says. "They are the fastest-growing market—76% of all regular exercisers are millennials—with a thirst for new products and technological advances that help them reach that next goal." To put it another way, Zumba teachers and martial arts instructors won't be going hungry anytime soon.

THE SPORTS-RELATED JOBS OF THE FUTURE

The sports of the future—along with the new sports bars and gyms—will give rise to several new jobs that don't exist today. There will be a need for robot engineers and technicians to look after athletes' artificial limbs, as well as doctors and nurses specializing in bionic medicine. The boundary between the human and the artificial parts of the athlete will be increasingly blurred as bionic prostheses—like the robotic legs being developed by Hugh Herr at MIT that we discussed in chapter 1—become more popular.

And sports medicine will no longer be a profession limited to working for professional teams with injured athletes. It will have a much broader appeal as more athletes will be using physical enhancers and new products derived from biomedical breakthroughs to improve their physical or psychological conditions. In the beginning, over the next five to ten years, these products will be used mostly by professional athletes. But later on, maybe in ten or twenty years, there will be a distinction between natural athletes and those who have been enhanced. In a prediction that might seem a bit farfetched—but perhaps is not—the Delaware North study suggests that natural athletes and those who have been "perfected" will play in separate leagues, the way amateurs and professionals do today. "But there will be a Super Bowl," the study says, because "who wouldn't pay to see if natural-born humans can beat ones we 'perfected' in the lab?"

THE RISE OF TOURISM

The widely expected increase in people's free time will also boost the tourism industry. According to the World Travel & Tourism Council (WTTC), the industry will generate 30 million new jobs over the next ten years, bringing the total number of jobs directly involved in tourism to 100 million worldwide by 2027. That will translate into 6.5 million new jobs in India, 4.5 million in China, 1.6 million in the United States, 934,000 in Mexico, 741,000 in Brazil, 390,000 in Germany, 248,000 in France, 218,000 in Great Britain, 153,000 in Spain, 102,000 in South Korea, and 94,000 in Japan.

WTTC president Gloria Guevara told me that the boom in tourism will take place not only because people will have more free time and a growing population of retirees will be looking to travel, but also because millennials—people born between 1980 and the start of the new millennium—are more excited about exploring the world than previous generations. "When you ask millennials about their personal wishes in life, 'traveling' is always one of the top three things they mention. In the past, when you asked people what their top priorities were, they would say paying off their house or buying a car. That's why the tourism industry is now growing at 4 percent a year," she said.

But won't people prefer to stay in the comfort of their homes and see the world through their virtual reality headsets? I asked her. "On the contrary, virtual reality is going to motivate and inspire people to travel more," Guevara replied. "Augmented and virtual reality will allow you to improve on your travel experience. You will be able to visit the Colosseum in Rome, for example, put on your VR viewer, and watch gladiators fight in that same place just as they did in ancient times." Guevara also told me that when she took her young son to the Colosseum, he was disappointed. "Mom, this is just a bunch of rocks," he said. Once children can combine the experience of being in a physical place with access to historical images through augmented reality—like visiting Mayan ruins and seeing how the people once lived—the whole travel experience will be much richer, she explained.

TRAVEL WILL BE MUCH EASIER

What about the threat of terrorism? Won't that, and the long lines at airport security checkpoints, quash people's desire to travel? I asked the WTTC president. Guevara conceded that "traveling has become increasingly complicated and invasive," but added that the industry is working with various governments to solve the problem. Over the next ten years, biometric face-recognition systems will be put in place in most airports so that people can enter and exit without the need to show a boarding pass or even a passport, making the whole travel experience much less tedious, she said.

Cameras with facial recognition technology will take your picture and compare it with your fingerprints, a technology that is already being tested among others in New York, Atlanta, Boston, and Chinese airports. Databases with the faces of billions of people will be able to identify passengers as they enter and leave airports. "Your face and your fingerprints will be your ID," Guevara said. "Nobody can forge that. Biometric data will revolutionize the tourism industry and make traveling a much more pleasant experience."

And you won't have to carry around heavy suitcases, because much of what you'll be wearing in the future—including clothes from the most famous designers—will be printed anywhere. "In the future, instead of carrying your shoes around in your luggage, you will be able to print them on a 3-D printer at your hotel room. You will download your shoes from your computer and print them out right there," Guevara assured me. "It's already happening," she added, pointing out that many of the shoes worn during 2017 Milan Fashion Week were produced by 3-D printers.

Asked whether business travel won't be hurt by new high-quality videoconferencing technologies—why travel if you can talk with a life-size hologram?—she told me that "on the contrary, business tourism is growing and will continue to grow." During the last six years, global spending on business tourism—which makes up nearly a quarter of world tourism—grew by 33 percent. And it's expected to continue growing by an average of 3.7 percent per year between 2017 and 2026, according to WTTC projections. While videoconferencing is on the rise and Skype is basically free, it will be a long time before technology can replace personal contact, Guevara said. People will continue to travel so they can look each other in the eye and close a deal in person, and will continue attending business conferences and conventions, because "there's an element of trust that can only be measured with personal contact," she added. "Once the deal is closed, you can use videoconferencing to follow up, but the initial deal will most likely continue to be made in person."

FUTURE CRUISES WILL BE BIGGER THAN EVER BEFORE

The demand for travel on cruise ships is growing so fast that "if this was Christmas and you were Santa Claus, I'd ask for nothing," said Frank J. Del Rio, president and CEO of Norwegian Cruise Lines Holdings, at a 2018 industry convention. According to the Cruise Lines International Association (CLIA), the industry is setting new passenger records every year, and was projected to serve 27 million people in 2018.

There are currently more than a hundred cruise ships under construction or on order to be built by 2028, and they are getting bigger than ever. Many are capable of handling over 6,000 passengers and are adding ever more amenities. When Del Rio was asked at the conference if ships will have new and unexpected features, like a racetrack, he said, "No idea is absurd anymore. These ships are big. Anything can fit on them, and they are only going to get bigger." And there are companies that are getting into the cruise business for the first time, like Ritz-Carlton, whose 300-passenger luxury ships will target the wealthiest tourists.

According to the United Nations World Tourism Organization, by 2030, international tourism—measured in international flights—will grow by 50 percent over its current levels, reaching 1.8 billion trips per year. And as with the film, music, and sports industries, the expansion of tourism will give rise to all kinds of new jobs. There will be a demand for developers of augmented reality content to complement the physical experience of tourism with scenes from either ancient times or the distant future, as well as for historians, political scientists, or experts in local cuisine who will be with us virtually or in person, ready to answer any tourist's question while walking the streets of Paris, visiting the ruins of Machu Picchu, or exploring the pyramids of Egypt.

Granted, there will always be some unemployed actors, musicians, sports commentators, and tour guides, but these will not be among the high-risk professions in the future. There will be fewer parents who will be concerned about their children's future when the kids inform them that they want to pursue a career in the entertainment business.

10

THE JOBS OF THE FUTURE

When I was finishing this book, something happened to me that—while it may not seem extraordinary—momentarily left me in a state of shock. It was the overnight disappearance of the lady who worked as the cashier at the parking garage of the 200 South Biscayne Boulevard building in downtown Miami. She was a Cuban lady named Irma—I remember her name because it was embroidered on her uniform—and she was replaced by a machine from one day to the next. My brief chats with Irma had become part of my weekly routine, when I would go out for lunch with my son every Thursday and leave my car in his office building's garage. Irma had recognized me from television, and after meeting me in person, she had become a loyal viewer of my TV show, or so she said. Every Thursday, she had a comment about something she had seen in one of my shows or a question about the news of the day.

At first, when I was spiraling down the parking ramp toward Irma's ticket booth, I would be awaiting her comments with a mixture of resignation and curiosity. But as time went on, I realized that even her most sarcastic comments about the guests on my show or a particular tie I had worn on TV were all in good fun. And soon enough, I began to enjoy our regular little conversations. It even got to the point where I started asking her about what topics interested her, turning her into an informal one-woman focus group for my show or my newspaper columns. Until one day, after I circled my way down the parking ramp, ready for my weekly meeting with Irma, I found that she had vanished, along with the glass booth where she worked. In their place was a tower-shaped machine into which I had to insert my ticket and credit card.

The sudden automation of Irma's job shouldn't have caught me by surprise because I had been seeing it happen all over for several years. Cashiers, phone operators, receptionists, and even cameramen had been disappearing around me for a long time. But almost all of them had made their exit more gradually, with prior warning signs. Usually they were reassigned to perform a different task, and then another, before they finally disappeared without a trace. But Irma had been replaced by a machine overnight. The suddenness of it shocked me, and it led me to see more clearly than ever what is happening to millions of other people around the world.

THE NEW CONSENSUS ABOUT THE FUTURE OF JOBS

During the five years I spent researching this book, there has been a major shift in the consensus among tech leaders and futurologists about the future of jobs. In 2013, when I started interviewing leading experts on this subject, there was a general sense of optimism that technology would create more jobs than it destroyed, as had always been the case. At around that time, Peter Diamandis, cofounder of Singularity University and one of the most passionate Silicon Valley techno-optimists, had published his book *Abundance*. The subtitle said it all: *The*

Future Is Better Than You Think. In that book, Diamandis and his coauthor, Steven Kotler, predicted that—as has been the case since the Industrial Revolution—robots would not have a negative effect on employment. On the contrary, they will take some of the thankless tasks that humans are currently doing—like repetitive and physically demanding factory work—and allow us to devote ourselves to new and much more rewarding occupations. For every parking lot attendant like Irma who is replaced by a machine, new and more pleasant job opportunities will crop up, they argued.

Nowadays, Diamandis still has a largely positive view of the future, but he isn't as convinced as he once was that technology will create more jobs than it will destroy. In fact, he is concerned that the speed of automation could result in a social earthquake. When I saw him at a conference at Singularity University, four years after I had first interviewed him, Diamandis had significantly changed his tune. To my surprise, after reiterating his optimistic view of the future—he recalled that the average human life-span has nearly doubled in the last hundred years, and that the cost of food is now thirteen times cheaper than it was thanks to technological advancements—Diamandis pointed out that "technological unemployment is coming fast, and it has the potential to lead to significant social unrest."

Furthermore, he added, "while the magnitude of the coming change doesn't bother me, it is the speed of the change I'm worried about. A lot of people are going to be very upset, a universal basic income will probably have to be created, but that won't be very helpful if people's mentality is still centered on their jobs. The truth is that I don't have an answer. All I can say is that I'm very concerned about the issue." Diamandis was openly accepting what Bill Gates, Mark Zuckerberg, and Stephen Hawking, among others, had recently acknowledged: that technology is advancing at such a dizzying pace that—

unlike what has happened in the past—it will kill millions of jobs before they can be replaced with new ones.

MARK ZUCKERBERG: "WE LIVE IN AN UNSTABLE TIME"

In his commencement speech to the Harvard graduating class of 2017, Zuckerberg highlighted the growing concern shared by other Silicon Valley tech moguls about the social impact of automation. "We live in an unstable time," the Facebook founder told the young graduates. "When our parents graduated . . . purpose reliably came from your job, your church, your community. But today, technology and automation are eliminating many jobs. . . . Many people feel disconnected and depressed, and are trying to fill a void."

During his travels, Zuckerberg said, "I've met factory workers who know their old jobs aren't coming back and are trying to find their place." To counter rising unemployment, he suggested that we "explore ideas like a universal basic income to give everyone a cushion to try new things." And his advice to the young graduates was to find a purpose in their lives, to take on "big meaningful projects," and to be both idealistic and persistent.

Just as other generations went down in history for putting a man on the moon, immunizing children against polio, building the Hoover Dam, and countless other public accomplishments that required millions of workers, the upcoming generations should take on challenges like finding a way to end global warming through the use of solar energy and overcoming preventable diseases, he said. "I know, you're probably thinking: I don't know how to build a dam, or get a million people involved in anything," he continued. "But let me tell you a secret: no one does when they begin. Ideas don't come out fully formed. They only become clear as you work on them. You just have to get started."

DEVELOPING COUNTRIES WILL BE THE MOST AFFECTED BY AUTOMATION

Contrary to what many might believe, the countries that will be most threatened by the automation of jobs won't be the United States, Germany, Japan, and other highly industrialized countries. Rather, it will be developing countries in Asia, Southeast Asia, Latin America, and Africa. The reason for this is that developing countries tend to have the highest percentage of workers in manufacturing jobs, doing manual labor that will be increasingly automated. As wages continue to rise in China, Mexico, and other manufacturing nations, and the price of industrial robots continues to fall, it will be increasingly profitable for U.S. and European multinationals to replace these workers with robots in their own territories, closer to their home markets.

In 2017, as noted earlier, Adidas announced that it would be closing up a factory in China and shifting production of its footwear there to automated factories in the United States and Germany. This announcement came nearly thirty years after Adidas and many other manufacturing firms started moving their factories to Asia to take advantage of cheap labor. In its new roboticized factory in Bavaria, Germany, Adidas can churn out shoes in five hours, whereas in Chinese factories with human workers it took several weeks. It should be no surprise, then, that the company decided to pack up its plant in China.

Even Bangladesh, which became a magnet for the global textile industry thanks to its supply of cheap labor, is automating its factories. According to *The Wall Street Journal,* the Mohammadi Group, located in that nation's capital, has already laid off around 500 workers and replaced them with robots. At the Mohammadi Fashion Sweaters factory, which produces pullovers for Zara, H&M, and other department stores around the world, there are now just a few dozen workers who oversee a fleet of 173 robots imported from Germany. They are much more efficient than human workers, and "it doesn't make sense for us to slow ourselves down," said Rubana Huq, managing director of the Mohammadi Group.

This new generation of textile robots can do very intricate tasks, like sewing belt loops to trousers, that only human workers were able to do until recently. "Even inexpensive workers in the world's developing countries are vulnerable to automation, now that machines and robots are reaching into trades that previously seemed immune," the newspaper said.

77 PERCENT OF JOBS IN CHINA, 69 PERCENT IN INDIA, AND 64 PERCENT IN ARGENTINA ARE AT RISK

The World Bank says that a country's competitive advantage to become an international manufacturing center will no longer be its availability of cheap labor, but its capacity to have the latest generation of robots, 3-D printers, and other technologies that are transforming industrial production. "The use of new technologies to produce traditional manufactured goods will be disruptive in developing economies," says Mary Hallward-Driemeier, senior economic adviser in the Finance, Competitiveness, and Innovation Global Practice at the World Bank Group and lead author of the report. "If labor represents a smaller share of costs, more production may happen in richer countries, closer to consumers. Fewer businesses may move to lower-cost locations and local firms will face steeper competition."

According to the World Bank, the percentage of jobs threatened by automation will be 77 percent in China, 69 percent in India and Ecuador, 67 percent in Bolivia, 65 percent in Panama, and 64 percent each in Argentina, Paraguay, and Uruguay. The average among industrialized nations is 57 percent, and in the United States the figure is 47 percent. These percentages can be misleading, however, because some of the countries that are most threatened by automation, like China and South Korea, are buying up industrial robots as fast as they can in order to stay competitive.

As early as 2014—the year before President Xi Jinping announced his ten-year "robotic revolution" plan—China increased its annual purchase of industrial robots by 56 percent. And in 2015, as we saw in chapter 8, South Korea already had an average of 531 robots per 10,000 manufacturing workers, more than any other country. Singapore has an average of 398 robots per 10,000 manufacturing workers, Japan 305, Germany 301, the United States 176, Spain 150, China 49, Mexico 33, Argentina 16, and Brazil 11. China, because of its huge population, is still in the bottom half of this list, but with its massive purchases of industrial robots—and its policy of encouraging "factories without workers"—it is taking drastic steps to become an automated industrial power.

The vast majority of Latin American countries, on the other hand, have fallen asleep at the wheel. Their leaders don't seem to be aware of the coming automation revolution and the impact it may have on their workforces. As part of my own job with the *Miami Herald* and with CNN en Español, I usually interview several dozen Latin American presidents and cabinet ministers a year, and I can count on one hand the number of those who are thinking about public policies to prepare for the growing threat of technological unemployment. In most countries in the region, robots are still seen as objects of curiosity or trivial news bits for techies. But these countries could suffer a rude awakening in the very near future when they realize their workers are no longer competitive with the increasingly cheaper and more efficient robots of the industrialized world. Unless they start thinking about solutions now, they will soon find it harder to diversify their economies away from raw materials and export more manufactured goods.

THE IDEA OF A UNIVERSAL BASIC INCOME

The theory that robots will be more productive, make the economy grow, and pay a salary to humans is gaining many followers, and not just among tech leaders like Zuckerberg. In 2018, the city of Stockton, California, planned to begin implementing an experimental, unconditional universal income of $6,000 to each of its residents. Ontario, Canada, launched a similar experiment in 2017, wherein some 4,000 residents would start receiving nearly $17,000 per year in the case of single people, and up to $24,000 in the case of couples. Other trials are being developed in Finland, Great Britain, and Kenya. Even techno-optimists like Diamandis are enthusiastically embracing this idea as a solution to technological unemployment.

It's far from a new concept. Back in the sixteenth century, European humanist Juan Luis Vives wrote a philosophical text titled *On Assistance to the Poor* in which he proposed regular payments for everyone. Other thinkers like John Locke, Maximilien de Robespierre, Immanuel Kant, and John Stuart Mill were also interested in the idea. One of the main arguments in favor of a universal basic income is that it would save governments a lot of money—especially in hospital costs and health care services such as alcoholism and drug addiction programs—if jobless people had enough money to study a trade and remake their lives.

An experiment conducted in the 1970s in Dauphin, Canada, found that thanks to a universal basic income, hospital admissions for accidents and mental health problems were significantly reduced, and that high school graduation rates had increased. An experiment that took place in 2009 in London yielded similar results. Thirteen homeless people in the British capital were given the equivalent of $4,500 in cash with no conditions attached. A year later, eleven of them had a roof over their heads. Instead of using the money to buy alcohol or drugs, as some may have speculated, most of the subjects used the money to pull themselves up out of poverty, whether by taking courses or entering rehab programs.

"Poverty is fundamentally about a lack of cash. It's not about stupidity," says economist Joseph Hanlon. "You can't pull yourself up by your bootstraps if you have no boots." In other words, if people have to put all the money they have toward getting their next meal, they can hardly be expected to look more than a few hours into the future and will never be able to break the cycle of poverty.

CAN POOR COUNTRIES AFFORD A BASIC UNIVERSAL INCOME?

GiveDirectly, the nongovernmental organization that has made regular payments of more than $100 million to 26,000 people in Kenya over the past decade, argues that social subsidies currently given out by governments are much more expensive and inefficient than money given directly to the people. Plus, such subsidies need huge bureaucracies, which eat up a significant slice of social services budgets. "So why not give a basic cash income directly to the people?" ask the directors of GiveDirectly.

Many development economists say that, contrary to public belief, poor countries can afford to pay universal basic incomes. The reason is that these nations currently waste much more money in subsidies for water, electricity, and transportation—subsidies that benefit mainly the rich—than they would be spending for a universal basic income. If the rich and poor each receive a $1 subsidy per cubic meter of water they use, as is the case in many developing countries, a millionaire with the Olympic-size swimming pool in his backyard benefits the most. In other words, the government is subsidizing the rich man's pool. Ideally, those resources would be redirected to the poorest, many economists argue.

WILL GIVING MONEY AWAY LEAD TO LAZINESS?

Critics, on the other hand, argue that people who receive a basic universal income will simply spend it on drugs or alcohol, or stop working, which would damage their self-esteem and overall health. Andrew McAfee and Erik Brynjolfsson, the MIT professors who coauthored the book *The Second Machine Age,* argue that a universal basic income would not only be difficult to implement in the United States for lack of funding but would also be counterproductive. The researchers, fearing that many people would take their basic income and stay at home, cite several studies showing that unemployment causes greater social problems than poverty, because people need a purpose in life. In many cases, the studies indicated that neighborhoods with high unemployment rates had more divorces, alcoholism, drug addiction, and suicide than other neighborhoods where people worked, even at menial jobs at minimum wage. "Of course, these social woes stem from many sources. But unemployment and underemployment no doubt contribute, and troubled communities would certainly benefit from more opportunities and incentives for work," the professors say. The two MIT academics suggest that, instead of a basic universal income, governments offer tax breaks to those who work in order to reduce unemployment.

So who's right? The answer might lie in improving a system of conditional cash transfers that started in Latin America about twenty years ago. Under social programs such as those adopted in Brazil, Mexico, and other Latin American nations, heads of households in poor neighborhoods were given a basic cash income under the condition that their children be vaccinated or attend school. Often these programs degenerated into thinly veiled political subsidies where the conditions existed only on paper. But according to Ferdinando Regalia, an economist with the Inter-American Development Bank, the concept has great potential.

Regalia told me that contrary to what the skeptics speculate, a significant number of beneficiaries of conditional cash transfer programs in Latin America didn't quit their jobs in the informal economy, nor did they spend their money on drugs or alcohol. Instead, they continue to work, selling tacos on the street or washing cars. If they aren't able to find more formal jobs, it is primarily because they don't have the necessary education. The solution, he said, is to enforce the conditionality of cash transfers and combine them with better education systems.

A GOOD IDEA: PAID COMMUNITY SERVICE

Why not give people a universal basic income in exchange for community service? I asked Regalia. He responded, "It seems fine at face value. My fear is that if it's administered by the state, it could have high administrative costs and create a lot of bureaucracy." However, it's an idea that's worthy of serious consideration. In many cases, it wouldn't be necessary to create legions of inspectors to police those who provide social services. The local park caretaker would be responsible for making sure that someone was raking leaves for five hours a week, and a student's parents or a teacher could sign off that someone had given private math lessons. It wouldn't be easy, but given the magnitude of the social challenges that come with automation, new and innovative solutions will have to be tried, however complicated they might seem at first.

ALTRUISM, LIKE COCAINE, IS PLEASURABLE

Some may argue that it's somewhat naive to believe that countries could require everybody to perform community services. But there are a number of scientific studies that show that doing good activates our brains' pleasure centers and that people actually enjoy—given the right circumstances—performing good deeds. One of these studies was featured in a *Nature* magazine article titled "It's Good to Give." It involved a neuroimaging test in which several subjects were asked to make decisions about whether or not to give money to various causes or charities while undergoing an MRI of their brains. The study showed that "charitable donations activate the same neural systems as those that respond to monetary reward." Translation: people liked donating money.

Facundo Manes, a clinical neurologist, neuroscientist, and author, told me that "being generous, being altruistic, activates the same brain reward systems that are stimulated by cocaine, or a cheeseburger, or money." There is extensive scientific literature showing that virtues such as solidarity and cooperation are present among social animals like ants and bees. And there are many anecdotal examples of altruism among apes, such as that of the gorilla who rescued a three-year-old boy who had fallen over the barrier protecting the gorilla pit at Chicago's Brookfield Zoo in 1996. The boy, who was unconscious after falling nearly twenty feet, was cradled by the female gorilla and carried to an access door where zookeepers and paramedics were waiting.

Other neuroscientific studies have found that human beings do good for reputational reasons. By helping others, we become admired, which in turn gives us pleasure. According to several experiments, we are more altruistic when a third party is witnessing our good deeds than when we are alone. Gilbert Roberts, a scientist at Newcastle University, showed that people who cooperate in a group setting are seen by other members of that group as being more attractive. So whether there are biological, psychological, or cultural reasons for altruistic behavior, why not take advantage of this phenomenon to promote community service as a way to help solve technological unemployment?

BILL GATES: ROBOTS SHOULD PAY TAXES

In order to finance a universal basic income or other ways to make up for jobs losses due to automation, Bill Gates has proposed taxing the robots. Gates sees robotics as a generally positive phenomenon, but he points out that if robots are doing jobs that people used to do, they should have to pay taxes on earnings, just as humans do.

"The human worker who does, say, $50,000 worth of work in a factory, that income is taxed and you get income tax, Social Security tax, all those things," the founder of Microsoft told the digital tech magazine *Quartz*. "If a robot comes in to do the same thing, you'd think that we'd tax the robot at a similar level." According to Gates, a workforce with a large number of robots would free up many human workers to perform social tasks that require warmth and empathy, which humans can still do better than machines. With more robots allowing more people to perform social work, we can "do a better job of reaching out to the elderly, having smaller class sizes, helping kids with special needs," he explained. If the jobs eliminated by automation can be channeled to this sort of task, "then you're net ahead," Gates said.

"THE NEW DIGITAL PROLETARIAT"

What will millions of workers do when robots take their places in factories and offices? Many will work remotely from their homes for online companies, becoming part of a new "digital proletariat." Several years ago, when the use of the Internet exploded, there were hopes that the new digital economy would save the world, giving people much more dignified and environmentally sound jobs sitting in front of computers. But many of the new jobs produced by the digital economy ended up being temporary positions that pay very little and offer no benefits. They can provide a nice extra income to people who already have a primary job, but not much more than that.

According to the World Bank, there is already a labor market of more than 5 million people using websites such as Upwork.com and Freelancer.com to get temporary jobs. But the real figure is likely much higher: in 2014, Upwork.com, based in Silicon Valley, boasted of having more than 8 million registered online workers on its platform, along with 2.5 million employers. Upwork.com connects people offering to do online work with employers. Among those offering their services are web designers, software programmers, graphic designers, blog administrators, text editors, translators, transcribers, virtual secretaries, vendors, accountants, and people who read and answer emails for others.

When I checked the Upwork.com website recently, I found a woman named Aymee from Oklahoma who was charging $30 per hour for her services as a graphic designer. A young man named Amat from Pakistan was offering the same services for $18. Their profiles on the website—along with those of thousands of others—included information about their previous projects, their fees, and the evaluations they had received for their past jobs. That way, an employer looking for a freelance graphic designer can go to Upwork.com, interview several candidates online, and hire them directly through the website. Upwork receives the payment for the project and holds it in escrow until the work has been done to the client's satisfaction.

One of the digital jobs that is growing fastest is that of social network administrators. In the United States, those jobs have multiplied since the fake news scandals that shook the 2016 U.S. elections. According to *The Economist,* Google already has over 10,000 people monitoring and rating videos, including those of its subsidiary, YouTube. Facebook has recently announced that it would be increasing its army of content auditors from 4,500 to 7,500. Until recently, only China, Cuba, and a few other dictatorships used thousands of censors to scan the Internet and remove political criticism. But now, with the scandals surrounding the Russian fake news farms that tried to influence the U.S. election, Western democracies need growing numbers of content moderators and digital police. In Germany, a new law imposes fines on social networks that don't delete Holocaust denial posts within twenty-four hours. And new technologies that allow digital pirates to produce fake videos—like the one that purportedly showed former president Obama saying things that he had never said—will create an ever-growing need for human filters to prevent the spread of fake messages, recordings, and videos.

But many of these digital jobs are far from the panacea they were once believed to be. In addition to not paying all that well, they are often more stressful than the old jobs in factories and offices. Sarah Roberts, a professor of information studies at UCLA, has conducted studies showing that many social media content moderators suffer from physical and mental exhaustion from spending too much time reviewing toxic posts. The new digital proletariat is not having an easy time.

YOUNG PEOPLE ARE GOING TO HAVE TO INVENT THEIR OWN JOBS

"My generation had it easy," *New York Times* columnist Thomas Friedman wrote in 2013. "We got to 'find' a job. But, more than ever, our kids will have to 'invent' a job. . . . Sure, the lucky ones will find their first job, but, given the pace of change today, even they will have to reinvent, re-engineer and re-imagine that job much more often than their parents if they want to advance in it."

The trend that Friedman was talking about has become a reality. Estimates cited by the World Economic Forum indicate that between 75 and 80 percent of the labor market in industrialized countries will be made up of independent or temporary workers by 2030. In this new market of independent workers and subcontractors, the knowledge that you acquired in school won't matter as much as it did in the past, because most of the things you learned in school will be obsolete by the time you graduate, and anyone can now look up anything with a Google search. Instead, what will determine your success will be your self-motivation and your soft skills, such as creativity and the ability to solve problems. The "Uberization" of the economy—the fact that an increasing number of people will become independent contractors—will force many of us to think and work as small-business entrepreneurs. Our work will be our company.

As more companies look for workers with soft skills that allow them to constantly adapt to new technologies, the motivational gap is likely to grow. Many workers who don't have the will or the discipline to expand their skills will lose their jobs, whereas those who have a passion or are constantly updating their skills through lifelong learning will fare much better in the job market. Self-motivation, along with education, will be the name of the game.

A WORLD OF INDEPENDENT WORKERS AND "FLASH ORGANIZATIONS"

Most of the jobs of the future won't have a single fixed employer or a nine-to-five daily routine, like in the past. They'll be independent jobs. Until recently, those of us who wanted to just work a few hours a day or a few months of the year—mothers of young children, for example, or retirees—had to be lucky enough to find an employer who was willing to allow us to do that. But today, thanks to websites like Upwork or Uber, any of us can find employers who are willing to hire people for flexible hours. And thanks to sales platforms like eBay or Etsy, any of us can become a self-employed salesperson and work whatever hours, days, or weeks we want.

These websites allow us to connect with people we never had access to before. As we discussed in a previous chapter, algorithms allow for a rock band from South Korea to find a huge fan base in Chile and perform sellout concerts there. In much the same way, sellers on eBay or Etsy can find out where the greatest demand for their products is and even what reviews other sellers have given to potential customers. The scope of our market is not our neighborhood, but the entire world.

The new digital economy is also giving rise to so-called part-time companies, modeled after Hollywood movie productions, which are created for a specific project and then dissolved. In Hollywood, producers, directors, writers, actors, costume designers, publicists, and other professionals come together to make a film that is sometimes worth hundreds of millions of dollars, and then they go their separate ways once the movie is completed. These sorts of companies used to be rare outside the film industry because the costs of setting up a working structure—including hiring and training new employees—were prohibitive. But with websites like Upwork .com and Freelance.com, which allow entrepreneurs to hire independent contractors from anywhere in the world, it is becoming much easier—and cheaper—to create what some are already calling flash organizations.

Business Talent Group, for example, brings together teams of independent experts to tackle specific projects in the pharmaceutical industry. Much like in the movie industry, when a pharmaceutical company launches a new drug, Business Talent Group brings together part-time public relations specialists, marketing experts, independent journalists, publicists, pollsters, and lawyers to launch the new product. "We're the producers," Jody Miller, one of the cofounders of the Business Talent Group, says. "We understand how to evaluate talent, pick the team."

Two Stanford University professors, Melissa Valentine and Michael Bernstein, have created the website Foundry.com, where the process of creating a flash organization can be done entirely online without the need for a single phone call. According to *The New York Times,* "There is some evidence that the corporate world, which has spent decades outsourcing work to contractors and consulting firms, is embracing temporary organizations" as a way to eliminate headhunters and middlemen and cut costs.

TODAY'S CHILDREN WILL BE WORKING IN JOBS THAT DON'T EXIST

"Sixty-five percent of children entering grade school this year will end up working in careers that haven't even been invented yet," wrote Cathy Davidson, professor of cultural history and technology, in her 2011 book *Now You See It.* Indeed, a child who was in elementary school in the early 1990s could not have anticipated ending up working as an iPhone app programmer, or a social media administrator for Facebook or Twitter, since neither the iPhone nor Facebook nor Twitter existed at the time. The iPhone was released in 2007, Facebook was born in 2004, and Twitter debuted in 2006. Today tens of millions of people designing websites or buying or selling things online are working at jobs that didn't exist when they were young. And with exponential technological acceleration, this will happen increasingly often in the future.

The big question, then, is what to teach our children so that they can acquire useful skills for the job market. It has become commonplace to say that it won't matter what you know—it's all available in your Google search engine or in your virtual assistant's memory—but what you do with that knowledge. But what does that mean in practical terms? Among other things, it means that schools will have to help children find their passion and teach them soft skills such as creativity, empathy, teamwork, and communication abilities, so they can turn knowledge into productive work.

Finland, a nation that always ranks at the top in international student tests, is changing its school curricula. Starting in 2020, it will be replacing traditional subjects with new ones that emphasize four key competencies: communication, creativity, critical thinking, and collaboration. In an automated world, where most people will be working independently either as contractors or entrepreneurs, these skills will be much more important than memorizing what year Columbus arrived in the Americas or who invented the printing press. The best-educated students will be those with the motivation and skills to reinvent themselves every so often so as not to be left behind in the wake of technological changes.

"FIND A BIG WAVE AND PUT YOUR SURFBOARD RIGHT ON TOP OF IT"

One of the most interesting people I interviewed about what advice to give to young people was Benjamin Pring, the cofounder and managing director of the Center for the Future of Work. I called him up to ask him what specific career he would recommend young people to pursue, considering that most higher education institutions don't have programs or degrees that emphasize soft skills. Pring, a fifty-five-year-old British-born philosopher turned technologist, has been spending much of his time looking into this issue in recent years.

Pring majored in philosophy at Manchester University, and later became a technology consultant for Coopers & Lybrand and other big firms. He became a leading analyst of cloud computing in the late 1990s. In 2011, he joined Cognizant, a consulting company with more than 250,000 employees, and was later appointed director of the company's think tank, the Center for the Future of Work. Perhaps because of its ties to Cognizant, the center is optimistic about the future of work, and predicts that, in coming years, many more jobs will be gained than lost.

When I asked Pring what career advice he was giving to his two children, who were then aged fifteen and seventeen, the futurologist said, "I tell them the best thing they can do—and what I did—is to find a big wave and put your surfboard right on top of it. When I was twenty, back in the mid-1980s, I wasn't really that focused on technology, but I knew that it was going to be a great big wave. I worked my way into it, and thirty-some years later, that's still my career, because the tech industry has grown so enormously that it has created huge opportunities and taken my surfboard along with it. If you're twenty now, find the big new waves of the future and go surf them."

So what will those great big waves of the future be? I asked. Pring specifically mentioned the fields of biotechnology, quantum computing, cybersecurity, virtual and augmented reality, space exploration, and—as life expectancy increases—preventive medicine and wellness programs that will improve people's physical condition. He said he wasn't too worried about his children not finding a place in the workforce of the future. "When you and I started working, we managed it, we figured it out. I don't see why my fifteen-year-old and seventeen-year-old won't be able to do the same. The world was changing a lot when we were young, and it continues to change today. The real trick is, as I said, finding those big waves. Don't get into an industry that's collapsing, don't go into an area or a skill set that's in decline."

At first Pring didn't want to single out which industries are collapsing—perhaps for fear of antagonizing some Cognizant customers—but said that they are in plain sight, and include many of those that have been disrupted by the Internet. My interpretation was that he was referring, among others, to the retail, music, and newspaper industries.

I told Pring that I was surprised that when he had mentioned the leading waves of the future, he had not included the sports and entertainment industries. Won't people have more free time to watch movies or read poetry or go to yoga classes, which will give a boost to the entertainment industries? I asked him. Pring didn't buy my argument. "Yes, people will have more time, and maybe people will be motivated to, as you say, read poetry and take yoga classes. That's great, but I don't think that's going to be a source of income. The notion that there will be a renaissance in the monetization of poetry I think is unlikely," he responded.

Pring cited an oversupply of labor in the entertainment business and said much of that industry faces an ominous future. He cited music as an example. "The real issue at the heart of the music business is that the economics don't work like they did back in the sixties, when there were probably a hundred rock and roll bands split between the U.S. and the UK, and they all sold a lot of records. But nowadays, there's thousands and thousands of bands out there. Demand plateaued, and so—on a purely supply-and-demand basis—there's more supply than demand. Unless you're a superstar, the money that each individual band makes just isn't there." He added, "I think we've almost reached this point where we've had peak music, peak poetry. There's just too much of the stuff, and I think that might be the danger with television in the next few years. There's so much on television . . . and I think the Netflix boom at the moment is unsustainable."

MY RECIPE: FIND THE WAVES YOU LIKE, PICK ONE THAT HAS A FUTURE, AND SURF IT

While I like Pring's advice for young people to seek out the big waves of the future and surf them, I find his examples of careers of the future a bit too techno-centric. He is probably wrong to exclude the entertainment industries, which are likely to thrive as people have more free time thanks to automation, and as we live longer lives. But more important, young people should prioritize the passion factor or at least put it high on their list of considerations when choosing a career. Before identifying the waves of the future, we should look for the waves that we like the most.

If I was to offer advice to a twenty-year-old, based on my own experience, I'd say that the first thing you should do is identify your passion. A person who isn't passionate about his work is much less likely to succeed than someone who is, even it's not in one of the industries of the future. Self-motivation will be the rule of the game in the new labor market, and it's hard to be motivated if you are not doing something that you love. So my recipe would be "find the waves that you like, pick one that has a future, and surf it."

How does one identify a passion? One good barometer is doing something you enjoy, even if you're not always entirely satisfied with the results. During my career, I've had the opportunity to interview thousands of famous people of all stripes, from presidents like Donald Trump and Barack Obama to megamillionaires like Bill Gates and Carlos Slim, to entertainers like Richard Gere and Shakira. And with a few notable exceptions—like Trump, an egomaniac who boasts about successes that in most cases exist only in his mind—the vast majority of these people are passionate about their work and yearn to do it better every day. Many of them are insecure overachievers: people whose self-doubts drive them to do their job better than anyone else. Perhaps the best yardstick for judging whether you are passionate about your work is to ask yourself whether you're doing it perfectly. Only those who aren't much interested in what they're doing or the charlatans are fully satisfied with their work. The most talented people are never completely happy with what they have achieved.

One of the most talented insecure overachievers I interviewed over the years was late Peruvian painter Fernando de Szyszlo, one of Latin America's foremost artists. At more than ninety years of age, he was still painting frantically eight hours a day. Szyszlo had both fame and money. At the time of his death in 2017, his work was among the collections of the Museum of Modern Art and the Guggenheim in New York, the Centre

Pompidou in Paris, and the Museum of Modern Art in Mexico. During an interview on my TV show, I asked him what motivated him, at his age, to be preparing four exhibitions of new works in the United States, Europe, and Latin America in the coming year. He could be traveling the world receiving honorary degrees or do anything else he liked, I told him. So why is it that, in your nineties, you are still working so hard? I asked.

Szyszlo looked straight into the camera and said, with a mixture of resignation and pride, "Because I still haven't painted the perfect painting I have always dreamed about." I thought it was a wonderful response. The same thing happens to most overachievers who dedicate themselves passionately to their job: they feel they are doing it well but have yet to do it perfectly. Perhaps it was not just coincidence or good genes that Szyszlo lived an active life until a fall down the stairs at his home resulted in his death at age ninety-two. He loved his work, and while the perfect painting never quite came, the quest for it kept him alive.

WE MUST HAVE A PLAN B, A PLAN C, AND A PLAN D

It's good to encourage young people to choose the career they like the most, but what about middle-aged people whose jobs will be increasingly threatened by automation? The answer is, at least in part, the same as it would be for young people. First, they will have to be flexible and constantly update their skills. As MIT president Rafael Reif told me, universities will become lifelong learning centers. People should not walk away from them after graduation. And second, we will all have to have a Plan B, a Plan C, and a Plan D and be ready to reinvent ourselves both in and out the jobs we're currently doing. Luckily, there are more opportunities to do that than ever.

Many of us know someone over the age of fifty who, after having spent all his or her life working in an office, suddenly reinvented himself as a reiki instructor or independent salesperson. Others indulge in things they were never able to do before, like Richard Erde, a seventy-five-year-old New Yorker who had always loved opera and who—after working nearly three decades as a computer programmer—retired in 2005 and auditioned to become an extra at the Metropolitan Opera. "I've been on stage at the Met literally hundreds of times with world-famous singers, and I never sang a word," the Brooklynite said, chuckling. "I've worn all kinds of costumes, from Buddhist priest to Russian soldier. It's ecstatic at times, plus I get paid to do it."

More important, Internet platforms that connect buyers and sellers of goods and services have opened a world of new possibilities for middle-aged people exploring new occupations. Currently, only 15 percent of the roughly 162 million independent workers in the United States and Europe have used digital platforms like Upwork, Freelancer, Etsy, or other related sites to find customers for their products or services. But the "on demand" economy is growing daily. Kickstarter, the crowdfunding platform where anyone can raise money to finance a creative endeavor, reported that in 2018 alone, over 138,000 projects had been funded by more than 14 million sponsors.

At the time of this writing, one of the projects looking to raise funds on Kickstarter is a book titled *The Photo History of the Black 95th Regiment in World War II,* which has already raised nearly two thousand dollars in online preorders. Most of the soldiers in the 95th Regiment have passed away, but Stuart Bradley, the project's creator, thought their descendants would want to have a book documenting the service of their grandparents, who made up one of the few black regiments in World War II. Another project on Kickstarter is Taller Nu, which offers fashionable shoes and purses designed and manufactured by female prisoners in Mexico, and which has topped 170 preorders. Many of the projects posted on these crowdfunding platforms are relatively modest, but not all of them: the Professor Einstein teaching robot raised $850,000 in just a few weeks. And the Pebble smartwatch, promoted on Kickstarter as better than Apple's smartwatch for having a seven-day battery life, raised over $20 million from 78,500 buyers.

In the new digital economy, entrepreneurs no longer depend solely on bank loans, venture capitalists, or personal connections. Anyone with a good idea can offer it up to the world. And increasing numbers of people want to be their own boss. A recent survey showed that more than 70 percent of people who work independently, whether full-time or part-time, prefer working on their own to more traditional jobs. Respondents said that, in addition to having more flexible schedules, independent work gives them greater opportunities for growth. While automation will kill millions of jobs, more middle-aged people will be able to reinvent themselves as small-business owners and entrepreneurs in the expanding digital economy.

THE WORLD IS GETTING BETTER, BUT TURBULENT TIMES LIE AHEAD

When people ask me whether I'm a techno-optimist or a techno-pessimist, I try to avoid the cliché of saying I'm a techno-realist. I prefer to say that I'm pessimistic in the medium term, but optimistic in the long term. The world will continue getting better, but over the next two decades we are likely to go through turbulent times. Technological disruption will probably create significant unemployment among the lesser-educated segments of the population, and greater social inequality. Only those with the greatest motivation and best academic credentials or special skills will have access to the best jobs of the future. It will be hard for many of today's cashiers, servers, and cabdrivers to reinvent themselves as data analysts or video game programmers. There will be a huge mass of socially marginalized, hopeless, and frustrated people. Some will spend their lives getting high on drugs or watching movies in their virtual reality viewers, while others may join growing anti-robotization protest movements. It will be a traumatic transition, and—in some cases—even a violent one.

The anti-tech rebellion has already started, and it goes far beyond the taxi drivers who have burned Uber cars in foreign capitals. More than 50,000 hotel and casino workers from the Las Vegas Culinary Workers Union voted in 2018 to go on strike, stating among other things that their jobs were being threatened by robots. "I voted yes to go on strike to ensure my job isn't outsourced to a robot. We know technology is coming, but workers shouldn't be pushed out and left behind," said Chad Neanover, a cook at the Margaritaville Hotel. Las Vegas's Culinary Workers Union secretary treasurer Geoconda Argüello-Kline said, "We support innovations that improve jobs, but we oppose automation when it only destroys jobs. Our industry must innovate without losing the human touch."

When I asked the union's spokeswoman, Bethany Khan, whether they were demanding a ban on robots, she responded that "we don't oppose technology, but we want to have a say in how technology is implemented in our workforce." Among other things, the union was demanding that people displaced by technology be retrained "so that workers have the opportunity to grow with technology, versus being laid off," she said.

The Las Vegas labor union members had good reasons to worry. At the Tipsy Robot bar within the Planet Hollywood casino, two robots were already making and serving cocktails.

The bar's web page said its robots "have the capacity to produce 120 drinks per hour. . . . Our mechanical marvels use exact measurements, ensuring a perfectly crafted sip every time. They have killer dance moves, too." At the nearby Mandarin Oriental Las Vegas Hotel, a four-foot-tall Pepper robotic concierge had recently started offering assistance with hotel services and directions. Meanwhile, the Renaissance Las Vegas Hotel had started using two delivery robots to take food and drinks to the guests' rooms. A University of Redlands study in 2017 predicted that 65.2 percent of the jobs in Las Vegas—including servers, kitchen workers, cooks, and bartenders—risked being eliminated by automation within ten or twenty years.

On a larger scale, there has been a growing public reaction against big-tech companies following the Facebook scandal over reports that the Trump campaign–linked data firm Cambridge Analytica had inappropriately obtained private information of more than 50 million of the social network's users. More than 552 million people made Google searches under the words "delete Facebook" in the aftermath. While most of them probably didn't pull out from Facebook, many—including celebrities such as Apple cofounder Steve Wozniak, Tesla founder Elon Musk, and singer/actress Cher—did so. The European Union passed rules to protect privacy on the Internet. And an entire country, Papua New Guinea, announced it would unplug Facebook for one month to look into ways to eradicate fake news and pornography. The government wanted to make sure that "real people with real identities" used the network responsibly, the *Papua New Guinea Post-Courier* reported.

In addition, many tech companies that until recently were darlings of the media are now under fire for allegedly creating "tech addiction." There are "tech-detox" retreats across the country where people spend vacations with no access to Wi-Fi and where smartphones and other electronic devices are forbidden. Several television series that portray a skeptical view of big-tech companies, such as *Westworld* and *Black Mirror,* have drawn huge audiences. And there are increasingly more newspaper stories casting doubts about the true intentions of big-tech firms, such as an October 13, 2017, article in *The New York Times Sunday Review* titled "Silicon Valley Is Not Your Friend."

In Silicon Valley, a group of former executives and technologists from Google, Facebook, and other technology firms have recently launched an initiative called Truth About Tech to fight against tech addiction. They announced they had collected $57 million in cash and donated advertising time to promote their cause. Tristan Harris, a former Google design ethicist who is one of the group's leaders, told me that big-tech firms intentionally try to keep us glued to their platforms for as long as they can because their stock valuation depends on viewers' engagement time, the time we spend in front of our screens. Netflix, which previously asked you to press the yes button if you wanted to see the next episode of a TV series, now moves on to the next installment automatically, without asking for your permission. Twitter, likewise, uses casino gambling techniques to keep you hooked, he said.

"The people who designed Twitter made it so that when you pull down to refresh, it's like playing with a slot machine. There is a variable reward, because sometimes you have new tweets and sometimes you don't. And that makes it intrinsically addictive," Harris told me. Tech addiction is causing isolation, attention deficit problems, and depression among young people, and causing adults to sleep less, he added, citing several studies. Besides educating the public, Truth About Tech and other advocacy groups are demanding that big-tech companies and the government fund studies to look into the impact of tech addiction on youngsters.

EVENTUALLY, AUTOMATION WILL MAKE THE WORLD A BETTER PLACE

But in the long term, two or three decades out, many of today's big-tech excesses are likely to be under control, and automation is likely to increase productivity and allow countries to pay a universal basic income to all their citizens, perhaps in return for community service. People will live better, much like what happened after the initial traumas of the Industrial Revolution and the agricultural revolution before it. After a transition that may result in massive job losses and anti-robotization protests, we may see a re-accommodation of the workforce, with more people doing better and safer jobs. In the United States, as we saw earlier in this book, the percentage of people working in agriculture fell from 60 percent of the population in the mid-nineteenth century to just 2 percent today. Similarly, the percentage of people working in the manufacturing sector fell from 26 percent in 1960 to less than 10 percent in 2017. And yet the standard of living is much better today than it was when most Americans were working in the fields or in factories.

The same thing happened in China and India, where hundreds of millions of people climbed out of poverty thanks to the economic modernization that began in the late twentieth century. Greater productivity resulting from automation will also allow people to work fewer hours, as has been the trend for centuries now, and in less boring and repetitive tasks. This greater amount of leisure time will allow us to rediscover the lost arts of conversation, reading, and good music, and hopelessness will give way to new and previously unimagined possibilities.

I'm not ending this book on an optimistic note to be politically correct, but because I'm convinced that in the long term, the world will be a better place. Of course there will be ups and downs, as there have always been. Terrible wars will occur, and there will be horrendous natural disasters produced by global warming, but the general trend over time will be positive. We are likely to see a continuation of the overall progress that humankind has been making since the time when we were living in caves. Just take a look at the amazing achievements of the past two hundred years:

- *Life expectancy:* The average life expectancy has risen from only thirty years in ancient times to nearly seventy years today and has increased at an exponentially rapid pace over the past two centuries. As Oxford University economist Max Roser reminds us, even in low-income countries, people are living longer than ever. And this increase isn't due solely to a dramatic reduction in infant mortality rates. If we just take into account children who reach the age of five, average life expectancy has gone up from fifty-five years in 1841 to eighty-two years nowadays. By the same token, a generation ago, a fifty-year-old person could expect to live another twenty years, whereas today that person can be expected to live another thirty-three years. We have managed to either limit or eradicate several diseases that devastated entire populations two hundred years ago, like polio, smallpox, and measles, and we are making great strides in combating many other illnesses.
- *Poverty:* The percentage of the world population living in absolute poverty has fallen from 84 percent in 1820 to 10 percent nowadays. Famines, which were common in the time of our great-grandparents, are now rare. Today, obesity is a bigger killer than famine. In 2010, obesity killed roughly 3 million people worldwide, whereas famines and malnutrition together claimed the lives of about a million people. As Oxford's Roser says, technology is helping even the poorest among us. Nathan Rothschild,

the wealthiest man in the world at the time of his death in 1836, died from an infection that can now be easily treated with an antibiotic that costs pennies and is available in just about every hospital on the planet.

- *Infant mortality:* It wasn't very long ago that mothers used to lose one or more children. In 1820, 43 percent of children died before reaching the age of five. In eighteenth-century Sweden, every third child died before turning five, and in nineteenth-century Germany, the infant mortality rate was one in two. Today, in developed nations, the rate is less than one in a hundred, and in emerging countries, it has fallen to 1.07 percent in China, 1.2 percent in Argentina, 1.3 percent in Mexico, 4 percent in South Africa, and 4.7 percent in India. There are only a few nations, such as Angola, where the rate hasn't yet fallen below 15 percent.
- *Education:* Whereas only 12 percent of the world's population knew how to read in 1820, that figure has now risen to 85 percent. In the United States and most European nations, 99 percent of children can read and write, and literacy rates have reached 98 percent in Argentina, 95 percent in China, 94 percent in Mexico, 90 percent in Brazil, and 63 percent in India. There are only a few nations in sub-Saharan Africa where the literacy rate continues to hover at around 30 percent.
- *Freedom:* Despite big bumps on the road, such as World War II and the recent rise of authoritarian populism across the globe, there are more people around the world today who enjoy basic freedoms than ever before. The wave of decolonization in the nineteenth century and the breakup of the Soviet Union in 1989 contributed to the birth of many democratic nations. While there was just one democracy in the entire world in 1811, today there are eighty-seven. Freedom House, the U.S. watch-

dog organization, reported in 2017 a global reduction in basic civil liberties for the eleventh straight year, but the trend over the past two centuries has been clearly positive. According to the organization's ranking of 195 nations, 87 can currently be considered "free," or 45 percent of the total, while 59 are classified as "partially free" and 49 are listed as "not free."

- *Wars:* Contrary to what we might believe if we rely only on the news of the day, there are fewer wars in the world. In ancient times, human-caused violence accounted for 15 percent of all deaths in the world. During the twentieth century, that figure had fallen to 5 percent, and at the beginning of the twenty-first century that figure stands at less than 1 percent. In 2012, about 620,000 people died from acts of violence across the globe, but the vast majority of them were victims of murders. Only 120,000 of the total number of violent deaths were due to armed conflicts. Comparatively, 1.5 million people died from diabetes. As Israeli historian Yuval Noah Harari has put it, "sugar is now more dangerous than gunpowder."
- *Quality of life:* Medical advances have allowed us to make great progress in alleviating, if not eliminating, pain. Can you imagine what it must have been like to go to the dentist and have a tooth pulled before anesthesia was invented? Painkillers as we know them today have been around only since the mid-nineteenth century. Until just a few decades ago, going to the dentist was torture. Today, while it's not exactly something we look forward to doing, we often don't even feel the sting that numbs our mouth, because the dentist uses a local anesthetic at the site of the injection. Aspirin, the most common painkiller today, didn't exist before 1899. People often had to suffer chronic pain throughout their lives from things that today are easily treated with an aspirin. And air conditioning,

which has become so essential to those living in hot climates, was invented only in the early twentieth century. Would you want to go back to a time where there was no anesthesia, no aspirin, and no air conditioning?

Many of those who say the world is going from bad to worse are forgetting other key facts, such as that slavery was a common practice in the United States and many other countries until the mid-nineteenth century. Or that half the world's population—women—were considered second-class citizens until relatively recently, though they still are denied basic rights in some parts of the world. Most women today are living better not only because they have been able to assert their rights, but also because of technology. In the 1920s, many people—especially women—spent nearly twelve hours a week washing clothes. But with the invention of washers and dryers, that has fallen to less than two hours per week. This might seem trivial, but it's not. Washing machines and microwave ovens have simplified our lives, leaving us with more leisure time to watch TV or do whatever else gives us more satisfaction. Our ancestors never had that luxury.

Will this positive trend continue in the future? Probably, and most likely we will eventually live even longer and more enjoyable lives. But in the immediate future, things will get rocky. While we make the transition into an increasingly automated world, we will have to adapt, update, and reinvent ourselves, and look for new opportunities in what will be a constantly evolving and sometimes chaotic workplace. Until automation brings about enough prosperity to provide a basic income for everyone who is left behind, or we find other ways to take care of technological unemployment, our motto may just have to be *Watch out . . . the robots are coming!*

EPILOGUE

THE TOP TEN JOB FIELDS OF THE FUTURE

When young people ask me for career advice and I tell them to study whatever they like most, I speak from my own experience. When I was a teenager trying to find my place in the world, I knew that I wanted to be a journalist. I was aware that it wasn't a well-paying profession then—and it's become even less lucrative nowadays—but it was my passion. When I was thirteen, I started writing imaginary travel books in notebooks, inspired by *National Geographic* magazine, which we used to get at home. My passion for journalism and politics had probably started when I was a child growing up in Argentina and spent a lot of time at my grandmother's place, which was midway between my parents' home and my school. She was a widow and was living with a relatively well-known journalist and politician, who at that time was serving in the Argentine National Congress. I went to their house almost every day after school and was fascinated by the books and newspapers piled up everywhere in his home office. And I was awestruck by his lifestyle. He wrote in the mornings, took a nap after lunch, and several times a week he would have visitors for dinners with whom he would have passionate discussions about current events until late into the night. To me, it seemed much more fun than working from nine to five at a bank or in any other business.

I was just fifteen years old when my father died, and I felt at the time that I would never overcome the grief. I sought refuge in the world of books and became a somewhat withdrawn, introverted teenager. Years later, without knowing what career path to follow—no major university in Argentina had a journalism program at the time—I studied law and took an internship at a current affairs magazine. When I turned twenty-three, I told my mother I wanted to be a journalist. She reacted with obvious concern. "What will you live on?" she asked. She reminded me that journalism was one of the worst-paying jobs around. She wanted me to enter the family business—a medium-size factory that produced chocolate and other raw materials for bakeries—hoping that one day I would become a top executive at the firm. I refused to follow her advice. And when I look back in time, it was one of the smartest decisions I ever made. I decided to go with my passion.

If you are a young person and fortunate enough to have found a passion in life, pursue it. Whatever you do, if you enjoy it, you'll be more motivated and committed to doing it well. When I left Argentina in 1976 and two years later graduated from Columbia University's Graduate School of Journalism, I found myself unemployed in a country that wasn't my own. On top of that, I had an accent that identified me as an immigrant. But I never entertained the notion of doing anything other than journalism. I decided I needed to get into a media company, no matter how, and work my way up to a job in journalism. So I got a job as an English-to-Spanish translator working the night shift at the Associated Press news agency's headquarters in New York.

It was a tough job—the shift was from midnight to

eight A.M., and I sometimes had to pull two or three shifts in a row—and it was well beneath the qualifications of someone who had just graduated from one of the best journalism schools in the world and already had a thick folder of published articles. But it was the only job I could get. I worked as a night-shift translator at the AP for three years before I was finally able to get transferred to the day shift. There I started to have direct contact with my bosses, whom I had hardly met, and let them know about my desire to become a reporter. Eventually they started sending me out to cover routine events when the regular reporter was on vacation or out sick. Little by little, I went from being an occasional substitute to a regular one, and that opened my way to starting a career as a journalist in the United States.

So to this day, whenever students ask me about how to get their first job, I always tell them, "Get your foot in the door of whatever company you would like to work for. Either that, or be the founder of your own company. If you want to work for an existing company, just get a job inside the building. Any job you can get, the closest to what you want to do. If you have the credentials and are motivated, and if you are already inside the building, sooner or later there will be an opening in a position that you will be interested in." But the key condition in either case—whether you get into an existing company or start one of your own—is that you have to have found something you're passionate about. In my case, I never would have been able to work the graveyard shift as a translator for several years if I didn't have a passion for and a dream of working as a journalist.

But what if you are a young person without a clearly defined passion? In that case, I recommend you take a look at the following list of occupations where we are likely to see the greatest job opportunities in the near future. It's not exhaustive by any means—we don't know what new jobs will arise from future technologies—but it summarizes the predictions made by many futurologists I interviewed for this book. In the long term, past 2030, many of the new frontiers in the world of work will be in the field of space exploration—will we be gardeners on Mars?—and genetic engineering. But in the short term, in the 2020s, most of the jobs are likely to be within the following ten fields:

1. *Health care assistants:* The increase in life expectancy and an aging world population will require increasingly more health-related professionals, including physicians, nurses, psychologists, nutritionists, massage therapists, physical trainers, and counselors. There will also be several new kinds of health workers with interdisciplinary skills, such as robotic medicine specialists, who will be in charge of handling the robotic surgeons in operating rooms; medical engineers, who will, among other things, use 3-D printers to create new skin from the cells of patients undergoing reconstructive surgeries; and genetic engineering specialists, who will help create personalized medications tailored to each individual patient.

And among health care workers in general, those who work with the elderly will be in highest demand. Between 2014 and 2030, the world's population aged sixty-five and over will increase by 300 million. And these people need the help, empathy, and human warmth that robots and algorithms won't be able to offer for quite some time. In countries like China, Germany, Italy, and Japan, roughly 25 percent of the population will be sixty-five years of age or older by 2030. While the elderly in Japan already have robotic pets that can be caressed and simulate joy by moving their tails, they won't replace—at least in the foreseeable future—the human touch of health care workers who can look someone in the eye, hold their hand, and convey a sense of affection.

Health care workers will also be needed to fight an epidemic of loneliness. In the United Kingdom, Prime Minister

Theresa May appointed in 2018 a minister for loneliness to address the needs of the estimated 9 million British citizens living solitary lives. This represents about 14 percent of the population, though in some sectors, like the elderly, the figure goes above 33 percent. According to Sir Simon McDonald, the head of the British Diplomatic Service, one of the primary reasons for the creation of this new position was to help save on government health expenses through social activities that give a sense of purpose to elderly people's lives. "Loneliness destroys lives, and it costs the public treasury an enormous amount of money" in health expenditures, McDonald told me. The parliamentary commission that recommended the creation of this new agency had stated that loneliness can be more damaging to people's health than obesity and even smoking.

I wouldn't be surprised if one of the most common jobs of the future will be that of "people walkers." I'm not kidding. The Center for the Future of Work, the research wing of the tech firm Cognizant, ranks "walker/talkers" among the nearly two dozen jobs that will be needed most in the upcoming decade. The study, titled "The 21 Jobs of the Future," says that with the increase in longevity and oncoming technological unemployment, walker/talkers will be employed both by government agencies and by the elderly and their families.

There will be numerous websites offering companionship for elderly people who find themselves alone. Just as Uber puts drivers in touch with people who need a ride, these websites will allow the elderly to hire a walker or a conversational companion at an hourly rate to spend time together and chat. "Academic research has demonstrated that engaged and energized seniors are twice as healthy as those who spend most of their time alone; health cost savings generated by our services more than pay for themselves," the center's study says.

To provide this service to the elderly, people will have to pass a rigorous background check. For many people, it will be an ideal job. Like Uber drivers, they will be able to choose their working hours and decide which jobs to accept or reject. And thanks to these online platforms, they will be free to choose which clients to work for. Any professional walker/talker who receives a request will be able to see who else has spent time with the potential client, and what rating the customer received, before accepting an assignment. Also available online will be what topics of conversation the customer recently enjoyed, so that any new walker/talker can pick up the dialogue where a previous colleague left off.

Does that sound crazy? No crazier than it would have sounded if someone had told you a few decades ago that there would be dog walkers or personal nutritionists. Plus, there's no reason why the elderly should spend their golden years like many do now, crammed into overcrowded nursing homes where a handful of caregivers must look after large numbers of older people. Paying individual attention to the elderly—whether through home visits, hour-long walks, or virtual conversations—will be one of the jobs that will be most in demand.

2. Data analysts, data engineers, and programmers: Data will be the most valuable commodity in coming years—the oil of the twenty-first century—and there will be plenty of jobs for those exploring and analyzing digital information. Already, all sorts of industries—from banks to stores—are recruiting as many data analysts and engineers as they can to identify potential new customers and keep their current ones. According to some estimates, the growth of the middle class in China, India, and other emerging countries will result in an increase of a billion consumers across the world by 2025. That will mean a lot of work for data analysts.

Restaurants will need a data manager to create client profiles with the birthdays and favorite dishes of their customers.

Movie production companies—big and small—will be hiring data analysts to explore social media and identify potential new viewers or to look to see what people thought of a particular movie so they can offer similar films. Most businesses will also employ data analysts to track our social media habits and find out exactly what time of day we are likely to be on Facebook or Twitter, in order to send us personalized advertising at just the right moment.

This sort of data work used to be done by well-paid engineers or scientists with master's degrees or Ph.D.s. But with the growing use of data mining platforms like Tableau.com or Domo.com, more people with basic computer skills will be able to do this sort of job for all types of companies. Many of these analysts will be digital detectives who will try to identify trends and rumors in social media. If reports are popping up on Facebook and Twitter about people getting sick from eating tomatoes, data analysts working for supermarkets will immediately send an alert to their bosses, perhaps recommending to avoid using the color red in their ads for the next six months. Data managers will become—and in some cases, already are—top advisers to CEOs.

3. Digital security guards: As the economy moves further into the digital world, there will be even more of a need for companies to protect themselves from cyber attacks. Just as most office buildings have an armed guard at their door, companies will also need a digital security guard—or many—to make sure that their data are not stolen by some mischievous teenager in America, a professional spying group in Russia, or the government of North Korea. According to U.S. officials, China has a special military agency, known as PLA Unit 61398 of the People's Liberation Army, specifically to hack into foreign governments and companies.

Cyber pirates are getting ever more ambitious. Emails stolen from Hillary Clinton's 2016 presidential campaign—which the CIA, the FBI, and the National Intelligence Agency attributed to people with ties to the Russian government who later passed the data along to WikiLeaks—destabilized elections in the most powerful nation on earth and helped elect Donald Trump. The 2013 hacking of Yahoo, which didn't become known until three years later, put the personal data of more than a billion people at risk. The 2017 cyber attack on Equifax, one of the three largest U.S. credit reporting agencies, resulted in personal information of 143 million Americans being stolen. Not even Saudi Aramco, the world's largest oil company, has been safe from hacking. In 2012, a group of cyber pirates connected to the Iranian government introduced a virus into the company's servers that affected 30,000 computers and temporarily paralyzed its operations.

Global cybersecurity expenses—or investments, if you prefer—are expected to double from $3 trillion in 2016 to $6 trillion by 2021, and jobs in this field will more than triple from 1 million to 3.5 million over the same period, one study says. As the world becomes increasingly dependent on the Internet—the global online population doubled from 2 billion individuals in 2015 to 3.8 billion in 2017 and is expected to reach 6 billion by 2022—there will be more cybercrimes and a greater need for cyber police.

4. *Sales consultants:* Thanks to increased productivity and the growth of the middle class worldwide, global consumption will increase by more than $23 trillion. And as an increasing number of physical stores are replaced by e-commerce, growing numbers of specialists will be needed to advise the public about the pros and cons of all kinds of products. Sales consultants will replace what we now call salespeople, and will become known as specialists or geniuses, as customer service reps are already known at Apple stores. They will have to have a stronger aca-

demic background and better communication skills than many current salespeople. Instead of pushing sales as fast as they can, they will be expected to educate consumers and build trusted relationships in order to earn long-term client loyalty. If they don't have what you need, they may refer you to a competitor. One of their primary job requirements will be to have a contagious smile and to radiate good vibes, something that humans will continue to do much better than robots for quite some time.

5. Robot maintenance technicians and programmers: Worldwide sales of industrial robots are expected to increase fivefold, from the 253,000 units sold in 2015 to nearly 1.3 million units in 2025, which will require many more mechanics and engineers to provide them with technical support. Robotic engineers will be needed to keep the robots oiled up and running, and programmers will have to constantly update the robots' software.

Virtual assistants such as Siri, Alexa, and Google Home will need programmers to help them answer increasingly more sophisticated questions. Also, self-driving cars will need humans to oversee algorithm reactions to unforeseen factors and exceptions to the rules, such as when there is a detour sign on the road that autonomous cars' sensors may not be able to detect because of bad weather.

In addition, there will be a need for human designers and inspectors of the Internet of Things, the system through which all kinds of objects will be connected with one another. Thanks to the Internet of Things, the sensor on a milk carton will notify our refrigerator that it's running low on milk; the fridge will then send a message to the supermarket ordering a replacement, which in turn will communicate with a taxi service that will deliver the product to our home—all of that without any human intervention. This phenomenon will require people who can monitor and maintain the millions of sensors that will be everywhere and on everything.

Cities across the world are already installing sensors in their water and gas pipes to alert them about leaks, helping them avoid accidents and reducing waste. With self-driving cars, there will be more sensors at bridges and tunnels to warn vehicles about potential dangers. The city of Barcelona already has an energy-saving system of public lighting that turns on only when a car or pedestrian approaches, instead of having the lights on all night.

A world in which all things are digitally interconnected means people will be needed to install sensors, maintain them, integrate them, and inspect them to make sure there are no flaws that could lead to chaotic or even dangerous situations. Just as good airplane maintenance can be a matter of life and death today, maintaining urban infrastructure sensors will be critical in the future. Nobody will want to risk having a broken sensor on a highway send the wrong signal to self-driving cars and steer them off a cliff.

6. Teachers and professors: With the growing automation of jobs, we will need more teachers and professors to instruct people on how to run and maintain robots, how to work with them, and how to perform the sophisticated tasks that intelligent machines won't be able to perform. There will be two types of jobs: those in which robots will supervise humans, and those in which humans will supervise robots. The latter will require better education and will pay better salaries. The current education system whereby young people study a subject and then apply what they have learned in school for the rest of their lives has become obsolete. What we majored in in college ten, twenty, or thirty years ago is prehistoric as far as today's jobs are concerned. As we move forward, we'll have to study throughout our lives, reinventing ourselves from time to time, depending on the demands of the labor market. Those who don't keep learning for life or don't have an exceptional skill will be left in the dust.

Granted, robots like Professor Einstein will replace some educators, but there will be a greater need for elementary and preschool teachers to help children find their areas of interest and teach them soft skills such as ethics, empathy, teamwork, persistence, and a tolerance for failure. University professors will also be needed to meet the lifelong educational needs of hundreds of millions of people. Robots and tablets will eventually take over the role of transmitting information to students, but they won't be as effective as humans in developing young people's sense of curiosity and helping them find their passions, and in keeping adults constantly updated and motivated.

7. *Alternative energy specialists:* The growing threat of natural disasters caused by climate change and the lower costs of clean energy will give rise to dozens of new green energy–related careers. There will be a need for more scientists specializing in renewable energies, such as those using solar panels or wind turbines, and more architects and engineers who can design energy-efficient plants, buildings, and vehicles, or can convert existing ones into greener ones. The U.S. International Energy Agency estimates that between 2015 and 2030, global investments in clean-energy factories and projects to reduce greenhouse gases will reach $16.5 trillion.

And while Trump's 2017 decision to pull the United States out of the Paris Agreement on climate change could delay some investments in clean energy, his unfortunate decision may not succeed in keeping America from meeting the Paris Agreement's goals. Key state and local U.S. governments are vowing to abide by the Paris Agreement's targets, whether Trump likes it or not. As former U.S. vice president and Nobel Prize winner Al Gore told me in an interview, "In California, New York,

Washington, and many other states, and in many cities, they have made a commitment to do what Trump has refused to do. And many of these states and local governments have the tools available to them to start reducing emissions." Some cities such as Georgetown, Texas, have already decided to rely 100 percent on renewable energy, he added. China has already announced big investments in alternative energy, and India has set a goal for itself of getting 40 percent of its energy from renewable sources by 2030. With or without Trump, global investments in clean energy will continue to grow, and that will mean millions of new jobs for workers to fill.

8. Artists, athletes, and other entertainers: As more people work flexible hours, have temporary jobs, or spend fewer hours a week on their jobs, there will be more leisure time. This will mean a greater need for workers in creative industries like moviemaking, music, art, and literature. The shrinking work-week, which we're already seeing in countries like the Netherlands, will create a greater demand for content to entertain the population. The increase in the number of television series produced by Netflix, HBO, and Amazon is already proof of this phenomenon. And the same thing will happen with sports. There will be an explosion of local and school sports leagues, and their games will be broadcast live to our smartphones. With more free time, we will have a greater desire to spend it the best way we can, and that will increase the demand for more and better entertainment.

9. Product designers and creators of commercial content: As e-commerce grows, and as more consumers make their choices based on what they see online, companies will need more people to create virtual content—including web designers, bloggers, social media writers, and virtual reality artists—to promote their products. As pointed out in chapter 3, restaurants will be hiring their own designers, writers, artists, and videographers to promote their menus. They will tell the story of each plate and will give us a detailed analysis of its nutritional benefits. Companies, athletes, and artists alike will increasingly rely on their own designers and content creators to reach their audiences. In the auto industry, for instance, most potential buyers used to go to a dealership to check out a car, whereas now they can preview everything online or with augmented reality goggles and go to the showroom only to confirm their decision. Websites and augmented reality showrooms will be more important than salesroom floors, which will create a need for ever more talented content creators.

Also, the shift from mass production to individualized production with 3-D printers will trigger a greater demand for product designers. Today, a shoemaker produces hundreds of thousands of copies of the same shoe in China. But in the future, many of us will download a custom shoe design we like on our computer and produce it using a 3-D printer in our own home. Instead of one designer for hundreds of thousands of shoes, there will be thousands of them.

And designers won't just be creating looks, they'll be creating lifestyles. Thanks to the Internet of Things and smart homes in which all the devices and appliances are interconnected, lifestyle designers will be needed to create our own environment. They will help us coordinate the intensity of the lights in our foyer with the music we might like to hear when we enter our homes, with the air conditioning's temperature, with whatever task we want to assign to our robotic home assistant. The supply of interconnected devices will be so immense that most of us will feel too overwhelmed to set up all our machines without the help of a professional lifestyle designer.

10. Spiritual counselors: Priests, imams, rabbis, and all sorts of spiritual gurus will enjoy job security for quite some time because our existential questions will not go away. As we have already seen happen for several years now, the disintegration of families and the growing loneliness of many people despite—or because of—an increasingly connected digital universe will generate a greater need for spiritual guides who can help us find meaning in life. It will be hard for robots and algorithms—regardless of how much information they might have—to replace the warm, personal touch of a spiritual guide. Spiritual retreats and mindfulness classes will keep growing and multiplying. And they won't be led by virtual assistants, but by real people, many of whom will be relying on stories and words of wisdom that have been around for thousands of years.

ACKNOWLEDGMENTS

I would like to thank my editors Cristóbal Pera, Ricardo Cayuela, and Juan Ignacio Boido for the excellent recommendations they gave me after reading the first draft of this book; my *Miami Herald* editor, Nancy Ancrum, for her support; and my colleagues Juan Camilo Gómez, Ismael Triviño, Gaston Volpe, and many others who helped me in the research process over the past five years. My agent Kris Dahl from ICM in New York gave me excellent advice, and Angelina Peralta in Mexico and Annamaria Muchnik in Argentina supported me with ideas and contacts. My friends Ezequiel Stolar and Juan Carlos Parodi reviewed the book or parts of it before it went to press, and Alberto Ibargüen of the Knight Foundation helped me open several doors. My son and biggest source of pride, Thomas Oppenheimer, a partner with a major U.S. law firm, helped me navigate the chapters about lawyers and bankers. And Dr. Sandra Bacman, my wife, a scientist at the University of Miami, helped me understand many of the latest scientific discoveries and saved me from making more mistakes than I would have otherwise done. To all of them and many others, my deepest gratitude!

ACKNOWLEDGMENTS

NOTES

PROLOGUE

5 **"today, technology and automation":** Hayley Tsukayama, "Mark Zuckerberg Tells Harvard Grads That Automation Will Take Jobs, and It's Up to Millennials to Create More," *Washington Post,* May 25, 2017, www.washingtonpost.com/news/the-switch/wp/2017/05/25/mark-zuckerberg-tells-harvard-grads-that-automation-will-take-jobs-and-its-up-to-millennials-to-create-more/?utm_term=.a460e968567e.

5 **"technology over time":** Julie Bort, "Bill Gates: People Don't Realize How Many Jobs Will Soon Be Replaced by Software Bots," *Business Insider,* March 13, 2014, www.businessinsider.com/bill-gates-bots-are-taking-away-jobs-2014-3.

1. A JOBLESS WORLD?

10 **"the clearest indication yet that Google":** John Markoff, "Google Adds to Its Menagerie of Robots," *New York Times,* December 14, 2013, www.nytimes.com/2013/12/14/technology/google-adds-to-its-menagerie-of-robots.html.

10 **new technologies would leave:** McKinsey Global Institute, "Disruptive Technologies: Advances That Will Transform Life, Business, and the Global Economy," www.mckinsey.com/~/media/McKinsey/Business%20Functions/McKinsey%20Digital/Our%20Insights/Disruptive%20technologies/MGI_Disruptive_technologies_Full_report_May2013.ashx.

12 **this will change the world:** Lin Wells, "Better Outcomes Through Radical Inclusion," November 1, 2014, quoted in Thomas L. Friedman, *Thank You for Being Late: An Optimist's Guide to Thriving in the Age of Accelerations* (New York: Picador, 2017).

13 **"It worked great":** Michael Osborne, interview with the author, Oxford, England, July 8, 2016.

15 **"We were surprised to see that servers":** Ibid.

16 **"Anything that relies on storing and processing information":** Carl Benedikt Frey, interview with the author, May 23, 2016.

16 **"the probability of automating an occupation":** Frey, interview with the author via Skype, May 23, 2016.

17 **"if your job can be easily explained":** Anders Sandberg, interview with the author, Future of Humanity Institute, Oxford, July 18, 2016.

18 **the number of people working in agriculture:** McKinsey Global Institute, "Jobs Lost, Jobs Gained: Workforce Transitions in a Time of Automation," December 2017, www.mckinsey.com/~/media/McKinsey/Global%20Themes/Future%20of%20Organizations/What%20the%20future%20of%20work%20will%20mean%20for%20jobs%20skills%20and%20wages/MGI-Jobs-Lost-Jobs-Gained-Report-December-6–2017.ashx; and McKinsey Global Institute, "A Future That Works: Automation, Employment and Productivity," January 2017, www.mckinsey.com/~/media/McKinsey/Global%20Themes/Digital%20Disruption/Harnessing%20automation%20for%20a%20future%20that%20works/MGI-A-future-that-works-Executive-summary.ashx.

18 **There were only 700,000 farmers:** World Bank Development Report, 2016, http://documents.worldbank.org/curated/en/896971468194972881/pdf/102725-PUB-Replacement-PUBLIC.pdf.

25 **singularity—that moment in time:** Alec Ross, *The Industries of the Future* (New York: Simon & Schuster, 2016).

26 **"I would bring a hammer":** Erik Brynjolfsson and Andrew McAfee, *The Second Machine Age: Work, Progress, and Prosperity in a Time of Brilliant Technologies* (New York: Norton, 2014), 189.

30 **"Uber moment":** Steve Slater, "World's Banks May Halve Jobs and Branches Within 10 Years—Barclays Ex-Boss," Reuters, November 24, 2015.

31 **Whereas in 2004 there were twenty-five banks:** Citi GPS, "Digital Disruption: How FinTech Is Forcing Banking to a Tipping Point," March 2016, ir.citi.com/D%2F5GCKN6uoSvhbvCmUDS05SYsRaDvAykPjb5subGr7f1JMe8w2oX1bqpFm6RdjSRSpGzSaXhyXY%3D.

31 **"The return on having a physical network":** Ibid.

32 **REX Real Estate Exchange:** "Artificial Intelligence Is the Last Competition for Real Estate Agents," Helen Zhao, CNBC, March 20, 2018.

36 **an automatic sedation system called Sedasys:** Ross, *Industries of the Future.*

37 **a pharmaceutical robot:** Christopher Steiner, *Automate This: How Algorithms Came to Rule Our World* (New York: Penguin, 2012).

38 **This is no joke:** Shai Danziger, Jonathan Levav, and Liora Avnaim-Pesso, "Extraneous Factors in Judicial Decisions," *Proceedings of the National Academy of Sciences,* 108 (17), 6889–6892, http://dx.doi.org/10.1073/pnas.1018033108.

41 **"My ultimate dream for the world":** Hugh Herr, interview with the author on CNN's *Oppenheimer Presenta,* June 7, 2016, www.youtube.com/watch?v=ZeIgIm3DjFU.

42 **"But very soon we will be replacing them":** Junku Yuh, interview with the author in Seoul, March 31, 2017.

43 **"Turn back," it says:** Simon Parkin, "Killer Robots: The Soldiers That Never Sleep," BBC.com, July 16, 2015, www.bbc.com/future/story/20150715-killer-robots-the-soldiers-that-never-sleep.

44 **it took humanity 119 years:** Citi GPS Global Perspectives and Solutions, "Disruptive Innovations: Ten More Things to Stop and Think About," 2016, https://privateclientsolutions.citi.com/globalassets/pcs/insights/downloads/161013_citi_usa_insights_citi_gps_disruptive_innovations_iv.pdf.

44 **While the United States began using electricity:** Ibid.

45 **In the 1980s, 8.2 percent of U.S. jobs:** Charles Arthur, "Artificial Intelligence: 'Homo Sapiens Will Be Split Into a Handful of Gods and the Rest of Us,'" *The Guardian,* November 7, 2015, www.theguardian.com/business/2015/nov/07/artificial-intelligence-homo-sapiens-split-handful-gods.

46 **In 1964, when AT&T:** Derek Thompson, "A World Without Work," *The Atlantic,* July 2015, 53. The Alphabet's employment data are from the 2017 Fortune 500 Ranking.

47 **Even in the United States:** World Bank, World Development Report 2016.

48 **"While innovations in robotics produce":** Martin Ford, *Rise of the Robots: Technology and the Threat of a Jobless Future* (New York: Basic Books, reprint ed., 2016), 108.

49 **"The predictions that can be extracted":** Ibid., 94–95.

49 **According to data from the United Nations:** "World Bank: 'Extreme Poverty' to Fall Below 10% of World Population for First Time," *The Guardian,* October 4, 2015, www.theguardian.com/

society/2015/oct/05/world-bank-extreme-poverty-to-fall-below-10-of-world-population-for-first-time.

50 **"That's the outcome that":** Martin Ford, interview with the author on CNN's *Oppenheimer Presenta,* October 30, 2015.

52 **the number of textile workers actually quadrupled:** *The Economist,* Special Report: "The Return of the Machinery Question," June 25, 2016, https://www.economist.com/special-report/2016/06/25/the-return-of-the-machinery-question.

52 **"the means of labour passes through different metamorphoses":** Karl Marx, *Grundrisse: Foundations of the Critique of Political Economy,* trans. Martin Nicolaus (New York: Penguin, reprint ed., 1993), 614.

52 **A 1928 headline in *The New York Times*:** Evans Clark, "March of the Machines Makes Idle Hands," *New York Times,* February 26, 1928.

52 **"due to our discovery of means of economising the use of labour":** John Maynard Keynes, "Economic Possibilities for Our Grandchildren," in his collection *Essays in Persuasion,* 1931, cited in "The Future of Employment: How Susceptible Are Jobs to Computerization," by Carl Benedikt Frey and Michael A. Osborne, Oxford University, 2013, page 2, https://www.oxfordmartin.ox.ac.uk/downloads/academic/The_Future_of_Employment.pdf.

52 **"to maintain full employment":** President John F. Kennedy, News Conference 24, February 14, 1962.

53 **"This stream of innovation":** McKinsey Global Institute, "A Future That Works," 31.

54 **in 1985, there were 60,000 ATMs:** "Are ATMs Stealing Jobs?" *The Economist,* July 15, 2011: www.economist.com/blogs/democracyinamerica/2011/06/technology-and-unemployment.

55 **"Why didn't employment fall?":** James Bessen, "How Computer Automation Affects Occupations: Technology, Jobs, and Skills," November 13, 2015, www.bu.edu/law/files/2015/11/NewTech-2.pdf.

56 **When news of this broke:** Vanessa Bates Ramirez, "How Robots Helped Create 100,000 Jobs at Amazon," SingularityHub.com, February 10, 2017, singularityhub.com/2017/02/10/how-robots-helped-create-100000-jobs-at-amazon/#sm.001tjanh93bldio11bc1q1wj3dxe2.

57 **"There is good news":** Michael Mandel and Bret Swanson, "The Coming Productivity Boom," Technology CEO Council, www.techceocouncil.org/clientuploads/reports/TCC%20Productivity%20Boom%20FINAL.pdf.

59 **"With a 3-D printer in our house":** Author's telephone interview with Bret Swanson, April 14, 2017.

60 **"Today 99 percent of Americans":** Peter H. Diamandis and Steven Kotler, *Abundance: The Future Is Better Than You Think* (New York: Free Press, 2012), 13.

60 **"People are concerned":** Peter Diamandis, "Why the Cost of Living Is Poised to Plummet in the Next 20 Years," SingularityHub.com, July 18, 2016, https://singularityhub.com/2016/07/18/why-the-cost-of-living-is-poised-to-plummet-in-the-next-20-years/#sm.0014mrsd312ucetuwrj19ml3zr0f4.

61 **"In the U.S., in 2011":** Ibid.

62 **"When Uber rolls out":** Ibid.

64 **"automation is very good for growth":** Andrew Berg, Edward F. Buffie, and Luis-Felipe Zanna, "Should We Fear the Robot Revolution? The Correct Answer Is Yes," IMF Working Paper, May 2018.

64 **"a future of continued polarization":** Carl Benedikt Frey, interview with the author via Skype, May 23, 2016.

65 **"when we examined which jobs":** Ibid.

67 **The number of horses in the United States plummeted:** Nick Bostrom, *Superintelligence: Paths, Dangers, Strategies* (New York: Oxford University Press, 2014).

68 **"My main fear":** Nick Bostrom, interview with the author, Oxford, July 8, 2016.

75 **Apprehensions of undocumented immigrants along the Mexico border:** U.S. Customs and Border Protection, Stats and Summaries, www.cbp.gov/newsroom/media-resources/stats.

75 **"The swing to Republicans between 2008 and 2016":** Daron Acemoglu, quoted in Thomas B. Edsall, "Robots Can't Vote, but They Helped Elect Trump," *New York Times,* January 11, 2018.

2. THEY'RE COMING FOR JOURNALISTS!

77 **the number of reporters, correspondents, and editors:** Alex T. Williams, "Employment Picture Darkens for Journalists at Digital Outlets," *Columbia Journalism Review,* September 27, 2016, www.cjr.org/business_of_news/journalism_jobs_digital_decline.php.

78 **"in 2005, for every one digital-only journalist":** Ibid.

79 **"The algorithm changes":** Sapna Maheshwari and Sydney Ember, "The End of the Social News Era?" *New York Times,* January 11, 2018, www.nytimes.com/2018/01/11/business/media/facebook-news-feed-media.html.

81 **"The A.I. system had demonstrated overnight improvements":** "The Great A.I. Awakening," Gideon Lewis-Kraus, *New*

York Times, December 14, 2016, www.nytimes.com/2016/12/14/magazine/the-great-ai-awakening.html.

83 **"computer keyboards will disappear":** Claudio Muruzábal, interview with the author, July 8, 2017.

84 **"We need to rely less on expert judgments and predictions":** Andrew McAfee and Erik Brynjolfsson, *Machine, Platform, Crowd: Harnessing Our Digital Future* (New York: Norton, 2017).

85 **A similar study:** Ibid., 40.

85 **"used 5,200 computer equipment purchases":** Ibid., 38.

85 **"a small group of scientists and thinkers":** Michael Linhorst, "Can a Robot Be President?" Politico.com, July 8, 2017, www.politico.com/magazine/story/2017/07/08/robot-president-215342.

87 **"the dispatch came":** Joe Keojane, "What News Writing Bots Means for the Future of Journalism," *Wired,* February 16, 2017, www.wired.com/2017/02/robots-wrote-this-story/.

87 **"From staff and wire reports, powered by Heliograf":** "Rep. Darrell Issa Elected to Represent California 49th Congressional District," *Washington Post,* updated on November 28, 2016, www.washingtonpost.com/news/politics/2016-race-results-california-house-49th/?utm_term=.29793664cb22.

88 **"the purpose of Heliograf":** Jeremy Gilbert, director of strategic initiatives at *The Washington Post,* interview with the author, July 7, 2017.

97 **"We're adding dozens of journalists":** Ken Doctor, "Profitable Post Adding More Than Five Dozen Journalists," Politico.com, December 27, 2016, www.politico.com/media/story/2016/12/the-profitable-washington-post-adding-more-than-five-dozen-journalists-004900.

98 **"This is the face of a modern newsroom":** Ibid.

99 **"In the twentieth century, the notion of journalism":** John Bracken, interview with the author, July 10, 2017.

102 **"Our goal is to significantly shift the balance":** Daniel Victor, "New York Times Will Offer Employee Buyouts and Eliminate Public Role Editor," *New York Times,* May 31, 2017, www.nytimes.com/2017/05/31/business/media/new-york-times-buyouts.html.

102 **"did a very, very good job":** Kinsey Wilson, interview with the author, July 21, 2017.

106 **"TV as a delivery channel":** Joi Ito, interview with the author, July 14, 2017.

108 **"Today, I'm happy to announce":** "YouTube Says Its Primetime Audience Is Bigger Than the Top 10 TV Shows Combined," Ben

Popper, TheVerge.com, May 6, 2016, www.theverge.com/2016/5/6/11608036/youtube-bigger-than-tv-brandcast-sia.

109 **The most successful YouTube star:** Nathan McAlone, "These Are the 18 Most Popular YouTube Stars in the World," *Business Insider,* March 7, 2017, www.businessinsider.com/most-popular-youtuber-stars-salaries-2017/#no-4-smosh-226-million-subscribers-15.

112 **"This is going to revolutionize the industry":** Matthew Caruana Galizia, interview with the author, July 28, 2017.

112 **"technology changes, journalism doesn't":** "The Future of Augmented Journalism: A Guide for Newsrooms in the Age of Smart Machines," Associated Press, insights.ap.org/uploads/images/the-future-of-augmented-journalism_ap-report.pdf.

3. THEY'RE COMING FOR SERVICE WORKERS!

117 **"it does wonders":** Leslie Patton, "Sushi Robots and Vending Machine Pizza Will Reinvent the Automat," Bloomberg, June 7, 2016, www.bloomberg.com/news/articles/2016–06–07/vending-machine-pizza-made-fresh-for-you-is-coming-to-america.

117 **In 2018, four recent:** Luke Dormehl, "In Boston's Newest Restaurant, All the Chefs Are Robots," Digitaltrends.com, May 30, 2018.

118 **"Our device isn't meant to make employees":** Jason Dorrier, "Burger Robot Poised to Disrupt Fast Food Industry," SingularityHub.com, August 10, 2014, singularityhub.com/2014/08/10/burger-robot-poised-to-disrupt-fast-food-industry/#sm.00001r7lrz1dkmeycpt9dfp3cwm5a.

119 **"we want to help the people":** Ibid.

119 **"What we are doing is leveraging":** "Is a Pizza Chain Run by Robots the Future of Fast Food?" Gretel Kauffman, *Christian Science Monitor,* October 2, 2016: www.csmonitor.com/Business/2016/1002/Is-a-pizza-chain-run-by-robots-the-future-of-fast-food.

120 **"Whether people like it or not":** Patton, "Sushi Robots and Vending Machine Pizza."

120 **"Research shows that many appreciate":** Andy Puzder, "Why Restaurant Automation Is on the Menu," *Wall Street Journal,* March 24, 2016, www.wsj.com/articles/why-restaurant-automation-is-on-the-menu-1458857730.

121 **"This is not a vending machine":** Patton, "Sushi Robots and Vending Machine Pizza."

121 **"Millennials, accustomed to apps":** Ibid.

122 **Altogether, they generate annual sales of over $60 billion:** Harri-

son Jacobs, "Japan's Vending Machines Tell You a Lot About the Country's Culture," *Business Insider,* January 23, 2017: www.businessinsider.com/why-so-many-vending-machines-in-japan-2017–1.

124 **"Listening to a recitation of the specials":** Andrew McAfee, "Future Restaurant Waiters Will Respond to Taps Instead of Tips," *Financial Times,* September 10, 2015, www.ft.com/content/88e2a58a-57b2–11e5–9846-de406ccb37f2.

125 **"the low-labor Eatsa concept":** Puzder, "Why Restaurant Automation Is on the Menu."

128 **In 2017, Macy's:** Hayley Peterson, "The Retail Apocalypse Is Creating a 'Slow Rolling Crisis' That Is Rippling Through the U.S. Economy," *Business Insider,* April 17, 2017, www.businessinsider.com/retail-job-losses-are-hurting-the-economy-2017–4.

129 **Amazon could have annual revenue:** Rex Nutting, "Amazon Is Going to Kill More American Jobs Than China Did," MarketWatch.com, March 15, 2017, www.marketwatch.com/story/amazon-is-going-to-kill-more-american-jobs-than-china-did-2017–01–19.

129 **"every job created at Amazon destroys":** Ibid.

129 **Amazon needs many fewer workers:** Ibid.

130 **"No lines. No checkout":** "Introducing Amazon Go," YouTube, December 5, 2016, www.youtube.com/watch?v=NrmMk1Myrxc.

132 **"we were afraid that people would get scared":** Marco Mascorro, interview with the author, San Jose, California, May 8, 2017.

133 **"Before, employees had to spend hours":** Ibid.

136 **"the one device to disrupt and rule":** "Future Reality: Virtual, Augmented, and Mixed Reality," Bank of America/Merrill Lynch, September 22, 2016.

137 **Amazon . . . went from having:** Todd Bishop, "Amazon Soars to More Than 341K Employees," Geekwire.com, February 2, 2017.

137 **e-commerce created 355,000 U.S. jobs:** Michael Mandel and Bret Swanson, "The Coming Productivity Boom," Technology CEO Council, March 2017, www.techceocouncil.org/clientuploads/reports/TCC%20Productivity%20Boom%20FINAL.pdf.

137 **"Production and non-supervisory workers":** Michael Mandel, "How E-commerce Is Raising Pay and Creating Jobs Around the Country," *Forbes,* April 3, 2017, www.forbes.com/sites/realspin/2017/04/03/how-e-commerce-is-raising-pay-and-creating-jobs-around-the-country/#a60a78f6dff5.

138 **"Look at the way the Apple store":** Bret Swanson, telephone interview with the author, April 14, 2017.

140 **"we're not building a mega-mall":** Douglas Hanks, "Nation's Largest Mall Wins County Approval," *Miami Herald,* May 18, 2018.

141 **"He said, 'Ron, you might have'":** Roger Fingas, "Steve Jobs Initially Blasted Genius Bars at Apple Stores, Says Former Retail Head," Appleinsider.com, March 6, 2016, appleinsider.com/articles/17/03/06/steve-jobs-initially-blasted-genius-bars-at-apple-stores-says-former-retail-head.

4. THEY'RE COMING FOR BANKERS!

147 **"nonhuman contact":** Citi GPS, "Digital Disruption: How FinTech Is Forcing Banking to a Tipping Point," March 2016, www.nist.gov/sites/default/files/documents/2016/09/15/citi_rfi_response.pdf.

147 **And in 2015 alone, the largest banks:** Laura Noonan and Martin Arnold, "Thousands More Bank Jobs Under Threat," *Financial Times,* December 13, 2015, www.ft.com/content/5b8c94e0–9f8f-11e5–8613–08e211ea5317.

148 **A study by Citi Global Perspectives & Solutions (GPS):** Portia Crowe, "The 'Uber Moment' for Banks Is Coming—and More Than a Million People Could Lose Their Jobs," *Business Insider,* March 30, 2016, www.businessinsider.com/bank-layoffs-are-coming-2016–3.

148 **"that figure could easily double":** "Retail Banking: Withdrawal Symptoms," *The Economist,* July 29, 2017, www.economist.com/news/finance-and-economics/21725596-banks-have-shuttered-over-10000-financial-crisis-closing-american.

148 **"We agree with Antony Jenkins' comment":** Citi GPS, "Digital Disruption."

149 **The experiment worked so well:** Author's telephone interview with Gastón Bottazzini, CEO of Banco Falabella, March 3, 2018.

149 **"Roughly 60 to 70 percent of retail banking employees":** Citi GPS, "Digital Disruption."

150 **"branches and associated staff costs":** Ibid.

150 **Bills and coins now represent:** Liz Alderman, "In Sweden, a Cash-free Culture Nears," *New York Times,* December 26, 2015, www.nytimes.com/2015/12/27/business/international/in-sweden-a-cash-free-future-nears.html.

151 **"Cash isn't necessarily expensive":** Anette Broløs, telephone interview with the author, April 29, 2016.

152 **"We've had cases where the robbers":** Michael Busk-Jepsen, telephone interview with the author, May 9, 2016.

152 **By 2016, virtual banks:** Citi GPS, "Digital Disruption."

154 **Goldman Sachs had acquired:** Jonathan Marino, "Goldman Sachs Is a Tech Company," *Business Insider,* April 12, 2015, www.businessinsider.com.au/goldman-sachs-has-more-engineers-than-facebook-2015–4.

154 **But now Kensho's algorithm:** Nathaniel Popper, "The Robots Are Coming for Wall Street," *New York Times,* February 25, 2016, www.nytimes.com/2016/02/28/magazine/the-robots-are-coming-for-wall-street.html.

155 **"I'm assuming that the majority":** Ibid.

156 **"We've created, on paper at least":** Ibid.

157 **"would have taken days":** Ibid.

157 **"while the data-crunching can be automated":** EY.com, "Transforming Talent: The Banker of the Future," www.ey.com/Publication/vwLUAssets/ey-transforming-talent-the-banker-of-the-future-global-banking-outlook/$FILE/ey-transforming-talent-the-banker-of-the-future-global-banking-outlook.pdf.

157 **"algorithms will become":** Karl Meekings, telephone interview with the author, October 19, 2016.

158 **"when it comes to investing in real estate":** John Garvey, interview with the author, September 16, 2016.

158 **"There's always the chance":** Karl Meekings, interview with the author, October 19, 2016.

159 **"I got into this business":** Jon Stein, "The Digital Future of Finance and Banking," Techonomy.com, May 30, 2016, techonomy.com/conf/nyc/videos-finance/jon-stein-digital-future-of-finance-banking/.

159 **"your broker might have a bad day":** Ibid.

159 **"Ultimately, this technology is going to be":** Ibid.

160 **projected to skyrocket to $1 trillion by 2025:** Joe Myers, "Should We Be Worried About the Growth of Peer-to-Peer Lending?" World Economic Forum, February 10, 2016, https://www.weforum.org/agenda/2016/02/should-we-be-worried-about-the-growth-in-peer-to-peer-lending/, and Statista.

161 **founder and CEO, Renaud Laplanche:** Oscar Williams-Grut, "LendingClub, the Poster Child of Online Lending, Is in a Life-Threatening Crisis—Here's What You Need to Know," *Business Insider,* May 17, 2016, www.businessinsider.com/lendingclub-faces-doj-and-sec-investigations-could-buy-more-of-its-loans-2016–5.

162 **Prosper.com announced:** Michael Corkery, "As LendingClub Stumbles, Its Entire Industry Faces Skepticism," *New York Times,* May 9,

2016, www.nytimes.com/2016/05/10/business/dealbook/as-lending-club-stumbles-its-entire-industry-faces-skepticism.html.

164 **"The blockchain could provide a much lower-cost solution":** Alec Ross, *The Industries of the Future* (New York: Simon & Schuster, 2017), 115.

164 **"a Ponzi game":** Ibid.

165 **"will undoubtedly be the most important innovation":** Salim Ismail, telephone interview with the author, January 20, 2017.

165 **"Consumer banking as we know it":** Ibid.

166 **"to understand a customer's need":** "Retail Banking 2020: Evolution or Revolution," PwC, 32, www.pwc.com/gx/en/banking-capital-markets/banking-2020/assets/pwc-retail-banking-2020-evolution-or-revolution.pdf.

166 **"areas of significant effort":** Ibid., 23.

167 **"The technological areas of the banking industry":** Karl Meekings, telephone interview with the author, October 19, 2016.

167 **"Banking the unbanked (urban and rural)":** "Retail Banking 2020: Evolution or Revolution," PwC, 32.

167 **"we will see a democratization":** John Garvey, interview with the author, September 16, 2016.

170 **"the banker of the future":** EY.com, "Transforming Talent."

171 **Globally, women control 65 percent:** Ibid.

171 **"there is a positive correlation":** Ibid.

5. THEY'RE COMING FOR LAWYERS!

174 **"ROSS is not a way to replace our attorneys":** Karen Turner, "Meet 'Ross,' the Newly Hired Legal Robot," *Washington Post,* May 16, 2016, www.washingtonpost.com/news/innovations/wp/2016/05/16/meet-ross-the-newly-hired-legal-robot/?utm_term=.56448fc96274.

174 **"goal is to have ROSS":** Ibid.

175 **in the United Kingdom alone, 31,000 law-related jobs:** "More Than 100,000 Legal Roles to Become Automated," *Financial Times,* March 15, 2016, www.ft.com/content/c8ef3f62-ea9c-11e5–888e-2eadd5fbc4a4.

175 **"two-thirds of lawyers":** Victor Li, *ABA Journal,* "What Will Lawyers Be Doing in 5 to 10 Years?" May 18, 2016, www.abajournal.com/lawscribbler/article/what_will_lawyers_be_doing_in_5_to_10_years.

176 **"we really haven't been impacted":** Abraham C. Reich, interview with the author, February 6, 2017.

177 **"Despite not being a lawyer":** Twitter account of @JBrowder1, December 11, 2017.

178 **by the end of 2017:** John Mannes, "Donotpay Launches 1,000 Bots to Help You with Your Legal Problems," Techcrunch.com, July 12, 2017.

178 **"As part of the funding":** "Joshua Browder's Donotpay Gets $1.1 Million Investment from Top VC Funds," artificiallawyer.com, November 6, 2017, www.artificiallawyer.com/2017/11/06/joshua-browders-donotpay-gets-1–1m-investment-from-top-vc-fund/.

179 **There are already three times as many:** Richard Susskind and Daniel Susskind, *The Future of the Professions: How Technology Will Transform the Work of Human Experts* (New York: Oxford University Press, reprint ed., 2017), 1.

181 **"Right now, Modria promises":** Benjamin Barton, "Modria and the Future of Dispute Resolution," October 1, 2015, Big Law Business, biglawbusiness.com/modria-and-the-future-of-dispute-resolution/.

181 **"There were huge piles of paper":** Alec Ross, *The Industries of the Future* (New York: Simon & Schuster, 2017), 116.

183 **"a struggle between the past and the future":** Joe N. Dewey, interview with the author, October 3, 2016; Josias "Joe" N. Dewey, "Warning to Law Firms: The 'Uberization' of Law Is Coming . . . and Fast," Medium.com, March 1, 2016, legal-tech-blog.de/warning-to-law-firms-the-uberization-of-law-is-coming-and-fast.

183 **"In a 'technology-based Internet society'":** Susskind and Susskind, *The Future of the Professions,* 2.

186 **"Imperfection is the norm":** John O. McGinnis and Russell G. Pearce, "The Great Disruption: How Machine Intelligence Will Transform the Role of Lawyers in the Delivery of Legal Services," *Fordham Law Review* 82 (May 15, 2014): 3047, fordhamlawreview.org/wp-content/uploads/assets/pdfs/Vol_82/No_6/McGinnisPearce_May.pdf.

187 **"the advantage of predictive analytics":** Ibid.

188 **which law firm or particular lawyer:** "Lex Machina Releases New Law Firms Comparator and Courts & Judges Comparator Apps," September 20, 2016, lexmachina.com/lex-machina-releases-new-law-firms-comparator-and-courts-judges-comparator-apps/.

191 **"Lawyers do more than undertake legal analysis":** McGinnis and Pearce, "The Great Disruption," 3047.

191 **"The overall effect of the machine invasion":** Ibid.

192 **the four largest accounting firms:** "Lawyers Beware: The Accountants Are Coming After You," *The Economist,* March 21, 2016, www.businessinsider.com/lawyers-beware-the-accountants-are-coming-after-your-business-2015–3.

193 **"there's good news and bad news":** Mark L. Silow, interview with the author, February 6, 2017.

194 **websites that offer automated tax returns:** "Robots Will Soon Do Your Taxes: Bye, Bye, Accounting Jobs," *Wired,* February 2, 2017.

194 **"If you're a journalist in California":** Sean Captain, "H & R Block's Watson-Powered Robots Are Here to Help with Your Taxes," fastcompany.com, February 1, 2017, www.fastcompany.com/3067800/hr-blocks-watson-powered-robots-are-here-to-help-with-your-taxes.

195 **"reviewed the claim":** "Peer-to-Peer Insurance: When Life Throws You Lemons," *The Economist,* March 11, 2017, www.economist.com/news/finance-and-economics/21718502-future-insurance-named-after-soft-drink-new-york-startup-shakes-up.

196 **"The industry is still astonishingly reliant":** "The Future of Insurance: Counsel of Protection," *The Economist,* March 11, 2017, https://www.economist.com/news/finance-and-economics/21718501-technological-change-and-competition-disrupt-complacent-industry-coming.

6. THEY'RE COMING FOR DOCTORS!

204 **"robots will not replace surgeons":** Moshe Shoham, interview with the author, Caesarea, Israel, December 26, 2016.

206 **Watson can digest information:** Jonathan Cohn, "The Robot Will See You," *The Atlantic,* March 18, 2013, www.theatlantic.com/magazine/archive/2013/03/the-robot-will-see-you-now/309216/.

207 **"Most doctors couldn't possibly read and digest":** Vinod Khosla, "Technology Will Replace 80% of What Doctors Do," *Fortune,* December 4, 2012, fortune.com/2012/12/04/technology-will-replace-80-of-what-doctors-do/.

210 **"We're moving from an intermittent":** Daniel Kraft, Skype interview with the author, January 30, 2017.

216 **"serve as a filter":** Vivek Wadhwa and Alex Salkever, *The Driver in the Driverless Car* (Oakland, CA: Berrett-Koehler Publishers, 2017).

220 **while an experienced pathologist:** Yun Liu et al., "Detecting Cancer Metastases on Gigapixel Pathology Images," drive.google.com/file/d/0B1T58bZ5vYa-QlR0QlJTa2dPWVk/view.

221 **operations performed by robots:** "Rise of the Surgical Robot and What Doctors Want," Reuters, July 28, 2016, fortune.com/2016/07/28/surgical-robot-development-intuitive-surgical-medtronic-google/.

228 **"Technology is the next phase":** Deepak Chopra, interview with the author, Miami, February 12, 2017.

7. THEY'RE COMING FOR TEACHERS!

234 **"When children find something interesting":** Andy Rifkin, interview with the author, January 23, 2017.

235 **"It's great to have a tutor":** Randall Bass, telephone interview with the author, March 18, 2017.

239 **"This tool turns teachers into superheroes":** Benjamin Schrom, interview with the author, Mountain View, California, May 8, 2017.

240 **"We also identify longer-term risks":** "Future Reality: Virtual, Augmented and Mixed Reality," Bank of America/Merrill Lynch, September 22, 2016, 38.

240 **a group of children who had participated:** Ibid.

240 **"role-play VR games can exacerbate social isolation":** Ibid.

243 **"what was once done in the classroom":** Andrés Oppenheimer, *Innovate or Die!* (New York: Penguin Random House, 2016), 227.

245 **"I've done things to make my parents happy":** Peter Diamandis, at an executive conference of Singularity University, May 8, 2017.

245 **"You'd be amazed at how many people don't":** Peter Diamandis, "Reinventing How We Teach Our Kids," Tech Blog, www.diamandis.com/blog/reinventing-how-we-teach-our-kids.

247 **"'Become an expert in quantum physics'":** Peter Diamandis, at an executive conference of Singularity University, May 8, 2017.

251 **"The employers told us":** Gabriel Sánchez Zinny, director of INET, interview with the author, February 4, 2017.

252 **"expand apprenticeships and vocational training":** Sarah Kessler, "What You Should Know About Apprenticeships, Trump's Answer to the Skills Gap," Quartz.com, June 15, 2017, qz.com/1005062/trumps-plan-for-job-training-involves-apprenticeships-heres-what-you-should-know/.

253 **That helps Germany maintain:** Katherine S. Newman and Hella Winston, "Make America Make Again: Training Workers for the New Economy," *Foreign Affairs,* January 2017, www.foreignaffairs.com/articles/2016–12–12/make-america-make-again.

253 **"our population is getting older":** Shin Sang-yeol, interview with the author, March 30, 2017.

255 **"I get up at six-thirty in the morning":** Surim Kim, interview with the author, Seoul, South Korea, March 30, 2017.

255 **among the top scorers:** Andrés Oppenheimer, "Why South Koreans Are Richer Than Latin Americans," *Miami Herald,* April 5, 2017.

258 **"While it's true there are successful college dropouts":** Jonathan Wai and Heiner Rindermann, "The Successful College Dropout Is a Myth," The Conversation, theconversation.com/the-myth-of-the-college-dropout-75760.

258 **"The occupations with the highest estimated automatability":** Ljubica Nedelkoska and Glenda Quintini, "Automation, Skills Use, and Training," *OECD Social, Employment, and Migration Working Papers* No. 202, OECD Publishing, Paris, http://pmb.cereq.fr/doc_num.php?explnum_id=4268.

259 **there are around 78 million people:** Dhawai Shah, "By the Numbers, MOOCs in 2017," January 18, 2018, www.class-central.com/report/mooc-stats-2017/.

260 **"In some fields, the ratio":** Rafael Reif, interview with the author, June 10, 2016.

261 **"There's an educational revolution going on":** Julio Frenk, interview with the author, June 10, 2016.

262 **"Historically, all five of those roles":** Randall Bass, telephone interview with the author, March 18, 2017.

8. THEY'RE COMING FOR FACTORY WORKERS!

264 **"Any cars that are being made":** Cadie Thompson, "Elon Musk: In Less Than 20 Years, Owning a Car Will Be Like Owning a Horse," *Business Insider,* November 4, 2015, www.businessinsider.com/elon-musk-owning-a-car-in-20-years-like-owning-a-horse-2015-11.

265 **"Since robots generally don't drink":** Brad Templeton, interview with the author, Palo Alto, California, March 11, 2013.

267 **"Few people seem to fully grasp":** Vivek Wadhwa and Alex Salkever, *The Driver in the Driverless Car* (Oakland, CA: Berrett-Koehler Publishers, 2017).

267 **Today, about 60 percent:** *The Economist* Special Report, "Reinventing Wheels," autonomous vehicles, March 1, 2018, media.economist.com/news/special-report/21737418-driverless-vehicles-will-change-world-just-cars-did-them-what-went-wrong.

268 **according to BCG consulting firm projections:** Ibid.

271 **"The car is now ready to drive":** Lauren Barriere, interview with the author, Mountain View, California, May 8, 2017.

272 **"ultimately self-driving will improve safety":** Dara Khosrowshahi, interview with the author, Miami, April 5, 2018.

273 **more than a third of the trucks:** Farhad Manjoo, "For the Debaters: What Shall We Do About the Tech Careening Our Way?" *New York Times,* September 21, 2016, www.nytimes.com/2016/09/22/technology/for-the-debaters-what-shall-we-do-about-the-tech-careening-our-way.html.

273 **"The truck is always productive":** Ibid.

274 **"It would make the job not worth doing":** Ibid.

275 **"It's going to be a real learning experience":** Neal F. Boudette, "There's a Pizza Delivery in Ford's Future, by Driverless Car," *New York Times,* August 29, 2017, www.nytimes.com/2017/08/29/business/ford-driverless-pizza-delivery-dominos.html.

276 **"Uber and Lyft Have Devastated":** Laura J. Nelson, "Uber and Lyft Have Devastated LA Taxi Industry, City Records Show," *Los Angeles Times,* April 14, 2016, www.latimes.com/local/lanow/la-me-ln-uber-lyft-taxis-la-20160413-story.html.

278 **"This isn't just a test":** Rohan Roberts, interview with the author, December 20, 2016.

280 **"Movable warehouses are a really nice idea":** Matthew Boyle, "Wal-Mart Applies for Patent for Blimp-Style Floating Warehouse," Quartz.com, August 18, 2017, https://www.bloomberg.com/news/articles/2017–08–18/wal-mart-s-amazon-war-takes-to-skies-with-floating-warehouses.

281 **annual sales of industrial robots:** World Robotics Report 2016, International Federation of Robotics, Frankfurt, September 2016.

282 **"as human beings are also animals":** John Markoff, "Skilled Work, Without the Worker," *New York Times,* August 18, 2012, www.nytimes.com/2012/08/19/business/new-wave-of-adept-robots-is-changing-global-industry.html.

282 **"Robots are not people":** Karel Čapek, *RUR (Rossum's Universal Robots),* translated by Paul Selver and Nigel Playfair, preprints.readingroo.ms/RUR/rur.pdf.

283 **South Korea had an average of 531 robots:** World Robotics Report 2016, Worldwide Distribution of Industrial Robots, 60.

283 **the overall density of industrial robots in Japan's:** Ibid., 60.

283 **"Right now, robots in car factories":** Kei Shimizu, interview

with the author, Yaskawa headquarters in Tokyo, Japan, March 29, 2017.

284 **"Imagine you are a manager":** "Disruptive Technologies: Advances That Will Transform Life, Business and the Global Economy," McKinsey & Company, McKinsey Global Institute, May 2013, 69, www.mckinsey.com/~/media/McKinsey/Business%20Functions/McKinsey%20Digital/Our%20Insights/Disruptive%20technologies/MGI_Disruptive_technologies_Full_report_May2013.ashx.

285 **"For example, if a small bakery":** Atsushi Yasuda, interview with the author, March 27, 2017.

285 **There are already 67,824 Japanese citizens:** Chris Weller, "Japan Has a Record 68,000 People over 100 Years Old," *Business Insider,* September 15, 2017, www.businessinsider.com/japan-people-over-100-centenarians-new-record-economy-struggling-2017–9.

286 **"We need robots to assist our elderly people":** Takeshi Kobayashi, interview with the author, Tokyo, March 27, 2017.

288 **"China is by far the biggest robot market":** "China forecast 2020," International Federation of Robotics, press release, August 16, 2017, ifr.org/ifr-press-releases/news/robots-china-breaks-historic-records-in-automation.

289 **"We will make robots":** Tom Ortlik, "China's Future, Reshaped by Robots," Bloomberg, August 13, 2013, www.bloomberg.com/view/articles/2017–08–23/china-s-future-reshaped-by-robots.

289 **Luo Weiqiang, the company's general manager:** "First Unmanned Factory Takes Shape in Dongguan City," *People's Daily,* July 15, 2015.

290 **The robots make:** Ibid.

292 **"This is a milestone":** Emma Thomasson and Aleksandra Michalska, "Adidas to Mass Produce 3-D Printed Shoe with Silicon Valley Start-up," Reuters, April 6, 2017, www.reuters.com/article/us-adidas-manufacturing-idUSKBN1790F6.

293 **"What you can do is introduce":** Ibid.

293 **but it was another eleven years:** Ronald E. G. Davis, "The Birth of Commercial Aviation in the United States," *Revue Belge de Philologie et d'Histoire* 78(3), 2000.

294 **"Today, a third group has emerged":** Tom Davenport, "The Future of the Manufacturing Workforce, Report Two: The Rise of the 'Tech' in Manufacturing," www.manpowergroup.com/wps/wcm/connect/f28fd14c-0b04–4174-b311–46e3e0c7e516/Man

_Rise-of-Tech_021913.pdf?MOD=AJPERES&CACHEID=f28fd14c-0b04–4174-b311–46e3e0c7e516.

295 **"now we have lots of robots":** Ibid.

295 **"Perhaps the ideal situation":** Ibid.

9. THEY'RE COMING FOR ENTERTAINERS!

299 **In 1870, the average workweek:** "What the Future of Work Will Mean for Jobs, Skills and Wages," McKinsey Global Institute, November 2017, 44, www.mckinsey.com/featured-insights/future-of-organizations-and-work/what-the-future-of-work-will-mean-for-jobs-skills-and-wages.

299 **"the cultural and creative industries":** "Cultural Times: The First Global Map of Cultural and Creative Industries," December 2015, 5, unesdoc.unesco.org/images/0023/002357/235710E.pdf.

302 **"It was barely possible last year when we did it":** Tim Gray, "How the Furious 7 Visual Effects Team Worked to Honor Paul Walker's Legacy," *Variety,* October 15, 2015, variety.com/2015/film/awards/furious-7-visual-effects-paul-walker-1201618224/.

304 **"At first movies had maybe":** Carlos Arguello, telephone interview with the author, September 1, 2017.

305 **The 1956 film *The Ten Commandments*:** www.tasteofcinema.com.

305 **the studio created its own:** Alain Bielik, "Troy: Innovative Effects on an Epic Scale," May 25, 2004, www.awn.com/vfxworld/troy-innovative-effects-epic-scale.

307 **"before, we used to make films":** Richard Gere, interview with the author, Miami, March 3, 2017.

307 **"Now we just remove":** Stuart Dryburgh, interview with the author, February 18, 2018.

308 **Netflix spent $6 billion:** Jeff Dunn, "Netflix and Amazon Are Estimated to Spend a Combined $10.5 Billion on Video This Year," *Business Insider,* April 10, 2017, www.businessinsider.com/netflix-vs-amazon-prime-video-content-spend-estimate-chart-2017–4.

308 **"It's only a matter of time":** Nick Bilton, "Why Hollywood as We Know It Is Already Over," *Vanity Fair,* July 3, 2017, www.vanityfair.com/news/2017/01/why-hollywood-as-we-know-it-is-already-over.

309 **"Eventually it will":** Ibid.

309 **the number of movies that people watch:** Movie Box Office Results Per Year, 1980–Present, Box Office Mojo, www.boxofficemojo.com.

309 **"The number of online platforms":** Julia Jenks, "The Number of Online Services Continues to Expand, Benefiting Consumers and Creators," March 22, 2016, www.mpa-i.org/the-number-of-online-services-continues-to-expand-benefiting-consumers-and-creators/#.WvxnYi-ZPUI.

311 **"There's an explosion of possibilities":** Carlos Arguello, interview with the author, September 1, 2017.

311 **After fifteen years of declining sales:** "The Music Industry: Scales Dropped," *The Economist,* April 16, 2016, and IFPI, Global Music Report 2017, www.ifpi.org.

311 **According to a study by the investment bank Goldman Sachs:** itsthevibe.com/spotify-music-industry/, and www.goldmansachs.com/our-thinking/pages/music-in-the-air.html.

312 **In 2017, a song had to be downloaded:** Giselle Maronilla, "Is Spotify Killing the Music Industry . . . or Saving It?" itsthevibe.com/spotify-music-industry/.

313 **live concert revenues in the United States:** Dave DiMartino, "Live Nation Leads the Charge in Concert Business' Booming Revenue," *Variety,* variety.com/2017/music/features/live-nation-concert-business-1201979571/.

313 **"artists aren't limited":** Cherie Hu, interview with the author, October 13, 2017.

315 **"We cross-checked with social-media-channel statistics":** Jeff Benjamin, "What Does It Take for a K-Pop Band to Blow Up in South America?" *New York Times,* May 7, 2017, www.nytimes.com/2017/05/04/magazine/what-does-it-take-for-a-k-pop-band-to-blow-up-in-south-america.html.

316 **There will always be superstars:** Quoted from "What Will the Music Business Look Like in 2020? 5 Predictions from Industry Insiders," http://blog.sonicbids.com/what-will-the-music-business-look-like-in-2020-5-predictions-from-industry-insiders.

317 **"Independent artists and songwriters":** Ibid.

317 **"People will have bots":** Ibid., 258.

318 **"Major networks become increasingly boxed out":** Delaware North, "The Future of Sports," futureof.org/wp-content/uploads/The-Future-of-Sports-2015-Report.pdf.

320 **Since it began, nearly five hundred athletes:** Jasneel Chaddha, "The New Face of Sports Media," *Huffington Post,* August 28, 2017.

321 **"The world of video and connectivity":** Delaware North, "The Future of Sports."

321 **"The entire sporting complex":** Ibid.

322 **history shows that some of the biggest innovations:** Ibid.

325 **And BASE jumping:** Leo Benedictus, "Why Are Deadly Extreme Sports More Popular Than Ever?" *The Guardian,* August 20, 2016, www.theguardian.com/sport/2016/aug/20/why-are-deadly-extreme-sports-more-popular-than-ever.

325 **the partnership between his company and GoPro:** "Red Bull Takes Over Shares of GoPro," May 27, 2016, www.ispo.com/en/companies/id_77942246/red-bull-takes-over-shares-in-gopro.html.

326 **"the biggest sports upset story in recent memory":** Delaware North, "The Future of Sports."

326 **"it's no longer just wanting":** Ibid.

326 **Forty-two percent of the U.S. health club market's:** Ibid.

327 **Yoga classes:** Ibid.

327 **"Alt-athletes have little interest in sitting":** Ibid.

328 **"But there will be a Super Bowl":** Ibid.

328 **the industry will generate 30 million new jobs:** Data provided to the author by the World Travel and Tourism Council (WTTC) research director Evelyne Freiermuth on December 13, 2017.

328 **"When you ask millennials":** Gloria Guevara, interview with the author, Miami, December 5, 2017.

331 **"if this was Christmas and you were Santa Claus":** Chabeli Herrera, "Cruising Was More Popular Than Ever in 2017—Big Changes Are Coming," *Miami Herald,* March 7, 2018, www.miamiherald.com/news/business/tourism-cruises/article203796204.html.

10. THE JOBS OF THE FUTURE

335 **"technological unemployment is coming fast":** Peter Diamandis, at his conference at the Singularity University headquarters, May 8, 2017.

336 **"We live in an unstable time":** Mark Zuckerberg's speech to graduates of Harvard University, May 25, 2017, news.harvard.edu/gazette/story/2017/05/mark-zuckerbergs-speech-as-written-for-harvards-class-of-2017/.

337 **Adidas can churn out shoes:** James Shotter and Lindsay Whipp, "Robot Revolution Helps Adidas Bring Shoemaking Back to Germany," *Financial Times,* June 8, 2016, www.ft.com/content/7eaffc5a-289c-11e6–8b18–91555f2f4fde.

338 **"it doesn't make sense":** Jon Emont, "The Robots Are Com-

ing for Garment Workers. That's Good for the U.S., Bad for Poor Countries," *Wall Street Journal,* February 16, www.wsj.com/articles/the-robots-are-coming-for-garment-workers-thats-good-for-the-u-s-bad-for-poor-countries-1518797631.

338 **"The use of new technologies":** "Trouble in the Making? The Future of Manufacturing-Led Development," World Bank, September 20, 2017, www.worldbank.org/en/topic/competitiveness/publication/trouble-in-the-making-the-future-of-manufacturing-led-development.

338 **the percentage of jobs threatened by automation:** World Bank Development Report 2016, cited in "Technology at Work v2.0: The Future Is Not What It Used to Be," by Citi GPS and the University of Oxford, www.oxfordmartin.ox.ac.uk/downloads/reports/Citi_GPS_Technology_Work_2.pdf.

339 **China increased its annual purchase:** Adam Minter, "China Has a Robot Problem," Bloomberg, June 8, 2016, https://www.bloomberg.com/view/articles/2016-06-09/china-has-a-robot-problem.

339 **South Korea already had an average:** World Robotics Report 2016, Worldwide Distribution of Industrial Robots, ifr.org/img/uploads/Executive_Summary_WR_Industrial_Robots_20161.pdf.

341 **thanks to a universal basic income:** Raya Bidshahri, "Is a Universal Basic Income a Solution to Tech Unemployment?" June 26, 2017, singularityhub.com/2017/06/26/is-universal-basic-income-a-solution-to-tech-unemployment/#sm.00000rt8utaosce8tsev3hnaezwgj.

342 **"Of course, these social woes":** Andrew McAfee and Erik Brynjolfsson, "Human Work in the Robotic Future: Policy for the Age of Automation," *Foreign Affairs,* July/August 2016, www.foreignaffairs.com/articles/2016–06–13/human-work-robotic-future.

343 **Regalia told me that:** Fernandino Regalia, interview with the author, November 17, 2017.

344 **"charitable donations activate":** Rachel Jones, "It's Good to Give," *Nature Reviews* 7, December 2006.

344 **"being generous, being altruistic":** Facundo Manes, interview with the author, January 29, 2018.

345 **"The human worker":** Kevin J. Delaney, "The Robot That Takes Your Job Should Pay Taxes, Says Bill Gates," *Quartz,* qz.com/911968/bill-gates-the-robot-that-takes-your-job-should-pay-taxes/.

346 **there is already a labor market:** "Artificial Intelligence Will Create New Kinds of Work," *The Economist,* August 26, 2017.

346 **Upwork.com, based in Silicon Valley:** "53 Million Americans Now Freelance, New Study Finds," September 3, 2014, www.upwork.com/press/2014/09/03/53-million-americans-now-freelance-new-study-finds-2/.

347 **many social media content moderators:** "Artificial Intelligence Will Create New Kinds of Work."

348 **"My generation had it easy":** Thomas L. Friedman, "Need a Job? Invent It," *New York Times,* March 30, 2013, www.nytimes.com/2013/03/31/opinion/sunday/friedman-need-a-job-invent-it.html.

348 **between 75 and 80 percent of the labor market:** Peter Miscovich, "The Future Is Automated. Here's How You Can Prepare for It," World Economic Forum, January 12, 2017, www.weforum.org/agenda/2017/01/the-future-is-automated-here-s-how-we-can-prepare-for-it/.

350 **"We're the producers":** Noam Scheiber, "The Pop-Up Employer: Build a Team, Do the Job, Say Goodbye," *New York Times,* July 12, 2017, www.nytimes.com/2017/07/12/business/economy/flash-organizations-labor.html.

350 **"There is some evidence":** Ibid.

352 **"I tell them the best thing they can do":** Benjamin Pring, telephone interview with the author, December 4, 2017.

353 **"When you and I started working":** Ibid.

353 **"people will have more time":** Ibid.

357 **"I've been on stage at the Met":** Jane E. Brody, "Reinventing Yourself," *New York Times,* March 14, 2016, well.blogs.nytimes.com/2016/03/14/reinventing-yourself/.

357 **Currently, only 15 percent:** "Independent Work: Choice, Necessity, and the Gig Economy," McKinsey Global Institute, October 2016, www.mckinsey.com/~/media/McKinsey/Global%20Themes/Employment%20and%20Growth/Independent%20work%20Choice%20necessity%20and%20the%20gig%20economy/Independent-Work-Choice-necessity-and-the-gig-economy-Executive-Summary.ashx.

358 **more than 70 percent of people who work independently:** "Independent Work: Choice, Necessity, and the Gig Economy."

362 **the percentage of people working in agriculture:** "Jobs Lost, Jobs Gained: Workforce Transitions in a Time of Automation," McKinsey Global Institute, December 2017, www.mckinsey.com/~/media/McKinsey/Global%20Themes/Future%20of%20Organizations/

What%20the%20future%20of%20work%20will%20mean%20for%20jobs%20skills%20and%20wages/MGI-Jobs-Lost-Jobs-Gained-Report-December-6–2017.ashx.

363 **If we just take into account children:** Max Roser, "Life Expectancy," www.ourworldindata.org.

363 **In 2010, obesity killed:** Yuval Noah Harari, *Homo Deus: A Brief History of Tomorrow* (New York: HarperCollins, 2017), 16.

363 **Nathan Rothschild, the wealthiest man:** Max Roser, "Economic Growth," www.ourworldindata.org.

364 **Today, in developed nations:** Max Roser, "Infant Mortality," www.ourworldindata.org.

364 **In the United States and most European nations:** Max Roser and Esteban Ortiz-Ospina, "Global Rise of Education," www.ourworldindata.org.

364 **While there was just one democracy:** Max Roser, "Democracy," www.ourwoldindata.org.

365 **During the twentieth century:** Harari, *Homo Deus,* 25.

366 **In the 1920s, many people:** Steven Pinker, *Enlightenment Now: The Case for Reason, Science, Humanism, and Progress,* quoted by Bill Gates in "My New Favorite Book of All Time," January 26, 2018, www.gatesnotes.com.

EPILOGUE

370 **Between 2014 and 2030:** "Jobs Lost, Jobs Gained: Workforce Transitions in a Time of Automation," McKinsey Global Institute, December 2017, www.mckinsey.com/~/media/McKinsey/Global%20Themes/Future%20of%20Organizations/What%20the%20future%20of%20work%20will%20mean%20for%20jobs%20skills%20and%20wages/MGI-Jobs-Lost-Jobs-Gained-Report-December-6–2017.ashx.

371 **"Loneliness destroys lives":** Sir Simon McDonald, interview with the author, Miami, February 1, 2018.

371 **"Academic research has demonstrated":** "21 Jobs of the Future," Center for the Future of Work, November 2017, www.cognizant.com/whitepapers/21-jobs-of-the-future-a-guide-to-getting-and-staying-employed-over-the-next-10-years-codex3049.pdf.

372 **the growth of the middle class:** "Jobs Lost, Jobs Gained: Workforce Transitions in a Time of Automation."

374 **Global cybersecurity expenses:** Steve Morgan, "Top 5 Cyber-

Security Facts, Figures and Statistics for 2017," Cybersecurity Business Report, www.csonline.com, October 19, 2017.

374 **global consumption will increase:** "Jobs Lost, Jobs Gained: Workforce Transitions in a Time of Automation."

375 **Worldwide sales of industrial robots:** Andrew Murphy, "Industrial: Robotics Outlook 2025," Loupventures.com, June 5, 2017, http://loupventures.com/industrial-robotics-outlook-2025/. Graphic with data from Loup Ventures and the International Robot Federation.

377 **"In California, New York, Washington":** Al Gore, interview with the author, Miami, August 3, 2017.